PENGUIN BOOKS
KANSHIRAM

Badri Narayan is professor and director, G.B. Pant Social Science Institute, Allahabad, and has been professor in the School of Social Sciences, Jawaharlal Nehru University, New Delhi. His research interests range from popular culture, social and anthropological history to Dalit and subaltern issues.

Writing in English and Hindi, Narayan is the author of *The Making of the Dalit Public in North India: Uttar Pradesh, 1950–Present* (2011), *Fascinating Hindutva-Saffron Politics and Dalit Mobilisation* (2009) and *Women Heroes and Dalit Assertion in North India* (2006). He has also been the recipient of the Fulbright Senior Fellowship (2004–05) and the Smuts Fellowship, University of Cambridge (2007).

'This is a book in a rare genre: a well-researched and analytical political biography of an important political figure. It is a sympathetic, clearly etched portrait of Kanshiram. But it is much more than that. It opens up new horizons on many subjects: Dalit politics, the nature of political organizing and social mobilization, the nature of leadership and politics in UP. A very valuable contribution'—Pratap Bhanu Mehta

'[This] is the first scholarly attempt to chronicle the life of [Mayawati's] more celebrated mentor . . . It meticulously charts the growth of the movement founded by Kanshiram, his passionate concern for the miserable lot of the Dalits, his rainbow coalition, his innovative use of the Dalit myths, the tireless work he put in . . . Worth a read'—*The Hindu*

'A comprehensive and well-written book . . . [It] ably illustrates Kanshiram's abilities as an organization builder and master strategist. . . . Narayan draws attention to significant features of Kanshiram's thinking as constituting an "agenda beyond Ambedkar"'—*Indian Express*

'This book is the first major—and very rich—biography of Kanshiram . . . Must be read by every student of Indian politics' —*Business Standard*

'Well-researched and intelligently argued . . . The book is more than competent in etching Kanshiram as a unique organizer and ideologue of a community that may well be the most oppressed in the history of mankind. . . . The author is frank about [Kanshiram's] amoral opportunism, which was in contrast to Ambedkar's ethical approach to politics'—*Mint*

'[The book] fills a crucial vacuum by contributing to the understanding of a personality important to both Dalits and mainstream politics' —*DNA*

Badri Narayan

KANSHIRAM

LEADER OF THE DALITS

PENGUIN BOOKS

An imprint of Penguin Random House

PENGUIN BOOKS

USA | Canada | UK | Ireland | Australia
New Zealand | India | South Africa | China | Singapore

Penguin Books is part of the Penguin Random House group of companies
whose addresses can be found at global.penguinrandomhouse.com

Published by Penguin Random House India Pvt. Ltd
4th Floor, Capital Tower 1, MG Road,
Gurugram 122 002, Haryana, India

First published in Viking by Penguin Books India 2014
Published in Penguin Books by Penguin Random House India 2018

ISBN 9780143446651

Typeset in Garamond by Eleven Arts, Delhi

Printed at Manipal Technologies Limited, India

www.penguin.co.in

This is a legitimate digitally printed version of the book and therefore might not
have certain extra finishing on the cover.

To
Ramachandra Guha
for inspiring me
and
giving me strength

Dalit god Kanshiram
Gives mighty speeches
That leave all speechless
And set the Dalits' drums beating.
Hail, the Dalit god!

Terrified is the Centre of you
Mayawati, your disciple
Is declaring war
On Sage Vishwanath
Lord, the Centre is
Apprehensive.
Hail, the Dalit god!
                    —Hindi poet Nagarjun, 1998, just before his death

Daliton ko maangnewaalon ki jagah denewaali community ke roop mein
tabdeel hona hoga.[1]
(Dalits will have to transform themselves from a community
of beggars to one of givers.)
            —Kanshiram, lecture at SC/ST Parliamentary Forum,
                                        New Delhi, 17 June 1992

Ambedkar ne kitabein ikatthi keen, maine logon ko ikattha kiya.[2]
(Ambedkar collected books, I gathered people.)
            —Kanshiram, interview in *Abhay Bharti*, 27 May 1987

---

[1] A. Kumar, ed., *Bahujan Nayak Kanshiram Ke Avismarniya Bhashan* (Delhi: Gautam Book Centre, 2007), p. 19.

[2] A.R. Akela, *Kanshiram Ke Saakshatkaar* (Delhi: Manak Publications, 2007), p. 19.

Contents

Contents

Author's Note

Kanshiram emerged on the political scene in the 1980s and early 1990s, when I had just started my academic career. Watching the changing face of democratic politics in Uttar Pradesh (UP), beginning with the fracas over the *Mandal Commission Report*, then the liberalization policies and the demolition of the Babri Masjid, I closely followed the rise and growth of Kanshiram and the Bahujan Samaj Party (BSP). As a part of my study, I visited a large number of villages dominated by dalits, to observe the functioning of dalit politics and also to understand better the dalit psyche. In village after village, I found that dalits were no longer docile and submissive. Instead, they had metamorphosed into a group with a strong sense of confidence and identity and self-respect. All the dalits I spoke to acknowledged that it was Kanshiram who had inculcated these feelings in them. They hailed him as the messiah of the dalits after B.R. Ambedkar. He was the one who had socially, culturally and politically empowered them to fight against injustice and the everyday humiliation and oppression they faced from the upper castes and the police.

These comments only increased my admiration for Kanshiram. I was already deeply impressed by him, since I had been part of left politics in my student days and had a strong empathy for dalits, subalterns and other marginalized groups. I had closely followed his journey, whereby the dalits had been transformed into one of the most politically powerful communities of UP. The party formed by him, the BSP, represented freedom, respect and a completely new way of thinking for the dalits, who had been used to being treated as a captive constituency by the Congress for years. Kanshiram's BSP was to bring about a transformation in (mainly Hindu) society through the political empowerment of dalits.

A democrat to the core, Kanshiram believed in constitutional and democratic values. He tried to bring together the dalits, people from the scheduled tribes (STs), other backward castes (OBCs) and other minorities under the umbrella of '*bahujan samaj*' or majority community—they constituted 85 per cent of the votes in UP at that time.[1] He made them realize the value of their votes, explaining how they could change the face of democracy. He also constructed the idea of 'Manuvadi', that is, the follower of the *Manu Samhita*, the social code of the upper castes, as the 'other' or opponent against whom he would battle.

This attempt to raise the consciousness of dalits and backward castes and to empower them was, like Ambedkar's, for sustaining the state, not to upturn it. If Ambedkar can be credited with putting in place a constitutional edifice for Indian democracy, it was Kanshiram whose organizational devices and political stratagems shored up its legitimacy, by involving many of the marginalized groups in his politics.

The demolition of the Babri Masjid in 1992, a fallout of Hindu majoritarian politics, and the run-up to economic liberalization triggered a legitimacy crisis for the Indian state. This crisis saw the politics of religious identity gaining ground from the early 1990s onward. There was also an aggressive growth of caste-identity politics following the recommendations of the *Mandal Commission Report*, which brought reservations for the backward castes to centre stage. Political parties like the Janata Dal and the Samajwadi Party (SP) were also involved in evoking the backward caste identity in electoral politics.

V.P. Singh, in a bid to stall the growing political power of the Bharatiya Janata Party (BJP), the Vishwa Hindu Parishad (VHP), the Shiv Sena, etc., implemented the *Mandal Commission Report*. In popular terms, it was an attempt to checkmate the 'kamandal', a religious symbol of the Hindus, by the use of 'Mandal', a symbol of backwards and dalit mobilization. The Mandal politics saw the strengthening of caste identities of dalits and OBCs. OBC leaders like Lalu Prasad Yadav, Nitish Kumar, Sharad Yadav and Mulayam Singh Yadav belonging to the Janata Dal and Samajwadi Party emerged in the Hindi-speaking region and established their stronghold in different parts of it. They gave voice to the politics of caste identity based on the idea of the upliftment of the marginalized castes. The controversy around the Babri Masjid was thus the underlying reason for the rise of this politics of backward-caste reservation in northern India—for good and for worse. Over time, the issue of reservation would create schisms in northern Indian politics between the backward castes and the mainly upper-caste and secular-minded supporters of the anti-Mandal agitation.

Kanshiram took full advantage of the situation to catapult his party to power. Together with his protégé Mayawati, who remained his most trusted sentinel since he embarked on his mission of empowering dalits socially and politically, he joined hands with the Samajwadi Party to gain control over UP. By installing thirty-seven-year-old Mayawati, a woman and that too from a dalit caste, as chief minister in 1993, he cocked a snook at the feudal and patriarchal forces, infusing the marginalized sections at the same time with a strong sense of pride and self-respect.

Kanshiram also challenged the Brahman dominance of the leaders from UP in national and state politics. Top national political leaders at that time like Atal Bihari Vajpayee and Murli Manohar Joshi from the BJP, and even earlier, leaders like Govind Ballabh Pant and Jawaharlal Nehru belonging to the Congress, were Brahmans. The dalits were dependent on them for their political survival. It was Kanshiram who understood the contradictions of subaltern politics in UP and exhorted the dalits not to remain stooges or *chamcha*s of these political leaders, but to develop their own leadership through their own political party. These ideas, which had been the inspiration underlying the Backward and Minority Communities Employees Federation (BAMCEF) and the Dalit Shoshit Samaj Sangharsh Samiti (DS4), were subsequently theorized in his lone book *The Chamcha Age: An Era of the Stooges* and would ultimately form the ideological basis of the BSP.

In addition, by glorifying the cultural resources of various dalit communities—such as their proverbs, folklore, folk songs, etc.—venerating the heroes and saints of the different dalit communities and then attempting to unify dalits under one broad umbrella, Kanshiram built a sense of self-respect among them. He also popularized Ambedkar, who was largely unknown in UP, by installing his statues across the state along with those of other local dalit saints and heroes. In doing so, he succeeded in implanting and disseminating Ambedkar's ideas of dalit liberation in UP, though many people here were deeply rooted in the myths and legends of the Puranas and the Hindu mythological epics.

Kanshiram was regarded differently by different people. The Ambedkarites considered him a bahujan icon who was carrying forward Ambedkar's legacy. The Manuvadis saw him as a fanatical dalit leader. Those in power considered him to be a tough negotiator, who could stand up even to the prime minister, but a proponent of casteism. Political analysts found it difficult to understand his moves and found him totally unpredictable. Yet, in his lifetime, he had emerged as the tallest political leader of the dalits, making them a force to reckon with in electoral politics.

The people who were affected by his politics considered him crooked, but chose to ignore the new way of thinking about society and economy he brought with him. His vision of social transformation was complex, but it did bring about change. He had the capacity to turn remedial measures into long-term transformative politics. For example, his politics of 'opportunism', often criticized, was for the sake of acquiring power for the dalits. In the same way, the politicization of the dalit identity played a significant role in mobilizing them in north India.

Kanshiram was critical of the communists, but on several occasions he was found turning to communist ideology. He gave a new twist to socialist ideas. He maintained he would nationalize the major industries if his party came to power. He also claimed he would create conditions so that labourers could lead a good life. Natural resources should be under government control according to him. Today, when the government is selling these to private companies, his belief is still relevant. He believed wasteland should be acquired by the government and distributed among the landless. He held that his party would not support industrialists who set up enterprises with government money and demanded that they should fund themselves and give adequate benefits to labourers. He was not against private industrialists but was against the benefits given to them by the government.

Where does that leave the BSP on Kanshiram's twin objectives of making it the agency for social change and the political empowerment of dalits? At present, there seems to be divergence in the pursuit of these goals. The BSP has grown into a strong political party but it is at a crossroads. To some extent, Kanshiram's objective of ensuring the bahujan samaj's interaction with the upper castes and classes on an equal basis has been fulfilled, thanks to the political empowerment of the bahujans. Eminent political scientist Sudha Pai affirms that the party has constructed a strong dalit movement, based upon identity and consciousness, in a state which still has a rigid, conservative social structure. Yet, she points out that despite considerable politicization of dalits in UP by the 1980s and 1990s, the BSP has been unable to displace Manuvadi (upper-caste) forces and introduce social change. She also raises the pertinent question about whether the BSP is a movement with an agenda 'for a radical social change or a political party driven solely by the compulsion of achieving power'.[2]

Making Indian democracy more inclusive today will depend greatly on whether or not the mode of politics followed by Kanshiram proves to be emancipatory for the dalits. In order to understand whether the dalit–bahujan politics will succeed in providing space for the larger dalit community or be appropriated by the electoral market merely for votes, a re-look at Kanshiram's life and politics becomes critical.

There have been crises in dalit politics like when the bahujan unity that Kanshiram had tried to conceptualize—in which dalits, STs, OBCs and lower sections of the minority (*pasmanda*) would come together—did not take shape and the OBCs became the main oppressors of the dalits. The incident in Dauna village, post the demolition of the Babri Masjid, when Mulayam Singh and Kanshiram had joined forces to form the government is a glaring example.

Shivpatia, an old dalit lady of Dauna village near Allahabad, bore the brunt of aggressive OBC behaviour. She was made to parade naked on 21 January 1994 because her son had raised an objection to some Kurmi (OBC caste) boys plucking vegetables from her field. Dominant Kurmi villagers virtually ran amuck in the dalit locality of the village and took their revenge by stripping Shivpatia. The incident hogged the headlines in the national dailies, prompting Kanshiram and Mulayam Singh Yadav to rush to the spot together. However, Kanshiram publicly reprimanded Yadav for his inept administration in a meeting. Despite all promises to deal with the perpetrators sternly, the incident faded into the background. Though it was the first sign of growing strains between the Samajwadi Party and the BSP, the incident appeared to be a closed chapter for all political parties.[3] There have been other publicized instances of the OBCs' crimes against the dalits like those that occurred after the 2012 legislative assembly elections when they were openly humiliated and insulted, beaten, killed by firing, the huts of weak and marginalized castes like the Nats set on fire, and so on.

Through this book I would like to examine Kanshiram's vision of democracy and what role was played by electoral politics in his achieving that vision. This will reveal future possibilities and how far the BSP can succeed in the fight for the liberation of dalits, given that there is no other party with a predominantly dalit agenda.

Way back in the 1940s, the eminent Hindi poet Suryakant Tripathi 'Nirala' had portrayed his vision for India in these lines:

Jald jald pair badhao, aao aao
Aaj ameeron ki haveli kisano ki hogi pathshaala
Dhobi, Pasi, Chamar, Teli kholenge andhere ka taala [4]

(March quickly
The mansion of the rich
will become the school of the peasants
Washermen, toddy tappers, shoemakers and oil pressers
will open the cage of darkness)

Kanshiram also felt the same way about the bahujans in the 1990s and tried hard to provide them the master key with which they could open the cage of darkness.

~

Allahabad was where I pursued academics. It was also here that Kanshiram made his political debut when, still a novice, he was pitted against the two heavyweights V.P. Singh and Sunil Shastri in an election. Ever since then, I had dreamt of penning a biography of Kanshiram. The main challenge was to maintain a critical distance from my subject; the other was to pass the acid test of reaching out to my readers. The road was difficult but I gathered courage and decided to go ahead. How far I have succeeded is for the readers to say.

This was the start of my uphill journey. Historically, powerful and influential people have penned their memoirs, leaving an account of their lives for posterity. Nehru documented his struggles as well as his ideas for India in his letters to Indira, entitled *Letters to a Daughter*. We have autobiographies by almost all important present-day dalit intellectuals, narrating the travails they faced at the hands of the middle and upper castes. Mayawati, Kanshiram's protégé, too, has written her memoirs and is the subject of many biographies. Kanshiram has left behind nothing—no autobiography, no letters to Mayawati or to anyone else, except a foreword in a book titled *Iron Lady: Kumari Mayawati* (1999) by journalist Mohammad Jamil Akhtar.

Why has his life remained unrecorded either by others or by himself? Was it perhaps because he didn't want to peddle his sorrows or narrate his tale of oppression, using it as a means to uplift the dalits? Was it because he did not see himself as a sufficiently important role model? He never occupied any important government position, so there is no state archive documenting his life and struggles. The Bahujan Samaj Party also possesses no papers about his life in its archives. Kanshiram himself clearly did not believe in recording systematically the various milestones of his struggle. We have only a book by him titled *The Chamcha Age*, where he critically describes the relationship between dalits and Indian politics in independent India.

A portrait of Kanshiram, *Sant Charit Varnan*, was penned by his secretary, the BSP treasurer Ambeth Ranjan. Not unexpectedly, it venerates Kanshiram, portraying him as a saint free of all the worldly desires and vices.

Kanshiram's propaganda leaflets and his various statements to the press are the only media through which he reveals his philosophy. Given this situation, the only sources I could turn to for his biography were his family members, his political comrades, his admirers, his critics, besides the articles about him, his lectures and his interviews published in magazines and booklets. Naturally, these do not make for authenticity of the kind demanded by historians, nor can one totally agree with narratives based on such sources. Nonetheless, I have endeavoured here to recreate an authentic portrait of Kanshiram, based on the available oral and written sources.

Four kinds of sources were used for this study. Firstly, there were interviews with the people who were closely associated with Kanshiram: people like A.R. Akela, a BSP activist from

Aligarh who had collected and compiled all the lectures and interviews of Kanshiram over the years; Ramchet Ram 'Toofani', a seventy-two-year-old activist and a former employee of the department of post and telegraph, who stays in the dalit settlement at Sohbatiya Bagh, Allahabad; Guru Prasad Madan, social activist and writer from Allahabad; R.P. Ram, BSP activist from Raebareli; and R.B. Trisharan, social activist from Basti, UP. My colleague, Brijendra Gautam, also interviewed Kanshiram's brother Dalbara Singh and his sister Sabran Kaur from Ropar, Punjab, Ravindra Singh from Bunga Sahib village, Ropar, and Dr Omkar Mittal from New Delhi. Secondly, there were letters written by Kanshiram to various dalit activists like Dr Devi Singh 'Ashok', an active member of BAMCEF. Thirdly, there were the documents relating to Kanshiram's illness, like the summary of his medical report, Dalbara Singh's letter of appeal to the President of India and leaflets and pamphlets related to the disputes around his illness and death. Fourthly, I consulted a large number of newspapers and magazines like *Amar Ujala*, *Dainik Jagaran*, *Sunday Mail*, *Ambedkar in India*, *India Today*, *Ambedkar Today*, *Kameri Duniya*, etc., for reportage about Kanshiram's rallies and activities.

1

The Early Years

Becoming Dalit

'Manyawar Kanshiram is taller than the tallest peak of the Himalayas. He is determined to obtain justice for the *bahujan samaj* and he is continuously striving to achieve his goal. There is no limit to his efforts. It is due to his backbreaking efforts that today the *bahujan samaj* is emerging as a new force and is shaking the roots of the Brahminical society.'

—Mayawati[1]

Every year on 15 March, Kanshiram's birthday, known as Enlightenment Day, crowds of dalits and bahujans visit Kanshiram Prerna Sthal in Lucknow to offer him prayers, to alleviate their sorrows and to provide them succour. Such is the spell cast by the man whose journey epitomizes his lifelong dedication to the cause of bahujan and dalit upliftment and empowerment. Popularly called 'Manyawar' or 'Sahib' by the bahujans, it was he—a humble, village-bred and educated dalit—who carried forward the battle for social transformation that had saints like the Buddha, Siddha, Nath,

Kabir and Ravidas, and social reformers like B.R. Ambedkar (also known as Babasaheb), as leaders. What Ambedkar dreamt of, Kanshiram transformed into reality, but in his own way. He roused the dormant consciousness of the dalits and gave them a voice. Learning from his travels across the country about the dalits and marginalized communities, he developed a model for politics that would transform their lives. The magic of his words inspired them to wholeheartedly join the fight and they echoed the slogan coined by him, *'Jiski jitni sankhya bhari, uski utni hissedari'*—that their share in democratic politics should be proportionate to the size of their community. His mission made possible what had been impossible until then: the empowerment of dalits and bahujans.

~

The earliest expression of dalit consciousness against caste discrimination is seen in the teachings of the Bhakti saints from the fourteenth to the sixteenth century, especially in eastern UP and Punjab. The sants Kabir, Ravidas and Shiv Narayan and, in the early nineteenth century, Ghasidas, railed against the caste system and spoke about the equality of all human beings. Through the Kabir Panth, the Ravidasia Panth, the Shivnarayani Panth and the Satnami Panth founded by them, their message spread far and wide. Subsequently, the spread of anti-Brahmanism that crystallized as the non-Brahman movement of the nineteenth century across India served to sharpen dalit consciousness. The movement was an organized uprising, challenging Brahman supremacy and hegemony, against caste-based discrimination and brutalities. In Maharashtra, where it first emerged, this movement, essentially for social reform, was spearheaded by the social revolutionary Jyotiba Phule. His vision galvanized and invigorated the dalit movement deeply. One of the early proponents of this anti-Brahmanism, Shivram Janba Kamble, a dalit, was Phule's follower.

The British Raj proved to be a blessing for the dalits. The introduction of compulsory education and recruitment in the army provided them an opportunity to break the caste chains and move up. Dalits began to assert and organize themselves systematically from the late nineteenth century. By the 1920s, various sections of the dalits were up in arms and the movement started gathering momentum. These pioneering anti-caste movements that took the path of social reform fed this dalit assertiveness. The revolt against the Brahman dominance in Tamil Nadu and Maharashtra provided an important impetus to the dalit movement.

Jyotiba Phule, himself a non-Brahman, made the dalits, the marginalized and the downtrodden, conscious of their rights and needs. He kindled the fire of cultural freedom in them. As a pioneer of dalit revolt, he was the first Hindu to start a school for the untouchables in 1848[2] in Poona (now Pune), the citadel of Brahman orthodoxy in Maharashtra. They had unhindered and free access to a water tank outside his house. In 1873, he set up the Satya Shodhak Samaj, to liberate the non-Brahmans (low castes) from the stranglehold of the Brahmans, *purohits* (priests) and the rich. He also fought for equal rights for the peasants, promoted the education of the lowest of the low and, asserting the equality between men and women, wanted to eradicate gender discrimination. Equality and rationality marked his vision of a cultural revolution. He became one of the three mentors of Ambedkar, besides the Buddha and Kabir.

Such a change was needed, Phule pointed out, because the very concept of a nation was getting eroded when its citizens were discriminated against on the basis of caste, of lowly birth. An alternative culture that would emerge as mass culture was necessary. It is another matter that Phule's attempt at propounding such an alternative by way of a non-Aryan universalistic religion could not gain roots, and his voice was not effective beyond Poona, nor did the dalits gain concretely from his movement. But his message was clear.

After Phule's death in 1890, his followers carried his movement to the remotest parts of Maharashtra. Shahuji Maharaj was one such social reformer. He became the ruler of Kolhapur on 2 April 1894 and supported Phule's movement. Fighting for the emancipation of the untouchables all his life, he established schools, colleges and hostels for the dalit and backward castes. This earned him the ire of the upper-caste people. But determined to fight against oppression, he launched a movement for spreading equality. So strongly was he influenced by the works of Phule that in 1911 he became a patron of the Satya Shodhak Samaj that his mentor had set up.[3]

There were other social reformers like Vitthal Ramji Shinde who established a mission for the depressed classes in 1906. He also set up hostels and educational institutions for them. For the Satara Mahars, Bhaurao Patil founded a hostel Sahuji Boarding.

Another reformer of Maharashtra, inspired by Phule, was

Gopalbaba Walangkar. He had retired from the British army. He dedicated himself to the cause of dalit emancipation. Shivram Janba Kamble succeeded Gopalbaba in the movement. In 1902, in a Mahars' conference, at Saswad, Janba Kamble asserted their right, through a petition to the Governor of Bombay, to be recruited in the police and military services. In Vidarbha, Kisan Faguji Bansode, Ganesh Akkaji Gavai and Kalicharan Nand Gavali were likewise engaged in fighting for dalits. These dalit leaders prepared the ground for Babasaheb Ambedkar's ideology to take root.

It was from the 1920s, when Ambedkar came on the scene, that the dalit movement gained a huge impetus. Educated in Britain and the United States, he had a modern outlook and brought fresh insight to the dalit movement, which served to infuse self-esteem in dalits and make them conscious of their rights. His vision of social change through education transformed the dalits and provided them an ideological framework for resistance. He brought modernity, criticality and the zeal of emancipation to the dalit consciousness.

The 1920s were a period of consolidation of dalit power throughout the country. They organized themselves effectively and independently in many parts of India. Among the early dalit uprisings were the Ad-Dharm movement in Punjab, the Namsudra movement of Bengal, the Adi-Dravida movement in Tamil Nadu, the Adi-Andhra movement in Andhra Pradesh, the Adi-Karnataka movement and the Adi-Hindu movement centred around Kanpur, in UP. The Pulayas and Cherumans in Kerala, too, had organized themselves. Pandit Iyothee Thass, a Tamil pariah, spearheaded the Buddhist revival movement, one of the most important movements for the dalits' social and political rights. Essentially non-Brahman movements, they all gave a fillip to dalit protest movements.

The Ad-Dharm movement, founded by Babu Mangu Ram Mugowalia in 1926 at Mugowal village of Hoshiarpur district (Punjab),[4] stressed on a distinctive dalit identity, independent of Hindus, Sikhs, Muslims and Christians.[5] When the Ad-Dharm movement appropriated the figure of Ravidas, it gave the lower classes—especially the Chamars, who later became associated with the Ravidasia movement—a religious and cultural identity.[6] The Namsudra movement, started in 1872, was the first protest against the social authority of the higher castes in Bengal. The Adi-Andhra movement, led by Bhagya Reddy Varma, began in 1917 in the coastal parts of Andhra Pradesh in the Madras Presidency. The Adi-Hindu movement started in Uttar Pradesh in 1922, under the leadership of Swami Achhutanand, also contributed significantly to the construction of dalit identity during this period. The Adi-Andhra, Adi-Karnataka and the Adi-Dravida movements in south India developed ideologies similar to that of the Ad-Dharm movement in Punjab.[7]

Such social-reform and non-Brahman movements significantly exposed the irrationalities of untouchability.

The religious discourse is thus a common feature of all the anti-caste movements. For example, the Satnami movement of the Chamars in the Chhattisgarh plains in Eastern Madhya Pradesh eventually became an independent religious sect (Russel 1916); the [Dravidar] Kazhagam movement of Periyar

EVR Ramaswamy Naicker which created a stir by publicly burning the effigy of Rama and celebrating the virtuousness of Ravana; the Nadar Mahajana Sabha was significant in [Tamil Nadu] (Hardgrave 1969); the Ezhava movement of Narayana Guru which culminated in establishment of a new religious sect called Sree Narayan Dharma Pratipalana Yogam in Kerala (Thomas 1965; Aiyappan 1944; Samuel 1973).[8]

The Adi-Hindu movement in UP wanted to eradicate 'irrationalism, sub-casteism and superstitions from among the depressed classes'.[9] It in fact preceded the Ad-Dharm movement. It also projected the untouchables as being the highly civilized and peaceful original inhabitants of India, rather than the Hindus. Achhutanand argued that 'the Aryan invaders had forced the Adi Hindus to follow Vedic Hinduism and had thus deprived them of their Bhakti religion, which they supposedly practiced before the coming of the Aryans'.[10] Interestingly, Achhutanand, who grew up in a military cantonment, where his father worked, was 'taught by missionaries' and at a young age became well versed with the religious texts.

Like in Punjab, the Arya Samaj enjoyed immense popularity in UP, and was engaged in facilitating the social upliftment of lower castes, through schools, hostels and scholarships it established. It hoped for the entry of the untouchables into 'the Hindu caste hierarchy through "purification" or shuddhi'.[11] The Arya Samaj organized religious discourses and processions. Swami Achhutanand also participated in these activities and strongly subscribed to its philosophy and became an active member of the Shuddhi Sabha.[12]

Over time, the few literate untouchables who had joined the Arya Samaj grew disillusioned with it. They saw through its strategy, which in fact preserved the hold of the high castes over the untouchables, rather than 'eradicated untouchability'.[13]

Swami Achhutanand now turned violently against the Arya Samaj. In April 1924, a five-day Jatav conference was organized in Tofapur village, Meerut district, UP. He was one of the chief guests of this conference.[14] In a lecture he delivered there, he said, 'It is a trickery of the Vedic religion weaved to save the Brahamanical religion from attacks by the Christians and Muslims. Its philosophy is hypocritical and principles lopsided . . . Its [aims] are to declare enmity with Muslims and Christians, enslave the Hindus and put them under the control of the Vedas and Brahmins . . .'[15]

In a largely attended meeting in Delhi in 1922, Achhutanand now announced the name he had coined for his movement: Adi-Hindu. To further its cause, he undertook a tour across India, especially of northern India. He established Adi-Hindu committees at various places through which the untouchables exerted pressure for fulfilment of their rights.[16] In Punjab, this movement started under the banner of Ad-Dharm movement; in the south it took the name of Adi-Dravida movement.

The dalit movement in Punjab was quite strong. There were a number of notable dalit leaders like Sant Brahma Das (Ludhiana), Lala Santram BA (Hoshiarpur), Swami Shudranand (Jalandhar) and Thakur Chand (Jalandhar).[17]

In fact, though Babu Mangu Ram founded the Ad-Dharm movement, the idea was conceived by Vasant Raj, Thakur Chand and Swami Shudranand. All three of them were active in the

Arya Samaj and went out to spread its message[18] even before they had joined the movement. Another important leader was Lala Santram BA. Born in Basti village of Hoshiarpur district in Punjab, his main aim was to bring an end to the social evils prevalent in the society. He wanted to bring down class–caste barriers and therefore founded the Jaat-Paat Todak Mandal in 1922 in Punjab. Through this organization, Santram did exceptional work in raising awareness of the dormant society not only in Punjab but also in various other states.[19] The Mandal was active in arranging and promoting inter-caste marriages.[20]

The Arya Samaj thus played an important part in dalit upliftment. It kindled the fire of social equality in the youth among the untouchables. Juergensmeyer points out that Arya Samaj sponsored organizations specifically concerned with the scheduled caste welfare. And in addition they provided scheduled caste young people access to education through Arya Samaj schools.[21] Not only that, the Arya Samaj sought to bring them back into its fold by offering them 'key roles' in the movement. It went about reconverting the Shudras from Islam, Christianity and Sikhism to Hinduism.[22]

In this context, the Ad-Dharm movement that Mangu Ram launched was like a search for a new religion. He sought social upliftment of dalits through a 'cultural transformation'. He distanced himself from Hinduism, wanting to counter the existing domination of Hindus, and to restore the dalits' dignity. According to Ad-Dharm mythology the untouchables were the original inhabitants of India, who were renowned throughout the ancient world. Then the Aryans came and destroyed it all with so much cruelty and injustice that the dalits forgot their own identity and rich cultural heritage.[23] It is another matter that the followers of Ad-Dharm were persecuted by Hindus and Sikhs and had to often flee to the countryside. Over time, the Ad-Dharma movement gained strength, strongly impacting the lives of dalits socially and politically.

Eleanor Zelliot, veteran scholar of dalit studies, points out that the most pervasive dalit movement led by Babasaheb Ambedkar, curiously reached its climax with a mass conversion to Buddhism.[24] Like the Ad-Dharm and Adi-Hindu movements, it sought a new religion for the untouchables or dalits. Propounding an alternate faith for their community signified the deep dalit hatred for the religious code of Manu. It also reaffirmed their rejection of the Brahmans who were felt to be the root cause of their torments and sufferings. Ambedkar's assertion about overthrowing of 'Hindu' religious ideological hegemony as a necessary condition for dalit liberation is a powerful expression of this understanding.[25]

Notwithstanding the difference in the time periods of the dalit pioneers and reformers and the variance in their dispositions and backgrounds, we have seen there are striking similarities in their understanding of society and the movements they led.

The revolutionary zeal and visions of these pioneers contributed in creating a sociocultural consciousness among the dalits. In this, big and small movements played an important role. They sharpened the dalits' demand for social justice. The resulting political discourse created the space for their mobilization and active participation in democratization of the state. Above all, these dalit assertions, with pan-Indian reach, prepared the ground for Kanshiram in semi-feudal Uttar

Pradesh. He realized the latent aspirations and dreams of dalits there. His Bahujan movement was to become a safety valve for dalit assertions and facilitate the development of a critical thinking for resistance against centuries-old social injustice.

∽

We have seen how Kanshiram left behind no memoirs, personal letters or any such evidence that could tell us about his life (see author's note). What we know of his early years is from the reminiscences of his paternal uncle Bishan Singh and from speaking to his brother Dalbara Singh and sister Sabran Kaur.[26] Dalbara Singh is around sixty years old and wears a safari suit. He sports a small beard, has little hair on his head and does not wear a *pagri* (turban). Sabran is elder to Dalbara and younger to Kanshiram. Ravinder Singh is the son of Sabran Kaur.

Kanshiram was born in Pirthipur Bunga village, Khawaspur, Ropar district, on 15 March 1934, to Bishan Kaur and Hari Singh. Ropar district is now known as Rupnagar and lies midway between Chandigarh and Jalandhar. Khawaspur village is three kilometres away from Ropar district on the Nangal road and has now grown into a town. Kanshiram's ancestral home is half a kilometre's walk westwards from the main road. The local dalits call his house 'Chann Sahib', '*chann*' meaning house and 'sahib' being a mark of respect (see plate 1).[27] Though located in a congested area, the building is recognizable from far off. A blue-coloured statue of an elephant adorning the terrace of the house catches the eye. Dalbara Singh lives along with his wife, two sons and a daughter in the three small rooms downstairs. In the two rooms constructed later upstairs are kept the documents and memorabilia relating to Kanshiram.

Fifteen kilometres from Khawaspur is Pirthipur Bunga, deep in the countryside. Kanshiram's birthplace is two kilometres away on the main road beside a wide canal. In 2005, it was designated as the samadhi *sthal* of Kanshiram by Mayawati. Sabran Kaur lives here now.

Kanshiram's family was Telasingh Ravidasia, *gotra* Chaukri, Ramdasiya Sikh Panth, and came from the once-untouchable Chamar caste. The fifth Sikh guru Ramdas had brought the Chamars into the fold of Sikhism. Despite being Chamars, the family was relatively well off. Unlike in UP, in Punjab the Chamars engaged in agriculture and earned better than they did in the rest of north India. The family owned a fair amount of land, so their main source of income was agriculture. Besides, they had a small tannery, and also took on lease a mango orchard and made money by selling the fruit.

Kanshiram's paternal grandfather, Dheloram, was a retired jawan from Lahore who had set up a cottage industry in tanning leather. He had three sons, Hari, Bishan and Rachan, and one daughter, Haro. While Bishan Singh and Rachan Singh joined the army like their father, Hari Singh took up leather tanning. In addition, he farmed on leased land to supplement his income.

Of Hari Singh's seven children, Kanshiram was the eldest. Kanshiram had three brothers and three sisters. Kanshiram's Hindu name has a story behind it. Apparently, a saint named Kanshiram had been visiting the village when Bishan Kaur was expecting the child. People in the village had great faith in him. They found his discourses pleasing and elevating; Bishan Kaur would regularly go to listen to them. The saint had predicted that Bishan Kaur would give birth to a son who would be a great leader, and whose name would resonate across India, bringing glory to his family. So when her son was born, the elders in the family suggested she name him after the saint.[28]

Kanshiram joined school at the age of five and studied at the Government Primary School in Malkapur, two kilometres from his own village, till class four. Dalit children faced a lot of discrimination at this school. They were seated separately and had a different pot for drinking water. Though their religion is egalitarian, there is a great deal of underlying social discrimination among the Sikhs. Every Sikh is allowed to perform all the religious rituals, regardless of his socio-economic status and caste, unlike among Hindus. But the situation is different when it comes to social interaction. Even today, there are separate cremation grounds for each community or sect among the Sikhs. These are built on land formally allotted by the village panchayat. Kanshiram's family, which belonged to the Ramdasiya community, was a victim of these social inequalities and so the entire family had converted to the Khalsa Panth. As Ramdasiyas, they were not considered a part of the Sikh community. They were treated like untouchables. Following Guru Nanak, the Sikh Panth, also called the Khalsa Panth, was conceptualized as a religious sect that gave due respect to the labouring castes by negating birth-based caste identities. This position was affirmed by the Adi Granth, considered the sacred book of the Sikhs, which includes the verses of Kabir and Ravidas, popular saints of marginal communities and dalits.

Hari Singh, Kanshiram's father, was also influenced by the

social reformist ideology of the Arya Samaj, which had emerged as a powerful force in Punjab at the time. He opposed the cult of Manuvad—discriminatory practices followed by the upper caste, as encoded in the *Manu Samhita*—and strongly disapproved of the caste-based prejudice at his son's school. He moved Kanshiram to the Islamiya School, Ropar, in class five. Kanshiram completed class eight at this school, moving to DAV Public School, Ropar, for classes nine and ten. At Islamiya and DAV schools, because of the presence of the Arya Samaj and Khalsa Panth, caste discrimination was not so obvious. He finally graduated in 1956, with a BSc from the government college in Ropar.[29]

Growing up, Kanshiram never wanted for anything. His family was warm and loving. His paternal uncle Bishan Singh, who was more than ten years older than Kanshiram, wrote in his reminiscences that his nephew was a good-looking, loving boy and his father loved him a lot. When he was around three or four years old, Kanshiram used to demand to be taken around the village on a cycle and Bishan Singh would happily comply. In his childhood Kanshiram loved the sports of kabaddi and wrestling. He wasn't naughty or mischievous and, though serious by nature, he was friendly with everyone. He used to help out with household tasks. Before going to college he would bathe the buffaloes. He'd also pick tomatoes and bhindis (okra) from the fields and sell them in the market. Extremely earnest towards his studies, he even rejected a film role that was once offered to him. But he loved to eat, sometimes polishing off a kilo each of sugar and ghee at one go!

Bishan Singh adds that Kanshiram would fly into a rage when someone was wrongly insulted or humiliated. Once, when he went to a restaurant in Ropar he overheard some landlords, who were also eating there, bragging about how they had beaten up some Chamars working in their fields, to teach them a lesson. Hearing this, Kanshiram got so angry that he picked up his chair and started beating those men with it, smashing all the dishes and plates laid out on the table in the process.[30]

Although the family was fairly well off, Kanshiram never depended on his father for money even as a school boy. To meet his educational expenses he would do various odd jobs during his summer vacations. According to his sister, 'he would take on lease entire mango orchards and, when the fruit was ready for plucking, hire some labourers to fill up sacks with mangoes. He would take sackfuls of the fruit to the market and make a neat profit. Besides all this, he helped his father with tanning leather and also in the fields.'[31] These activities did not deter him from focusing on his studies and, as he himself said, he usually topped the class in every subject. 'Kanshiram also took a keen interest in sports and his sister recalls that he won many sporting awards at school, especially in athletics. Every evening, the young boy would also be seen wrestling along with boys of various castes in the open field outside the village.'[32] Wrestling is a popular sport in most Indian villages, enabling young boys to display their physical prowess, compete with other boys and entertain themselves. 'Tall and well built, Kanshiram would successfully hoist every opponent on his shoulder, remaining undefeated in his village.'[33]

In 1956, after graduation, Kanshiram went to the Staff College, Dehradun, for higher studies and training. While preparing for the examination for joining the Union Public Service Commission (UPSC), he also worked for some time with the Geological Survey of India in Dehradun. The news of Dr Ambedkar's passing on 6 December 1956 came while he was still there. Sri Giani, one of his colleagues, went into deep mourning for three days. Kanshiram, who had heard of Ambedkar, had the opportunity to learn more about his life and achievements from this man.[34]

In 1957, Kanshiram cleared the Survey of India examination but refused to sign a bond, binding him to his job for a certain number of years. He said he did not want to be a 'bonded labourer'. A year later, in 1958, he got a job with the High Energy Materials Research Laboratory (renamed Explosives Research and Development Laboratory [ERDL] in 1960), Poona, as a research assistant.[35]

∼

The widespread presence of the Khalsa Panth and Arya Samaj acted as a check on orthodox Brahmanism in Punjab. Although Kanshiram did face some caste discrimination in his primary-school years, it was never as blatant as elsewhere. His family had become Khalsa Panth Sikhs a long time back and so were not compelled to perform the polluting activity designated to his caste, Chamar. Although the Jat Sikhs did not see dalit Sikhs of the Khalsa Panth as equals, the latter also did not silently endure the oppression faced by untouchable castes elsewhere in north India. In Punjab, Brahmans were not that prominent economically or culturally. It was the Jat Sikhs who constituted the dominant community. The Brahmans were below them in the social ladder. Sikhism never encouraged Brahmanism and the Brahmans could not find a footing in Punjabi society. Kanshiram once recalled in a lecture that as a small boy when he saw how some Brahman boys he knew lived, he thought that Brahmans were a very poor, backward community. Only much later did he come to realize that socially they were way above the dalits.[36]

Recalling his childhood and student days, Kanshiram had once said that while he saw many people around him who were affected by casteism and led pathetic lives, he himself was 'never overtly' a victim of this. Seeing the injustices that these people faced merely because they were poor and illiterate would anger him and make him restless.[37]

About his own family he said: 'All my brothers were physically very strong and always ready for a fight. Our family always rejected helplessness and we were so arrogant that no one dared to touch us.'[38]

Growing up, nonetheless, Kanshiram saw at close quarters the exploitation of downtrodden people, including that of his father. On 2 July 2001, while addressing a gathering of intellectuals at the community hall of the thermal plant in Ropar, he narrated a story from his childhood.

Once, when I was a school student, my mother asked me to go and deliver food to my father who was performing a menial job (*bagaar kar rahe the*) at the Ropar Canal Guest House. I asked her what *bagaar* meant and she replied that it meant serving the high-up officials, which we poor people were supposed to do. I took the food and set off for the guest house. It was intensely hot and when I reached the guest house I saw that my father was drenched in sweat. I could not bear to see his condition so I asked him to rest. But my father said that he could not do this as the senior officer was sleeping inside and he had to constantly tug the rope of the hand-pulled fan to keep him cool. Before electric fans, there used to be hand-pulled fans with long ropes and the rope-puller had to sit outside constantly working them to keep the fans moving. My father was doing that job in return for a small amount of money and explained that if he stopped pulling [the rope], the officer would wake up and punish him. I then told him to keep a small fan in his other hand to cool himself but my father said he would do no such thing.[39]

Kanshiram said that the incident had affected him deeply. His father was no longer a low-caste man after his conversion. Kanshiram wondered about the exploitation of his ancestors, who had been low caste besides being poor. He went on to tell his audience that thirty-five years later when, as a member of Parliament, he stayed at that same guest house, he woke up with a start in the middle of the night and, almost in a daze, opened the door to look out and see if his father was still pulling the ropes of the fan.[40]

Later, when he was working in Poona, Kanshiram saw and understood the plight of dalits in India, which awakened in him the recognition of his own dalit identity. And when he travelled across the country to awaken dalits to fight against injustice and oppression, it was almost as though he was trying to liberate his own father and other ancestors from the exploitation and subordination by the upper castes.

Initially, Kanshiram was satisfied with his job as a research assistant at ERDL and his ambition was to become a senior scientist. But around five years after he had joined the organization, his life took a completely different turn due to one incident. The laboratory used to be closed on Buddha Jayanti and Ambedkar Jayanti but, later, upper-caste colleagues replaced these two days with the days commemorating the birth of Bal Gangadhar Tilak and Gopal Krishna Gokhale. The lower-caste staff members were against this move but no one had the courage to come forward and protest. Only one Class IV employee called Dinabhana, who belonged to the Bhangi community of Jaisalmer, Rajasthan, submitted a written complaint to his superior officer protesting against the cancellation of the holidays on Buddha Jayanti and Ambedkar Jayanti. In response, employees were arm-twisted into submission, and asked to choose between their jobs and the holidays. Afraid of the consequences, the other employees— mostly Mahars of Maharashtra—backed down. Dinabhana alone remained undeterred. The self-respecting Bhana asserted that he wanted both, because both were his constitutional right. He was told to report to the office on Ambedkar Jayanti but he refused to comply, although he came to work on the other *jayanti*s. His superiors accused him of indiscipline and insubordination and fired him.[41]

Kanshiram closely watched what was happening. Seeing Dinabhana leave the office, dejected after being fired, Kanshiram asked him what he would do next. Dinabhana replied that he would go to court against the order. Kanshiram asked if he had enough money to fight an expensive court case. When he replied that though he had some savings, they would be inadequate, Kanshiram assured him that he would arrange the money to help him. He encouraged him to go ahead and file a case. Dinabhana had been misled by Kanshiram's fair complexion and well-built body and taken him for an upper-caste person. He was wonderstruck by this gesture of Kanshiram, who counselled him: 'Rights are to be seized, not requested for. Requests are only granted as alms. All those who fight for their rights, I consider as my own.'[42]

Dinabhana's incident opened Kanshiram's eyes to the Brahmanism embedded in society. He saw the extent to which the upper castes could go to maintain their hegemony. He started following the case personally and stayed up all night to study its intricacies. He also met many senior officers and ministers and apprised them of the case. Alongside, he also mobilized the Class IV employees around this issue and organized a rally to demand their rights.

When the movement reached its peak, Kanshiram also met the then defence minister, Yashwantrao Chavan, who ordered a high-level inquiry into the case. The culprits were pulled up and Dinabhana was reinstated. The order for the cancellation of holidays on Ambedkar Jayanti and Buddha Jayanti was withdrawn. All the dalit employees were delighted and they cheered Kanshiram, hailing him as their hero. At the same time, all the upper-caste officers tried to convince Kanshiram not to get involved with Class IV staff as he was an officer and had little in common with them. Kanshiram retorted that the similarity indeed existed as Dinabhana was a Bhangi and he himself was a Chamar; they both had the same problems and this struggle was not for the Class IV workers alone.[43]

The fault lines revealed by this incident changed Kanshiram's life forever. He began to ponder over questions such as: What is our identity in this country? Who will safeguard our rights? Who will listen to our problems if there is no judge, no officer and no minister of our community? He remained lost at work. Kanshiram now started asserting his identity as a dalit.

Seeking answers and to calm his troubled mind, he started reading *The Annihilation of Caste* by B.R. Ambedkar, gifted to him by his friend D.K. Khaparde. The book had a strong influence on him. The more he read about Ambedkar's life and mission the more a sense of rebellion against the existing social system began to take shape within him.[44]

Initially, Khaparde was close to Kanshiram and became a founder-member of Backward and Minority Communities Employees Federation. He worked for twenty-seven years to make BAMCEF strong and powerful and was even the national president. Khaparde named the dalit castes *moolnivasi*s (prime inhabitants of India). He founded the Khaparde Memorial Publication Trust to raise awareness among dalits against injustice and inequality. Over time he came to differ with Kanshiram, adopting a different path from his, though still working for the BAMCEF. Only after the formation of Dalit Shoshit Samaj Sangharsh Samiti did they actually split.

Kanshiram also read works by great social reformers like Mahatma Jyotiba Phule—for example, *Gulamgiri* (*Slavery*)—and Shahuji Maharaj, all of which made him realize that the Brahmanical system practised for thousands of years was benefiting only a handful of people and victimizing the vast majority of India's population that belonged to the lower castes. Most of those who controlled the administration and governance of the country belonged to the upper castes—constituting barely 15 per cent of India's population—while the majority of the population suffered misery and slavery.[45]

The system that Ambedkar and other social reformers had spent their lives changing had assumed a new and even more frightening form in the context of independent India, and the people whose responsibility it was to realize Ambedkar's vision were now singing a different tune. Gandhi and Ambedkar had 'signed the Poona Pact in 1932, which envisaged reserved seats [in the provincial legislature] and certain other special rights for the Dalits. The Constitution of India, which envisaged justice—social, economic and political—provided certain special safeguards to Dalits.'[46] These benefits, however, had been appropriated by a small layer of the dalit population, which had become a stooge of the Brahmanical system by relinquishing its self-respect and dignity. Ambedkar's national mission had become a weapon in the hands of a few people using it to fulfil their own desires, while the rest of dalit society sank further into the abyss of misery, poverty and illiteracy. While working in the ordinance factory in Poona, Kanshiram came into contact with several educated dalits. He also met a large number of them when he visited the different towns and cities of Maharashtra as a member of the Republican Party of India (RPI). He felt that these educated but prodigal dalits needed to be reminded about the plight of the majority of their caste fellows and consciousness about them had to be raised.

After a thorough study of these works, Kanshiram came to the conclusion that the majority of the dalit population was exploited and suffering because it was divided into a large number of small caste groups, with each group constituting a separate community. None of these small groups had the capacity to fight the Brahmanical system on their own. Kanshiram understood that unless they consolidated themselves into a single bahujan (majority) community, they would fail in staking a claim to India's governance and administration. And in this lay the route to dignity and self-respect.[47]

He decided to launch a mission to consolidate the fragmented lower-caste groups, but soon realized the enormity of the challenge he faced, as caste-based inequality was intrinsic to Hindu society. The change had to be gradual and could be brought about only through a strong organization of dedicated people who were sincere to the cause of uplifting the dormant dalit population and could fight against the inequality embedded in the social system. He now worked to form an organization of educated, employed dalits in Poona, which later became a national-level organization called BAMCEF.[48]

Once he had dedicated himself to this task, Kanshiram took the crucial decision of quitting his job as a Class I officer. Though he did not submit a formal resignation, he stopped going to office and did not even try to claim some money that was due to him.[49]

Besides this, he also decided to break all personal ties. He made several resolutions, which he spelt out in a twenty-four-page letter addressed to his family. Unfortunately, this historic letter has been lost but Sabran Kaur, his sister, recalled what some of the promises were. He had declared that he would never return home, never own a house, and that the homes of the poor, dalits, backwards and minorities would be his home; that he would be free of all family ties and would not have any contact with his relatives, since all dalits were now his relatives; that he would never marry as this would come in the way of his single-minded dedication to the cause; that he would never participate in social gatherings—birthdays, weddings, funerals, etc.; that he would never accept any family responsibility, since the responsibility of all society was on his shoulders; that he would never take up any other job; and, finally, that he would not rest in peace till Babasaheb Ambedkar's dream had been fulfilled.[50]

Kanshiram was the eldest child and, as he had a government job, the entire family had high expectations of him. Sabran Kaur recalls that this letter left them stunned.[51] They could not believe their eyes. They had even accepted a marriage proposal for him with the daughter of a popular dalit Congress MLA.

Still in shock, his mother left for Poona to convince her son to change his mind. She stayed there for two months, reasoning with him and trying in vain to persuade him to accompany her back to Punjab. Bishan Kaur found her son completely changed; he rarely spoke. He would sit up all night reading Ambedkar's books. One day she said to him, 'Kashiya, half the night has passed, now you go to bed,' but he did not stir. Angrily, she snatched the book from his hands and demanded, 'What exactly is written in these books that you stay up all night to read them?'

Lovingly and patiently Kanshiram replied, 'Ma, these books hold the keys to the doors of the country's *satta* [ruling apparatus]. I am looking for the keys.'

Bishan Kaur spent her entire stay trying to convince Kanshiram to give up his resolve but he was immovable. Defeated, she finally went back to Khawaspur where she broke off his engagement.[52]

Kanshiram was true to his word. He did not attend his sisters' weddings, nor did he go home when one sister died unexpectedly. He stayed away from his father's funeral, though he had been informed that his father was on his deathbed. A younger brother performed the duty that was Kanshiram's as the eldest son, of lighting their father's funeral pyre. Occasionally, the family got stray news of Kanshiram from friends or relatives in Delhi or Pune. His sisters waited for him every year when the festival of Rakhi came around and his mother yearned to see him. Kanshiram himself often admitted that his family had numerous complaints against him and objections to many of his decisions, but he was firm in his resolve.[53]

By that time, Kanshiram's name and dedication to his cause had become a byword in political circles. Interviews with his political friends like Ramchet 'Toofani', an activist of the Bahujan Samaj Party, who was seventy-two when I met him in Allahabad in October 2010, made it clear that Kanshiram never spent any public money on himself, using it all for the cause.[54] When he travelled around to mobilize people, he ate at the homes of workers rather than spending public money on hotel food. In this way he also developed a rapport with people at the grass roots and saved money that was better spent to further his cause. Kanshiram did not have any lofty ideas about his own greatness and discouraged people who sought to put him on a pedestal. Once when some people came to the central office of the Bahujan Samaj Party, just to get a darshan of him, Kanshiram told them, 'If you wanted to see me you should have informed me earlier. I would have shaved and bathed and kept myself ready for your visit. Go and look instead at the members of the Bahujan Samaj who need you. Explain to them how the people of the Bahujan Samaj can become rulers.'[55]

At the beginning of his political struggle, around 1984–85, Kanshiram did not have the sort of political support that Mahatma Gandhi, Jawaharlal Nehru, Atal Bihari Vajpayee or L.K. Advani had enjoyed. He also did not receive financial support from any industrialists like the Congress had in the early years, from the Sarabhais and the Birlas. All he had was the support of people struggling against poverty in the villages, city slums and the poorer areas of cities and towns. Consciously also, the BSP members kept themselves away from the media as they had instructions from the party that the media served only Brahmanical interests, that it was a Manuvadi media. None of these people had links with the media, although that might have made things easier for Kanshiram. In the absence of an organization, resources, education and urban support, it was simply his dedication to the mission that carried him forward.

With his band of painstakingly chosen, dedicated comrades, Kanshiram moved from place to place with just a bag containing a set of clothes and some items of daily use. He used to travel by rail in the general compartment, enduring all the dirt, dust, heat and cold. When very tired, he would put his slippers in his bag and use it as a pillow to take a nap.[56]

> He never distanced himself from his workers, sitting, eating and sleeping with them. He dressed simply in half-sleeve shirts and trousers—a striking contrast to Ambedkar, who was always seen in a suit and tie. Kanshiram did sometimes wear a safari suit. When it was extremely cold, Kanshiram would cover himself with a shawl. He also sometimes bought clothes cheaply from markets selling second-hand garments, not shrinking from even those recovered from corpses. He never addressed a rally or meeting of the common people dressed in a white kurta-pyjama—the hallmark of most politicians in India . . . His slippers he himself made out of rubber tyres.[57]

Kanshiram's dedication to his cause was the bedrock of the future dalit–bahujan movement in UP, the state where he chose to take forward his movement, as it had an appalling record of oppression against dalits. His emotional appeal and creative ideas relating to dalit upliftment not only led dalit and bahujan politics in UP in the 1970s and early 1980s, before he established the Bahujan Samaj Party in 1984, but added a new dimension to the dalit movements in India.

2

Seeking the 'Master Key'

From the RPI to BAMCEF

Passionate about uplifting dalits, Kanshiram channelled his entire creativity into achieving that goal. Ambedkar had said that political power was the 'master key' for attaining social equality, and Kanshiram fully concurred. In his own language, Punjabi, the 'master key' was known as the *guru killi*.[1] For Kanshiram, the 'guru killi' became 'an idea for capturing power slowly and steadily, at a tortoise's pace'.[2]

Before Kanshiram arrived on the political scene, bigger political parties used to view dalits as subordinates, to be used as mere vote banks. The lack of consolidation of the dalits under one political umbrella and the absence of an overall dalit consciousness, he was convinced, had led to their remaining divided into separate caste groups. This made it easy for bigger political parties to mobilize the groups individually and garner their votes. Kanshiram's attempt was to make people across the numerous dalit castes aware of their economic, social and cultural subordination and how they could jointly liberate themselves through political empowerment. As he put it:

'It is imperative to produce leadership among these castes. The other parties produce only stooges but we will produce leaders and the day that leadership is produced the dalits will be truly liberated.'[3]

Kanshiram's journey towards this destination was a long and winding one, spanning many years, from the late 1950s to the 1980s, and was divided into four main phases, each phase marking a milestone. The first phase, from 1958 to 1964, was when he started his career, by joining ERDL in Poona. The second phase began when he decided to work for the emancipation of the bahujan community and resigned from his job in 1964. He had joined the RPI around that time and in 1971 he formed the SC/ST/OBC Minorities Communities Employees Association (SMCEA) in Poona. Some years later, it was renamed Backward and Minority Communities Employees Federation. This was the beginning of the third phase of his life. Now Kanshiram worked day and night to make BAMCEF a national-level organization. It took him five years' labour to organize the employees under one roof and he succeeded in establishing BAMCEF as a formal organization on 6 December 1978. In 1981, he formed the Dalit Shoshit Samaj Sangharsh Samiti and a national-level party, the BSP, in 1984. This marked the beginning of the fourth phase of his life. After the formation of the BSP, Kanshiram worked tirelessly for its success in UP. This was the start of the political rise of the bahujans.

∼

Kanshiram had been working for the RPI while he was still in his job. When he decided to devote himself completely to the dalit cause, he also joined the People's Education Society established by Ambedkar in Poona. It was an important learning experience. He saw at first hand the decline of the dalit movement in Maharashtra. The leaders had become opportunistic, greedy and selfish, and the internal conflicts in the RPI had overshadowed its original objective. He found that they either ran study circles or spent their time putting down each other. Kanshiram gave an example of the sorry state the movement had been reduced to at the time. 'Once when he was chatting with the Congressmen Dadasaheb Gaikwad and Mohan Dharia in 1971, two members of the RPI commented that till then [1971] no compromise had been struck between Gandhi's party and Ambedkar's party.' Yet a few years later, Kanshiram pointed out the Congress and the RPI had struck a seat-sharing deal whereby, of the 521 seats in Parliament, 520 were allotted to Gandhi, that is, the Congress, while only one seat was granted to Ambedkar, that is, the RPI. Kanshiram was extremely disturbed by this situation.[4]

He was distressed that the land where Phule, Shahuji Maharaj and then Ambedkar had struggled for hundred-odd years did not even have social democracy. In the absence of this equality and respect people were still fighting on the basis of caste. Ambedkar Jayanti, he found, was celebrated by the followers of Ambedkar, but had turned into a festival and lost its mission. He asserted that he wanted to bring back this element of mission in the remembrance of Ambedkar.[5]

The RPI was formed in 1956 under the leadership of B.R. Ambedkar who, at the fag end of his life, conceived of a different kind of political formation for fulfilling dalit aspirations, bringing together all the non-communist progressive forces under a single banner. He 'visualized RPI as a liberal, mass-based political organization',[6] based on the principles of equality, liberty and fraternity, and purportedly for safeguarding the interests of the dalits. '[B]ut his sudden demise in 1956 left the party unprepared for future hurdles.'[7] Since its inception, the party struggled to spread its influence among the electorate but with limited success; it 'was mostly dubbed as a "Neo-Buddhist party". The Congress was [the] first to exploit such [a] situation. Influential leaders of the RPI were co-opted and an alternative Dalit leadership developed by the Congress.'[8] The road for the exodus was paved by Yashwantrao Chavan, leader of the Congress party in Maharashtra, who not only convinced the RPI leaders to form an alliance with the Congress but also invited some of the senior leaders to join the party. The first to leave was R.D. Bhandare in 1967, followed by K.M. Roopvate and B.C. Kamble.[9] Subsequently, the Congress formed a 'token alliance with the RPI to influence and mobilize the Dalit voters'.[10]

'[T]he rise of parochial, right-wing politics in Maharashtra (Shiv Sena was established in 1966)' gave a boost to the RPI–Congress alliance. They came together in a secular 'alliance to keep the SS-BJP combine out of power'. The RPI came to be mostly treated as an 'object to impress the Dalit voters rather than [as] a representative body of the Dalit constituency'. But, given the RPI's ideological commitment to anti-caste struggle, dalit voters pursuing the secular agenda 'rallied behind the Congress' until recently, when the alliance soured.[11]

By 2008 the RPI was divided into eleven factions, most of them being dominated by the leadership of the Mahars. The party is even more faction-ridden today, as for example in

UP. The party has been unable to carry with it the non-Mahar dalits, besides the backward castes and the Muslims. Forging 'opportunistic alliances', like the one with the ruling Congress party, for the sake of visibility, harmed the RPI. It was seen as a 'stooge' of the Congress and had thus become 'a negligible force in Maharashtra's politics'.[12]

The 1960s saw the emergence of a 'youth culture' in Maharashtra, with the rapid expansion of higher education and the limited number of employment opportunities for educated youngsters.[13] During that time, caste atrocities on dalits were increasing. The dalit youth in Mumbai responded by forming the Dalit Panthers, along the lines of the Black Panthers in the US. 'They tried to transcend caste and embrace all the socially oppressed and economically exploited people [as] "Dalits" and spoke a militant language of transforming society.'[14] Men like Namdeo Dhasal and Daya Pawar, who started the movement in 1972, and others who joined them subsequently, constituted the leadership of the movement.[15] Gail Omvedt, veteran scholar of dalit politics, points out:

[It] was an intellectual movement, which succeeded in establishing new cultural and religious values among the urban dalits. But at the peak of its popularity, [differences arose] between the two most dynamic leaders of the Dalit Panthers, Namdeo Dhasal and Raja Dhale, over the primacy of Buddhism in the movement . . . The movement split into two distinct camps, with one group (Dhasal) adopting the Marxist class perspective and the other (Dhale) adopting the Ambedkarite Buddhist model for bringing change. The movement also faced the problems of unavailability of infrastructural assets, sound political vision and a direct onslaught of militant Hindutva forces. Due to the divergent ideals of the leadership and other related problems, the Dalit Panthers [collapsed] after a half-won battle leaving behind a great legacy of vast revolutionary literature and culture.[16]

Both the RPI and Dalit Panthers tried to capitalize on the roused aspirations of the dalits who had assumed the newly created Buddhist identity, but they overestimated its value on the ground.[17] Here both fell short in understanding the 'dynamics of caste politics in Maharashtra . . . The non-mahar dalits refused the leadership of RPI and Dalit Panthers because of the impractical and self-centred attitude of the mahar leaders. Instead of developing Buddhism as a political philosophy', the latter turned it into an instrument of political ideology and thus 'alienated many dalit castes and their leaders from the RPI'.[18]

Kanshiram observed the entire process from close quarters. After a few years with the RPI, he was utterly disillusioned with its functioning. He realized that it would not be possible to consolidate the dalit community through this party. By then he had begun to organize educated dalits working in government offices all over the country along the lines of trade unions, attempting to bring them together to form a federation that would serve as the money, talent and intellectual bank[19] for the political party he planned to form in the future. A little later, as a precursor to bringing them under his political umbrella, he sought to reach out to illiterate and semi-literate dalits living in rural areas and urban slums and make them aware of their inferior socio-economic and cultural conditions under upper-caste hegemony. He organized seminars and conferences to mobilize thinking in favour of dalit unity, held cycle rallies in different parts of India, sent cultural squads to villages to stage songs and drama with a strong political content, and so on, all in order to unite dalits. Manohar Ate, a close friend and associate of Kanshiram during his Poona days, recalls two incidents which show, firstly, the latter's commitment to the bahujan cause, and, secondly, the importance of the cycle as an important resource to expand his mission. The stories also bring out how Kanshiram's future politics in UP were being shaped in Poona.

There is a statue of Dr Ambedkar in the park in front of the headquarters of the government of Maharashtra in Pune. Many workers of the Ambedkar movement of Pune gather here in the evening. In front of the statue there is a small Irani hotel. The tea here is very famous. Activists hold discussions here over cups of tea . . . In those days, one got all the information about dalit movements from here. On holidays, Kanshiram and I used to always meet in front of the statue and converse till midnight. We would have only about two to four rupees in our pockets. The tea used to cost very little and we consumed a number of cups while discussing. Our pockets used to be empty by the time we returned home.

Kanshiram liked this place a lot. His mind would soar when he sat in front of Ambedkar's statue. He used to think deeply about the bahujan samaj movement. After listening to his ideas,

I used to think that they were impossible to realize. But seeing his confidence I was forced to accept them.

One day, it was 11 p.m., and we were still talking. The Irani owner was going to close the place, so we headed for the BAMCEF office. We had locked our cycles in front of the hotel and I had locked Kanshiram's cycle myself. Reaching there, we found that Kanshiram's cycle was missing. Kanshiram was very upset when he saw that his cycle had disappeared. Tears welled up in his eyes. Agitated, he started looking for it here and there. He even scolded me for not taking better care of the cycle. I told him that I had myself locked it and even showed him the key. Someone told us that cycles were often stolen from that place. Our suspicion fell on the waiter of the Irani hotel. Kanshiram then went and vented his spleen on him, that if his cycle was not found he would report him to the police. The owner of the hotel also started arguing and a heated exchange ensued. After a great deal of struggle the cycle was finally found. It had been stolen by a waiter of the hotel and he returned it after the threat of the police being called in.

Seeing the cycle, Kanshiram's eyes again filled with tears, but this time of happiness. It was as if he had got back something precious that had been lost. But his anger had not abated. He beat up the waiter and took him to the police station. He filed a report and got him arrested. After he returned, I asked why he was so angry over the loss of a cycle. He replied, 'For me this cycle is not just an iron vehicle. It is the most important instrument for enhancing my movement. I try to spread the mission of the bahujan samaj riding on this cycle. That is why I was so upset when it had got lost. When the cycle was stolen I felt as if I had lost my life.' He said this while trying to hide the pain inside him. Listening to this, my heart filled with admiration for Kanshiram's dedication to the cause of the Bahujan Samaj.[20]

Another reminiscence of Ate goes like this:

In 1972 we opened our first tiny head office in Pune. This was probably the first office of the dalit movement. At that time I was working in the RMS [Railway Mail Service]. For my work I had to travel to Mumbai from Pune every day. Kanshiram used to travel with me. A red compartment of the RMS attached to the train became our office. Inside the running train, we would come up with schemes to expand the movement. Kanshiram had a rail pass between Pune and Mumbai. Both of us used to cycle to the Pune railway station, park our cycles there and then board the Mahalakshmi Express. On reaching Mumbai he used to meet other activists of the movement. In the evening we used to board the same train and return to Pune. We used to take our cycles from the stand, eat something on the way, and then go to our office and sleep on a *tripal* [tent tarpaulin] which we spread on the floor.

One day Kanshiram and I reached Pune from Mumbai. At around 10 p.m. we picked up our cycles from the stand. Our office was nearly fifteen to twenty kilometres from the station. We were walking with our cycles and talking. We used to eat at the Vandana Hotel near the Pune station which offered cheap food. That day I had no money in my pocket. I thought Kanshiram would have money and we would be able to eat. But even when we passed the hotel Kanshiram did not stop. I thought that Kanshiram was in the mood for eating mutton and we might be going to New York hotel. Kanshiram loved eating mutton. Whenever he had money to spare, he took me there for mutton. But when we passed New York hotel, Kanshiram looked at me and I looked back at him but neither of us stopped. I understood that Kanshiram did not have money that day and Kanshiram too understood that I had no money, but neither of us exchanged a word till we reached the office. That day we slept on empty stomachs, taking just water.

The next day was my off-day but Kanshiram had to go to Mumbai to meet the activists. He got ready in the morning while I continued to sleep. Picking up his small attaché case, Kanshiram said, 'Ate, I am leaving.' 'Okay just close the door, I want to get up leisurely,' I replied. Kanshiram closed the door and left the office. Barely five minutes later, he returned. He said to me, 'Arey bhai, Ate, do you have some money with you?' 'Not at all,' I said. 'Look around you, you might find some lying here and there,' he said. I knew that there was no cash in the office but even then I checked in the drawers, etc. As expected, I did not find a pie. 'No there is not a single paisa,' I told him. 'At least five paise might be there,' he urged me. I again searched the drawers but did not find anything. 'No, Sahib, there are not even five paise, but why do you need five paise?' I asked him. 'Arey yaar, there is no air in my cycle. I will need at least five paise to get the air filled in the tyres,' he said. I told him to take my cycle. 'I have checked your cycle too. Its tyres also do not have air. Never mind. I will go on foot,' he said. Standing on the terrace I saw Kanshiram running towards the station, hurrying to catch the train.[21]

The educated dalits he approached had taken advantage of the reservation policy, like he had, and were employed in both the government and private sectors. But Kanshiram always held that 'reservation should not be just for gaining jobs but for getting a meaningful share in political participation and through it a control in the power structure'.[22] He mentioned in one of his lectures (collected and compiled by A.R. Akela), that by a rough calculation, in 1971, nearly twenty lakh dalits were in jobs that ranged from posts of high-level officers to Class IV staff all over India. In April 1971, he organized a meeting at the Madrasi School in the Khadki region of Poona. This was attended by fifty to sixty government employees, including D.K. Khaparde, Tambakhe, Madhu Parihar, Bhimrao Dalal and Manohar Ate, who were important dalit activists at the time in Maharashtra. At the meeting, Kanshiram suggested that Ambedkar's dream could be realized by bringing together these lakhs of educated dalit workers, spread across India, to form a non-political organization. Enthused by this idea, some workers joined hands with Kanshiram. He had alongside also begun mobilizing other backward and minority communities.[23] Six months later, the SMCEA was formally launched. The organization held a meeting on 14 October 1971 at the Nehru Memorial Hall in Poona that was attended by nearly a thousand workers. Kanshiram was nominated the president of this association.[24]

In those days, Kanshiram was living in Poona's Deccan Gymkhana area. He would visit various government and private offices each day, trying to motivate dalit workers to join his organization. He ate wherever he was offered food and slept wherever he found place. Most of his meals were at Khaparde's house. He had also set up an office at 142, Rastapeth, just opposite the M. Phule Cotter Gauge School in the city. In 1972, Kanshiram organized a seminar called 'Employees' Problems and Their Solutions'.[25]

The Poona-level organization, however, was just a beginning; Kanshiram and his associates wanted to expand it to the national level. So they formed an association called BAMCEF, with the slogan: 'Become educated, become consolidated, and struggle.'

From the outset, Kanshiram wished to clearly delineate the role of BAMCEF.[26] He remembered what Babasaheb Ambedkar had once declared in a conference held in Agra on 18 March 1956: 'These people for whom I have struggled lifelong are now only concerned in filling up their stomachs.'[27] These words were an affront to his community, Kanshiram felt, and he made up his mind to wipe out this blot. In the BAMCEF conventions, he primarily addressed government employees and motivated them to contribute 2 per cent of their income for the welfare of the society, unlike Ambedkar who had asked them to contribute 5 per cent of it. To give BAMCEF a national face, Kanshiram began by meeting representatives of workers' associations in government offices in districts all over the country. Amazingly, Kanshiram got the total support of the government employees everywhere. He sought help of the employees of Indian Railways, the telephone office and the post and telegraph (P&T) office. Going by train from city to city, he interacted with the workers at railway stations and in dalit settlements. He gave a personal touch to these interactions, according to BSP activist Ramchet Ram 'Toofani', who had accompanied Kanshiram on several meetings in the initial period.

Kanshiram would go to meeting venues with an iron trunk. The trunk contained the portraits of important saints and leaders revered by the dalits like Ambedkar, Ravidas, Phule and Periyar. Since one could not find statues of these heroes at that time, Kanshiram used these portraits to create a visual memory among the dalits of the glorious past of these heroes. His meetings also had a mobile exhibition called 'Ambedkar Mela on Wheels' that contained Ambedkar's photographs, books and posters. Some of these posters contained life sketches of Babasaheb Ambedkar, while some had sketches of violence against dalits—unruly mobs attacking dalits, a teacher beating up a dalit boy for drinking water from the common water pot, a dalit walking on the road with a broom tied around his waist and people throwing stones at him, etc. There were also several pamphlets containing the life stories of Ambedkar, Shahuji Maharaj, Periyar and other dalit and backward-caste leaders. Some of the pamphlets also elucidated the history of the dalits and the exploitation that they had faced over the centuries. All these would be set up on a table and Kanshiram would talk to the people gathered around, showing them the posters and pamphlets. Most of the meetings were held under the shadow of the Ambedkar statues that had been installed in most dalit bastis. Kanshiram would often say in his meetings, 'I have learnt about the experiences of Ambedkar through his books. I have noted them down in my diary, and I have always tried to learn from his bitter experiences.'[28]

He would urge those attending the meeting to be inspired by Babasaheb and learn from his life. Ramchet Ram observed that by the end of the meeting, Kanshiram would invariably have made a place for himself in the hearts of the people. They got inspired and joined him.

An old associate from Nagpur, Govindrao Bankar, recalled that Kanshiram used to travel by third class in crowded trains. Invariably he would be standing, and would eat whatever food was packed for him by his associates. When a journalist once asked him whether he had visited the entire country, he smilingly answered that he had travelled across India not just once but twice and had also visited many of the places a number of times.[29]

On 6 December 1973, Kanshiram organized a meeting at Panchkuian Hall in Delhi. It was attended by thousands of workers including twenty-three from Poona. Here, a course of action was chalked out; it was called 'Pay Back to the Society'. It was resolved that the organization that would ultimately be set up would be non-political, non-agitational and non-religious. Further, that it would be formally established when at least two lakh workers had joined. A temporary office was set up at the residence of Daulatrao Bangar, a section officer in the labour ministry, in Delhi.

From time to time, Kanshiram would also attend the local meetings of BAMCEF, like the Vidarbha departmental workers' meeting held in Nagpur on 6 March 1975. Speaking about his work at that time, Kanshiram later said, 'All 365 days of the year I remained busy as I had [a] huge workload. In fact, I was so busy that I did not even have time to fall ill.'[30] Kanshiram was also fond of reiterating his motto for life: 'If you have the right desire, paths open up on their own; but if it is not right, then thousands of excuses come up.' (*Dil mein agar sahi tamanna hai, to raaste nikal aate hain; tamanna agar sahi nahi hai to hazaaron bahane nikal aate hain.'*)[31]

Kanshiram strove for the next five years to mobilize dalit workers all over the country to join BAMCEF. The activists carried on their mobilizational activities informally, but no formal organization was formed as such. Kanshiram also held numerous workshops to train activists for the organization. Exactly five years after the first meeting, Kanshiram formally established BAMCEF, on 6 December 1978, with its office in Karol Bagh, New Delhi.[32]

Kanshiram's decision to shift to Delhi from Poona had been prompted by the fact that the majority of Chamars, one of the lowest among the untouchable castes, to which Kanshiram himself belonged, lived in north India.

The Chamar belt stretched from Jammu to some parts of north India; in the east from Dhanbad (Jharkhand) to Madhya Pradesh; and there were Chamar *patti*s [settlements] in the south. But most Chamars were under the influence of the Congress since the party had a Chamar leader, Jagjivan Ram. His task was to keep the Chamars under the Congress banner and not be stirred into action by Ambedkar's revolutionary ideas. Kanshiram resolved to weaken this stranglehold of the Congress on the Chamars.[33]

And the BAMCEF was going to be his instrument. Kanshiram now travelled the length and breadth of the country, working relentlessly, not caring about his health. An incident reported in a newspaper at that time shows his dedication to the movement and his desperation to utilize each moment of his life for it. According to the story,

Once, Sahib had to undergo an angiography and was advised rest for twenty-four hours. But he had already fixed a seminar meeting in Pune and had to leave Delhi that very day. The doctors had forbidden travel but Sahib did not listen to them. He was about to leave for Pune with Anant Rao Phule when the doctor asked him to cancel his trip. Sahib then said, 'Doctor, I understand your feelings very well. If this had happened ten years back I would have obeyed you. But today the condition of our community is such that I have to utilize each second of my life. After a great deal of struggle people have started understanding me and so I have to work very fast.' Saying this he left for Pune.[34]

This compulsiveness in pursuing his mission is also affirmed by Anand Rahate, a journalist with *Bahujan Nayak* and a fellow member of the movement. He wrote about Kanshiram in glowing terms saying,

[M]any years after the death of Ambedkar the movement had got a capable leader. He does not take a moment's rest but works non-stop tirelessly. I was with him during the rally held in Kolkata, and I observed that before the rally he went to the rally ground in the evening, and till three in the morning personally inspected all the arrangements—whether the mikes had been fitted, seating arrangements were all right, the hospitality arrangements for the visitors, etc. Kanshiram is one leader who works like an activist. After returning [to his room], he took a blanket and lay down on the sofa and fell asleep without even taking off his shoes. Before sleeping he told me to wake him up at five in the morning.[35]

Even later, as president of the BSP, Kanshiram used to travel by train and distribute the election material himself, like any activist. Another story about Kanshiram in *Bahujan Media*, published from Nagpur, describes how he travelled under arduous conditions in a train, to further his cause.

In the beginning, an election was fought under the banner of DS4. [These were local elections in Haryana and Delhi.] At that time there was no publicity about the election as there were no funds and resources, but the confidence level was very high. Once, Kanshiram had to send posters for the election to a remote village. He also had to campaign in the village. Sahib himself took the bundle of posters and went to the village by train. The second-class compartment was very crowded and he did not get any place to sit. So he placed the bundle on the floor and sat down on it. Because of his hectic schedule, he was very tired and fell asleep there. A pickpocket took advantage of the situation. At the station when Kanshiram put his hand inside his pocket to show his ticket, he found that his pocket had been picked. He told the TC about it. The TC was a good man, and when he saw Kanshiram's torn pocket, he allowed him to go. Kanshiram had to travel fifteen kilometres from the station. Hungry and thirsty, he requested a tonga-wallah to give him a ride but the man refused. It being the rainy season, the weather was very bad. Lightning flashed in the sky. Any moment it would pour. It was foolhardy to travel in that weather, but Kanshiram was not the kind to stop. He covered his head with the bundle and started walking along a footpath.[36]

Ramchet Ram[37] recalled how he had waited at the railway station to receive the great leader in 1980, when Kanshiram came to Allahabad for the first time. Ramchet Ram had helped organize a meeting at the dalit settlement in Rajapur. He added that after the meeting Kanshiram went to Lucknow the same night. From there he went on to meetings at Basti and Gorakhpur. That evening at Allahabad, he initiated eighteen government employees into the movement and entrusted them with the responsibility of carrying it forward. 'He would listen to the woes of the workers and talk frankly with them,' Ramchet Ram said.

Kanshiram found that meeting the government employees in urban slums had many advantages. These people had their roots in the villages and this helped Kanshiram penetrate the rural dalit *patti*s and get a sense of their problems and issues as well. He and his loyal band of followers went to the common areas—fields, banks of ponds, *chaupal*s (spaces for informal and formal discourse), etc. Some charpoys were usually laid out for them there. The people living there would bring them *atta* (wheat flour), vegetables and other things for cooking. This method had three benefits: firstly, a sense of camaraderie and fraternity developed as the community came together on such occasions. Secondly, it did not create a circle of the 'favoured few', whereby others were excluded; and thus there were no hard feelings or jealousy. Thirdly, it was a pragmatic step, so that no single person would have to bear the burden of all the expenses of hosting them. Additionally, small differences among the patti dwellers too were resolved amicably. Kanshiram was the magnet that increasingly drew people who were aware and sensitized.

It is worth pointing out that Kanshiram's presence served to re-energize the foot soldiers of the Nara-Maveshi Movement (NMM) and the few cadres of the RPI, which had lost its base in UP. These scattered forces, highly aware politically and socially, would be later initiated as the cadres of the BSP.

The Nara-Maveshi was a lesser-known but major social movement of the Chamars which swept the villages of UP and Bihar between the 1950s and 1980s. The Chamars had risen up, seeking social dignity. The men refused to dispose the carcass of dead cattle (*maveshi*), which they skinned and tanned, while the women declined to cut the umbilical cords of newborn babies (*nara*), traditional caste-based professions that eroded their self-esteem. The upper caste and other dalit communities had joined hands to crush this uprising. Upper castes like Thakurs and Brahmans and OBCs like Yadavs and Kurmis, who were dominant castes in the village sphere, got support from other dalit castes like Bhangis, Pasis, Dhobis, etc., who were slightly better located in the Jajmani system. The Jajmani system was an economic system where the lower castes performed various functions for the upper castes—known as *jajmans*—and received grain in return. These dalit castes considered themselves to be above the Chamars in the caste hierarchy and so they aligned themselves with the upper castes. In addition, they feared that if the Chamars gave up their caste-based occupation, who would be able to do that job? The Chamars were thus totally isolated in this movement with no other dalit caste willing to support them. The national media also did not report the movement. The Nara-Maveshi Movement was rediscovered entirely through oral traditions and other sources.[38]

Kanshiram's charisma lay in the personal rapport he established with people, whether in the cities or villages. The same magic was found in his letters and notes. All his letters carried notes in his own hand. No matter how small, his personal touch and signature made a huge difference. We see this in the letter he wrote to Devi Singh 'Ashok' on 4 August 1977 on the BAMCEF letterhead. It was about a seminar to be held on 11 and 12 August 1977 in New Delhi. Below the typewritten formal invitation, he added in his own handwriting: 'NB: We want you in Delhi on 11th and 12th, signed Kanshiram' (see plate 8). It was this vision, insight, ability to mingle with people and the immense capacity to inspire them that helped Kanshiram prepare the scaffolding for the BSP.

~

With the BAMCEF office in Delhi, Kanshiram wanted to be close to the scene of action.[39] By the time the organization was formalized, it had over two lakh members, which included 500 PhD scholars, 3000 doctors, 15,000 scientists and 70,000 office staff. It was easy for him to mobilize lower-caste workers to join the organization: on the one hand they were all indebted to Ambedkar for securing their constitutional rights to education and jobs; and on the other they were humiliated and insulted by upper-caste colleagues at their workplace. They were more than willing to unite and fight against this kind of oppression.[40]

The first meeting of the organization was held from 7 to 10 December 1978 in Delhi. A large number of issues were discussed and the organization's objectives were chalked out. Work had already begun on the earlier objective, to 'pay back to society', and the organization then embarked on its chief non-political initiative—strengthening the roots of the dalit community. An intellectual bank, a monetary reserve and a skill pool was created to further strengthen the BAMCEF. A set of educated employees in the BAMCEF formed a group to help other members of the oppressed community. The work of these employees was to arouse their consciousness, help them in times of distress, protest against the atrocities committed on them, organize rallies, etc.

To further the mobilization of the dalits, under the aegis of the BAMCEF, a series of seminars on the topic 'Will Ambedkarism Revive and Survive?' were held in ten major Indian cities between 14 April and 14 June 1979. Their proceedings caused havoc among the so-called Ambedkarite intellectuals because of the way Kanshiram interpreted Ambedkar. At the same time the seminars enabled Ambedkarite youths to accept Kanshiram as their new leader. This was one of the different ways in which he began to successfully restore the ebbing confidence of Ambedkarites.[41]

Besides holding seminars in different places, he would also organize rallies on the themes of the present condition of bahujan samaj and the struggle they faced, and would coordinate the activities himself. He would personally write to guests, inviting them to speak and participate.

BAMCEF functioned through a membership fee of Rs 6–12 and, in times of need, they raised money for regular conferences. In every government office where BAMCEF had a presence, a person was picked as treasurer. He would collect money from the members working there and hand it over to the mandal coordinator, who then handed it over to Kanshiram. The treasurer was appointed by the coordinator, who was in turn appointed by Kanshiram. Apart from collecting money, the coordinator also had to recruit new members and convey Kanshiram's directives to the members from his own mandal.[42] The coordinators at the district level functioned as a link between the mandal and the state levels. The state coordinators, on the other hand, maintained a balance between all the district-level coordinators in their respective states.

After the establishment of BAMCEF at the national level, Kanshiram organized a number of conferences that were attended by members from across the country. They served as a platform for members to interact and discuss various issues facing the dalit community. The first national conference of BAMCEF was held in Nagpur from 2 to 4 December 1979. It was attended by over 10,000 participants, who were very impressed to see the BAMCEF sub-branches called Dattak Grahan (Adoption), BAMCEF Sehkarita (Cooperative) and BAMCEF Bhaichara (Brotherhood).[43] The BAMCEF Dattak Grahan was concerned with the welfare of the rural and poor people. Its work was to adopt a few villages from a particular district and implement the government welfare schemes and policies in those villages. It had to ensure the sincere execution of the budget allocated for the various plans, programmes and projects for the benefit of the rural poor. The BAMCEF Bhaichara was concerned with the migrant dalit community living in urban areas. The work of this unit was to bring together dalits who had migrated to cities and towns—in whatever circumstances, good or bad—and created a base for themselves there. BAMCEF Sehkarita was organized with the intention of encouraging the dalit community, forming one of the largest sections of consumers that do not possess capital, to create an economy of their own.

The conference saw the participation of Jagriti Dasta—a group of people who created awareness about the plight of dalits through songs. They sang of Phule, Shahuji Maharaj, Periyar, Ambedkar and Kanshiram and exhorted the dalits to rise against oppression. Here are a couple of those songs.

Kaam adhure pure karna, Bhim ne sikhaya hai
Padhna likhna gyani banna Bhim ne sikhaya hai
Sahas poorvak buddhimani, bharat maa ke lal vidvaani
Jan hit mein har kaam kiya hai, apne watan ka naam kiya hai
Marg khola gyan ka Bhim ne maano humein bataya hai
Padhna likhna gyani banna Bhim ne sikhaya hai

(Work half-done should be completed, Bhim has taught us
Reading and writing, for becoming wise, Bhim has taught us
Courageous and intelligent, India's erudite son,

Did everything for the welfare of people, did his country proud,
He opened the gates to wisdom, like he has told us,
Reading and writing, for becoming wise, Bhim has taught us.)[44]

Baba Bhim keh gaye humein samjhai
Lo Baudha dharma apnai mitwa

(Baba Bhim exhorted all of us.
Adopt Buddhism, my friends!)[45]

BAMCEF was also given the nomenclature of 'mission' at the conference by Kanshiram, who declared that Indian democracy was nothing more than 'the buying of the votes of the poor with the notes of the rich' and was thus a kind of 'active imperialism'.[46] BAMCEF's mission was to politically awaken the dalits so that their votes could not be bought. He further declared that in order to strengthen the political, economic and social forums of BAMCEF and to give it the momentum it needed, they would have to solicit the support of existing organizations that actively mobilized the dalits.

The second national conference of BAMCEF was held between 20 and 24 November 1980 in Delhi. The site of the conference was named Dr Ambedkar Nagar. Representatives of BAMCEF in twenty-two states presented encouraging reports about their activities at the state and local levels. The third national conference was held between 14 and 18 October 1981 at the Parade Ground in Chandigarh. Representatives from nearly 300 districts attended the conference. Its chief attraction was the presentation of the 'BAMCEF Volunteer Force' to the participants.[47]

The office of BAMCEF was on the top floor of a small building in an alley of a busy marketplace in Karol Bagh in New Delhi. The alley had tiny shops of shoemakers and bands that were hired for weddings and other functions. A board with 'BAMCEF' on it hung outside the office, which comprised two small rooms and whose walls were covered with photographs of Ambedkar, Periyar and other dalit icons. This was where Kanshiram planned the strategy for BAMCEF members. Although BAMCEF was a purely non-political organization, it was the money raised by it that helped to run the BSP after its inception in 1984, covering the monthly expenditures that ran up to nearly one crore rupees.[48]

Once the BSP was formed, Kanshiram channelled all his attention towards its growth. BAMCEF continued to offer critical support to the BSP behind the scenes. Many of the BSP members were also BAMCEF members. Several political leaders of the BSP, including Mayawati, were initially members of BAMCEF, and fulfilled their political aspirations through the party. BAMCEF was also involved in the functioning of the BSP in its early and formative years, helping to maintain its accounts and in deciding the political strategy of the party at the local level.[49] This association did not last very long, however, with the BSP growing more and more powerful. Differences came up between the BSP and BAMCEF, and also within BAMCEF, especially over the role of Kanshiram who remained president of the latter. Eventually, in the 1990s, there was a split in the organization.

BAMCEF was coming along well, but Kanshiram now felt the growing need for another body, a more political one. As BAMCEF members were government employees, they could not stand for elections. He envisaged them as a think tank and support structure for the bahujan samaj. The Dalit Shoshit Samaj Sangharsh Samiti that was now set up, on 6 December 1981, was not a full-fledged political party, but its activities were more political than BAMCEF. 'No government employee could become a member of DS4, which anyway targeted the common dalits to raise their awareness level and prepare them to participate in political activities. The annual membership fee of DS4 was Rs 3, and anyone who did not belong to the "twice-born castes" (kshatriyas, brahmins and baniyas) could become a member.'[50]

From its inception, the DS4 was divided into ten wings, each having a different role or responsibility. The first three were the Jagriti (Awareness), Mahila (Women's) and Chhatra (Students') wings. Of these, the most active was the Jagriti Wing. Its members travelled across villages and small towns of north India trying to sensitize common dalits to their social, cultural and economic condition. They popularized the message of Kanshiram and Ambedkar through speeches, music and theatre.[51] Activists of DS4 travelled all over the country on bicycles with blue flags fluttering above them. Kanshiram knew that unlike the powerful political leaders the bahujan samaj could afford to use only small vehicles. The best way to compete with them he felt was to use vehicles like bicycles, popular among the masses, on a big scale. He was convinced that the two wheels and two legs together could achieve a great deal.[52]

Cycling through the countryside, DS4 activists used to sing a number of songs to rouse the dalits. Kanshiram himself would sing along with the activists. They also chanted slogans like *'Tilak, taraju aur talwar, joote maro inko char'* (*tilak*, a symbol for the Brahmans; *taraju*, or scales, a symbol for the baniyas; and *talwar*, a symbol for the kshatriyas; 'Beat them up four times with shoes / Brahmans, Baniyas and Kshatriyas and all'). When the large group entered villages raising slogans and singing loudly, it electrified the dalits, helping even the poorest and most submissive among them to believe that they could confront the upper castes with the support of DS4. The rallies used to stop at various places en route where they would be accorded a big welcome and be honoured by the villagers. DS4 made great inroads in states like UP, Bihar and Haryana, where the oppression of dalits was the greatest.[53]

There was a major cycle rally organized by DS4 in 1983–84 to mobilize people in the countryside. The first cycle rally started from Kanyakumari on 6 December 1983, the next from Kargil on 18 December 1983, the third from Kohima on 19 January 1984, the fourth from Puri on 28 January 1984 and the last one from Porbandar on 22 February 1984. All these rallies converged at the Boat Club ground in Delhi on 15 March 1984.[54]

Nearly three lakh DS4 activists took part. They had instructions to address 7500 gatherings and make sure that at least ten crore people attended. Cycling along, the activists raised a number of slogans: *'Babasaheb amar rahein'* (Long live Babasaheb), *'Kanshiram Zindabad / Zindabad, Zindabad'* (Hail Kanshiram), *'Vote hamara raj tumhara: nahi chalega, nahi chalega'* (Our vote, your rule: won't do, won't do), *'Jiski jitni sankhya bhari, uski utni hissedari'* (The share in power should be proportionate to the size of the community), *'Kanshiram teri nek kamai, tune soti kaum jagai'* (Kanshiram, you have earned a good name; you've awoken a slumbering community), *'Baba tera mission adhura, Kanshiram karega poora'* (Baba, your unfulfilled mission will be completed by Kanshiram), *'Bharat ki majboori hai, Kanshiram zaroori hai'* (To alleviate India's plight, Kanshiram is necessary), *'Sare desh mein ek hi naam: Kanshiram, Kanshiram'* (The country echoes with just one name: Kanshiram, Kanshiram), *'Ab bahujan ki bari hai—ikkeesvi sadi hamari hai'* (It is now the turn of the bahujans; we will own the twenty-first century), *'Kshatriya Brahman baniya chhod, baaki sab hain DS4'* (Except Kshatriyas, Brahmans and Baniyas, everyone else is DS4), and so on.[55]

When the massive cycle rally entered Delhi's Red Fort grounds en route to the Boat Club ground, the city watched spellbound. Journalists had never covered such a gathering, where dalits and lower castes, all charged up, had come out in vast numbers to assert themselves. The rally, which was addressed by Kanshiram, received extensive media coverage.[56] Large numbers of dalit officers and workers were so moved that they left their work to attend the rally. Kanshiram wanted to prove that the dalits could be mobilized in hordes and he was attempting to make them politically visible.

After this rally, Kanshiram received invitations to address many gatherings. At the very outset he would lay down his conditions before the organizers: there should be no four-wheelers within a five-kilometre radius of the meeting; in proportion to his weight, he should be presented with a bag containing Rs 12,000, and 12,000 people should be present at the meeting, of which 3000 people should be cycle-borne. By then he had become a hero of the underclass, so all his conditions were readily accepted. He addressed nearly 100 meetings in UP, and when the demand for his presence rose further, he started addressing nearly three meetings a day. Thus he addressed nearly 36,000 people each day, also thereby collecting Rs 36,000 for the party. As he told his activists soon after the rise in his popularity, 'I started gaining this experience at the age of fifty. I started late. I am moving late in my life. At the age of fifty I decided to pit the poor against the rich and now that experience has lasted two years. I am now fifty-two years old and now I want people to gather not in proportion to my weight but to my age. That is why I [now] collect 52,000 rupees and 10,000 cycle-borne people.'[57]

Such was the magic of Kanshiram that people were willing to accept this new condition of his. He addressed forty meetings after this in UP. Seven of them had almost a lakh people each. From UP alone, on his own strength and without spending a penny from his pocket, he succeeded in collecting forty-seven lakh rupees. The large turnout of people at the meetings portended the dalits' need for a party of their own, since the reins of the seven major national parties were in the hands of the upper castes. The dalit leaders who contested and won elections from the reserved constituencies had no opinion, freedom or independent identity and were mere puppets in the hands of the upper-caste leaders of their parties. Exactly one month after the cycle rally, Kanshiram would launch the BSP.[58]

However, to test the political waters before launching the BSP, Kanshiram for the first time contested the Haryana assembly elections through DS4 in 1982. He referred to this as a 'limited political activity'. In these elections DS4 obtained

47,499 votes—1.11 per cent of the total votes. This was much better than the performance of three other political parties, the Communist Party of India (CPI), the Communist Party of India (Marxist) (CPI[M]) and Congress (Socialist). He was heartened by the result, since he was not really looking to win a seat. He declared that by 30 June 1983 DS4 would be in a position to form a national party for the dalits.[59]

In addition to its political activities, DS4 also worked to alleviate the social condition of the dalits. One such initiative was organized in UP, to curb alcohol consumption. Activists cycled from village to village to prevent the opening of liquor shops in dalit hamlets.[60] This and similar activities set the ball rolling for the dalits to establish their own political party, which Kanshiram formally launched in 1984. In his own words, 'DS4 was formed to prepare the weak dalits for political battle.' He also challenged the other political parties, saying that while they were free to try and fragment the bahujan community, he also had the right to give the dalits their due by consolidating them.[61] DS4 would almost go into oblivion after the formation of the BSP, but even today, the dalits of UP owe their self-awareness to it. They became conscious of their exploitation at the hands of the upper castes and sought to rebel against it politically once the BSP came into being.

One of the most significant events of Kanshiram's political life during these years was his meeting with Mayawati. She was to change the face of Indian politics by becoming the first woman dalit chief minister of one of the largest states of the country, UP—acknowledged as being the most divided of all states along caste and gender lines. And, as the president of the BSP, Mayawati was elected chief minister four times, achieving this each time by overturning the established electoral traditions of the state.

Like Mayawati, there were thousands who left their jobs, studies, homes and families and entered the movement, putting at stake their youth and joined BAMCEF, DS4 and eventually the BSP. She, too, joined BAMCEF in 1980, some three years after first meeting Kanshiram. Several other activists like Master Ram Samujh, Raj Bahadur, Balihari Choudhry, Dr Masood Ahmad, B. Ram, D.K. Khaparde, Ram Khobragade, Manohar Ate, Aman Kumar Nagra, Satnam Singh Kaith, Sardar Bhag Singh, Ramadheen Ahirwar, K.R. Shashi, Tejinder Singh Jhalli, Ramchet Ram 'Toofani' and Sunil Chittor were closely associated with the movement at that time. Selflessly they strived alongside Kanshiram. Among them were people who came out of the Nara-Maveshi Movement. Some had also worked for the RPI during 1956–70. When Kanshiram came, they associated themselves with him.

Kanshiram was looking out for a dalit with local credentials, preferably from the Chamar sub-caste, whom he could groom to carry forward his movement in UP, when he discovered Mayawati. He was convinced that this state held the key to his ultimate success, since society was deeply feudal here and dalits and backward castes were severely at the receiving end of oppression; if this state could be brought under control, the whole country would follow. He was aware, however, that he himself was not the best public face for such a mass movement in UP since he would always be seen as an outsider from Punjab. In Mayawati, Kanshiram found his ideal candidate, since she belonged to UP, was from the Chamar sub-caste and was extremely aware of dalit issues and the inequities of the caste system. She was a great admirer of Babasaheb Ambedkar and abhorred the social order that had humiliated people like her in numerous overt and covert ways. She had been deeply involved in radical dalit politics since her early youth, and when he first saw her, Kanshiram was impressed by her feistiness and excellent oratorical skills.

Kanshiram's first meeting with Mayawati took place in Delhi in 1977, when she was barely twenty-one years old. At the time, she was teaching at a government primary school, studying law at Delhi University and preparing for the Indian Administrative Service (IAS) examinations. She was also active in dalit politics and had already acquired a reputation as a fiery speaker who had the gift of 'calling a spade a shovel'.[62]

Describing the meeting, Mayawati later said:

My first meeting with Manyawar Kanshiram took place at the end of 1977 in Delhi. It so happened that the Janata Party had formed a government at the centre and Morarji Desai was the prime minister. Before the government was formed and the elections had taken place, the leaders of Janata Party had projected Babu Jagjivan Ram as the potential prime minister. After the elections, when the party secured the mandate, however, the casteism entrenched in the minds and hearts of the leaders led to Babu Jagjivan Ram being overlooked and

Morarji Desai being selected as the prime minister. As a result, the Scheduled Caste community of the country was extremely angry and upset with the party and started complaining that it was practising casteism. In order to dispel this notion, around September 1977, the Janata Party organized a three-day conference in Mavlankar Hall in Delhi called Jati Toro Sammelan (Break Caste Conference). Many eminent people had been invited to speak at the conference including Morarji Desai, Raj Narain and Charan Singh. In those days I was very fond of debating and participated in all debating events, usually speaking against the government. It was my record that I always stood first. Since I also used to speak on the occasion of Babasaheb's and Buddha Jayanti, the Janata Party invited me to speak at the conference on behalf of the All India Ladies Youth and Student Association. In my speech I lambasted the party, especially their leader Raj Narain. At that time Manyawar Kanshiram was in Pune but some members of BAMCEF were in the audience. My attack on Raj Narain was widely reported in the newspapers, which Manyawar Kanshiram read after his return to Delhi. When he asked the activists of BAMCEF about me they told him that I belonged to their own community. They also told him that I would soon be speaking at a debate in Karol Bagh and he could hear me there. Kanshiram came for the programme and was very impressed when he heard my speech. After the speech he spoke with me in great detail for almost two hours.

The next day Kanshiram came to my house with a few of his companions. It was eleven in the night. At that time Budh Nagar, Inderpuri, the place where we lived, did not have any electricity connection. Since I was a first-year student of law I was studying by the light of a lamp inside my room while the rest of my family was asleep. He knocked at the door of our house and woke my parents. He told them that he was Kanshiram, the president of BAMCEF and wanted to invite Mayawati to speak at some functions in Mumbai and Pune on behalf of the All India Ladies Youth and Student Association. My father replied that I was still studying. Kanshiram insisted on speaking to me. I had an inkling that someone important had come so I opened my door and Kanshiram entered my room. He asked me what my future plans were and I told him that I wanted to become a district collector after clearing the IAS exams, as my father had told me that it was a very important post. Kanshiram, however, said that I had good leadership qualities and if I wanted I could lead my community members and do a great deal for them. He then explained at great length about bureaucracy and politics. He also said that bureaucracy moves hand in hand with the government and if the government was of some other party then I would be able to do nothing for my community as a bureaucrat, even if I wanted to. I understood what Kanshiram was trying to tell me and immediately decided that I would no longer try to become a district collector but would work for my community and bring about social change.[63]

Kanshiram would now become her guru. Their relationship, which spanned two decades, was unique. Kanshiram himself was never interested in becoming the chief minister, but he mentored and tutored her. Mayawati acknowledged that it was because of Kanshiram she evolved into the skilled politician that she is today. In an interview she once said, 'I acknowledge Manyawar Kanshiram as my guru. He is much older than me. He entered politics much before me and he is closely associated with this movement. His blessings are with me and I am with him heart and soul. I continuously learn from him.'[64] She went on to say:

Since the last few years I have been constantly with him. It was because of the inspiration he received from Dr Ambedkar's books that Manyawar Kanshiram entered the social and political domains [of the struggle for power]. I have been in constant touch with him for many years now. I have found that he is highly sensitive about the oppressed bahujan samaj. The exploitations faced by the bahujan samaj fill his heart with pain and sorrow. He has an intense hatred for the Brahminical system. He feels terribly upset and agitated at the condition to which the bahujan Samaj has been reduced by a mere 15 per cent of the population, comprising brahmins, banias and big landlords . . . When he sees a helpless human being, it arouses his intense anger. I have seen him several times roundly scolding people who display helplessness. But behind this scolding there is a pure emotion. He wants that each person belonging to the bahujan samaj should attain such a high standing that no one has the courage to look at him with contempt.[65]

At the end of the interview Mayawati voiced her innermost desire, saying that she would be happy to see him as the prime minister of the country. 'If he becomes the prime minister of this country he will prove to be excellent,' she said, adding that it would chart a new chapter in the history of the country.[66]

Kanshiram had strong faith in Mayawati whom he groomed from the very beginning to become his second in command in the future, as the leader of the BSP and the chief minister of UP. The reminiscences of a journalist in the daily *Haribhoomi*, 10 October 2006, recorded Kanshiram's words at the time of declaring her as his heir. He had apparently said to one of his close associates, 'Mayawati did such a great thing by going around UP on a cycle to disseminate the BSP's message among the people that I can never forget it. That too at a time when there was not even a remote chance of the BSP winning the elections. The young girl cycled from Bulandshahar to Bijnore and was constantly by my side. If she had not worked hard along with me, I would never have been able to take the BSP ahead.' He added, 'It is Mayawati's responsibility to create a bahujan samaj, now that the BSP has been formed.'

Today Kanshiram's party is firmly in the saddle in UP and Mayawati, though no longer chief minister, is a force to reckon with in the state and, indeed, in national politics in a coalition era. She has been chief minister four times and her party swept the polls in 2007, which more than vindicates Kanshiram's judgement of Mayawati's leadership potential when she was only in her early twenties.

3

The Chamcha Age

An Agenda beyond Ambedkar

Kanshiram's stint with the Republican Party of India, as we have seen, was an important learning experience. The lessons he gained became the impulse for the ideology of the BAMCEF and DS4 and subsequently the basis for a book he penned in 1982 called *The Chamcha Age: An Era of the Stooges*. The book became the ideological foundation for the BSP, which he was to form later. Not just a critique of the Dalit movement till then, the book by implication also brought to the fore Kanshiram's fresh take on Ambedkar's ideas.

The Chamcha Age was a scathing attack on scheduled caste politicians who had sold out their community's interests in favour of personal advancement. According to Kanshiram, these were the chamchas (stooges, agents or tools) created by mainstream political parties to oppose and compete with the genuine champions of the dalit cause. All dalit leaders, including old-timers like Jagjivan Ram and Kanshiram's contemporary, Ram Vilas Paswan, were encompassed within this definition of chamcha. In addition to identifying the various kinds of chamchas, the book also outlined a plan for future action, both short-term and long-term, to challenge the caste system.

Of the various subjects covered in the book, the most significant was his description of the historic truce between Ambedkar and Gandhi called the 1932 Poona Pact. Ambedkar and Gandhi had totally disparate ideas about tackling the issue of untouchability. When Ambedkar sought separate electorates from the British, to safeguard the political interests of the untouchables, Gandhi went on a fast unto death to oppose this. Their compromise resulted in the Poona Pact, signed on 24 September 1932, whereby joint electorates were granted. This system shaped the electoral method by which reserved constituencies were defined. Ambedkar had sought the introduction of reservation for untouchables in jobs, education and scholarships through the pact, but Kanshiram felt that Gandhi's insistence only skewed the electoral process, as it made the election of a reserved candidate dependent upon the dominant-caste vote, defeating the very purpose for which reservation had been secured.

In fact, Kanshiram chose to release *The Chamcha Age* on the eve of the golden jubilee of the Poona Pact which the Congress was planning to celebrate with great fanfare. Contrarily, the book strongly condemned Gandhi who, by threatening Ambedkar with a fast unto death, blackmailed the dalit leader into giving up his demands. Kanshiram claimed that this single development had sealed the political fate of the scheduled castes and given birth to the 'chamcha age'.

He strongly criticized the people who glorified Gandhi and his successors in the Congress and accused the party of being the main enemy of the people. Since there was no constituency in India where dalits formed more than 30 per cent of the electorate, dalit candidates had to depend on mainstream political parties to attract caste Hindu and other voters. Thus the chances of victory for scheduled caste candidates depended heavily on their amiable relationship with individual upper-caste leaders. He added that all this had been designed by the Brahmanical order in such a way that only stooges could emerge. He was convinced that as and when India's high-caste Hindu rulers felt the need for them, or when the authority of the upper castes was threatened by genuine dalit leaders, chamchas or stooges had been brought to the fore.

After the Emergency of 1975, two important dalit leaders of north India, Jagjivan Ram of the Congress and Ram Vilas Paswan, were working to create a space for dalits' participation in the state. Anti-Congressism, so dominant at the time, had overtaken the dalit agenda in the politics of not only these two leaders but also, generally, in government. Jagjivan Ram, an eminent dalit politician, had been Union minister in the Congress government several times, but he now became critical of the excesses committed by it during the Emergency. Quitting the government in 1977, he founded the party Congress for Democracy (CFD), contested the general elections held the same year in an alliance with the Janata Party and later merged with it. Having been a key advocate of dalit interests, his departure cut into the support that the elite among the dalits had traditionally extended to the Congress. Again the Janata Party used him to woo the dalits, but he failed to become the prime minister of the new government. The idea of a dalit prime minister was simply not acceptable to some of the conservative politicians in the Janata Party coalition. (Interestingly, the Congress, too, had never made Jagjivan Ram the prime minister, which had been a long-held dream of the dalits.) This further added to the growing disillusionment of the dalits, especially the Chamars of north India (the caste to which Jagjvan Ram belonged).[1]

Ram Vilas Paswan, who emerged on the political scene in north India just before the Emergency, was a follower of Raj Narain and Jayaprakash Narayan. Paswan became the general secretary of the Lok Dal in 1974. When Emergency was proclaimed, Ram Vilas Paswan was arrested and spent two years in jail. On being released in 1977, he became a member of the Janata Party and won the election to Parliament for the first time on its ticket. He made a world record for winning an election by the highest margin. In 1983 he tried to prove himself as a dalit leader when he established the Dalit Sena, an organization for dalit emancipation and welfare. But Paswan was unable to bring dalit problems to the fore since he did not try to mobilize dalits at the grass roots.

It was a time of growing atrocities on dalits, especially in the countryside. The failure of the Indian state to provide protection also enhanced the sense of disillusionment among dalits. Incidents like the massacre in Belchi sharpened their disenchantment with mainstream politicians.

On 27 May 1977, just after the establishment of the Janata Dal government at the Centre, eleven dalit landless labourers in Belchi village in Patna district were burnt alive by Kurmi landlords. In 1980 in the Parasbigha village of district Gaya in

Bihar, a dalit tola was surrounded and burnt and many dalits were shot dead. Fourteen dalits died . . . Nineteen days after this incident, in Pipra village of Punpun thana near Patna, many dalits were massacred by Kurmi landlords who set a dalit basti on fire and shot dead thirteen dalits. Even as late as 1986, twenty-two landless dalit labourers were shot dead by the police in the Arval village of Bihar.[2]

Such incidents made the dalits feel insecure since there was no dalit leader to look after their interests. It was left to Kanshiram, who appeared on the scene around that time, to effectively fill the political vacuum.

There are several instances, cited by K.C. Das in his book, where Kanshiram criticized Jagjivan Ram and other 'stooges'. 'According to Kanshiram, the popular dalit figure Jagjivan Ram, who had been in the Congress party before moving to the Janata Dal, was not a leader but a stooge.'[3]

In December 1989 Kanshiram said, 'Later on the stooge wanted to become prime minister but no one will make a stooge the prime minister.'[4] Later, in April 1992, he said, 'Babu Jagjivan Ram was created by the forces of status quo and he was dropped by the forces of status quo.'[5]

Speaking in 1992, Kanshiram was also critical of Ram Vilas Paswan: 'Paswan is known among his own community people as "Thakur ka Thappa". When the Thakurs want Paswan to be elected, they do not allow Scheduled Caste people to vote; they go and stamp five or six lakh votes in favour of Paswan.'[6]

In this and other ways, *The Chamcha Age* exposed all the shortcomings of the post-Ambedkarite dalit leadership and emphasized that the pathetic condition of dalits in India even after so many years of Independence was chiefly due to the leaders themselves, who were mere puppets in the hands of the Congress.

~

In *The Chamcha Age**, Kanshiram first clarifies the meaning of the word 'chamcha'. He traces its origin to the terms 'tools of the Hindus', 'agents of the Hindus', and so on, which Ambedkar had used in the context of the scheduled caste officers. He writes:

The political scenario post-Independence had led to a proliferation of these agents and tools. Since the death of Babasaheb Dr Ambedkar in 1956, the phenomenon of generation of agents had increased to such an extent that such people are found not just in the political arena but in each aspect of human life and also in different relationships. Earlier these tools were only perceived by Dr Ambedkar's discerning eyes and after him the dalit intellectuals could distinguish them, but today these agents have become so all-pervasive in our everyday lives that any common person can recognize them in a crowd. The common people have their own vocabulary and in their lexicon tools, agents and so on are known as 'chamcha'. In this

---

* The Chamcha Age *was written in English by Kanshiram and published by him on 24 September 1982. It was later reprinted by Samta Prakashan in English in 1998. The Hindi translation by Michael Moses was published by Samyak Prakashan in 2008. These passages are free translations into English by the author from the Hindi edition and edited by him.*

book, I have decided to use the colloquial vocabulary of the common people and I believe that when we are struggling for the welfare of the common people it would be appropriate to use the informal vocabulary used by them. A parasite is a person who is not active himself but needs another person to be active.

This person always uses a 'chamcha' or stooge for his personal benefit or for the benefit of his own community—and this is always harmful for the stooge's community. In this book we will use the word 'chamcha' more than the words 'agent' and 'tool'. This will be more suitable in the Indian context and for the common person, since along with its meaning, it is also expressive in terms of its connotation. 'Chamcha', 'stooge', 'agent' and 'tool', all these words are almost synonymous but they differ slightly in connotation.[7]

Kanshiram further elucidates why it is necessary to create stooges. He says:

Any tool, agent or stooge is created so that he can be used against genuine and actual struggle. The demand for stooges arises only when a genuine struggle exists. When there is no struggle or revolution and neither is there any fear of a revolution, there is no demand for stooges. As we have seen in almost the entire country since the beginning of the twentieth century, the dalit community has been protesting against untouchability and the unjust social system. Initially they were ignored but later when the genuine leadership of the dalits became strong and independent, they could no longer be ignored. At this point the upper-caste Hindus felt the need for creating stooges against the dalit community. During the Round Table Conference, Dr Ambedkar fought for the dalits in the most trustworthy manner. Till that time Gandhi and the Congress believed that the dalits did not have a genuine leader who could fight for them. Around 1930–31 during the Round Table Conference, despite opposition by Gandhi and the Congress leaders the viceroy took the historic decision to create an independent electorate for the dalits on 17 August 1932. Between 1930 and 1932, for the first time Gandhi and the Congress felt the need for stooges.[8]

Narrating the history of the dalits in India, Kanshiram writes that no community anywhere in the world has faced the kind of oppression faced by the untouchables of India:

Even the oppression and humiliation of slaves, Negroes and Jews was nothing compared to that of the untouchables of India. When we think of the inhuman behaviour of one human being towards another there is no example like the orthodoxy of the Hindus against the untouchables. The untouchables of India have been the most miserable slaves for centuries. There is such a poisonous element within Brahmanism that it killed whatever desire there was of protesting against the worst kind of injustice. The period of misery suffered by the untouchables of India over centuries can be said to be the dark ages for them. During British rule the untouchables had a long association with Western education and civilization. This ignited the feeling of rebellion within them. This is why we could find instances of untouchables standing up to protest against the unjust social system since the beginning of the twentieth century. Since 1920, Dr Ambedkar had emerged as their leader and messiah and within ten years he raised the issue of the dalits at two Round Table Conferences in London. He fought successfully for the dalits in both the conferences and obtained various rights for them, especially the right to a separate electorate. On introspection about that period we can safely say that Dr Ambedkar was leading the dalits from the dark ages to the age of enlightenment. But unfortunately this did not happen because just before reaching the age of enlightenment the dalits slipped and fell and lost their way into the Chamcha Age.[9]

Kanshiram goes on:

[B]etween 1931 and 1932, Gandhi and the Congress together systematically destroyed Ambedkar's efforts to take the dalits from the age of darkness to the age of enlightenment. However, Gandhi and the other Congress leaders were together conspiring for something different, as Gandhi wanted to run society based on the caste-based social system in which each person performed his dharma as laid down in the caste system. By doing this he wanted to keep the untouchables mired in the dark ages just as the *chaturvarna* [four-strata division of society] had kept them for centuries.[10]

What Kanshiram wanted to underline was how negligible the representation of untouchables or dalits in politics had become. The ratio of untouchables to upper castes was pushed back to 1:10 in some places and 1:15 in others. That was why Gandhi agreed to provide two stooges instead of one true and sincere representative.' (The 'two stooges' here refers to two members nominated by Gandhi who Kanshiram believed were not real representatives and were not committed to the emancipation of the dalits.) But how could even a large crowd of stooges be a substitute for one single representative?

Kanshiram also believed that the demand of the upper castes for stooges had declined in the previous five decades when there was no true leader of the dalits, but it arose once again when a true leadership of the dalits emerged in the form of BAMCEF and DS4, causing a conflict between the oppressed and the oppressors. In his estimation, these organizations would not need more than ten years to put a final end to the chamcha age.

The book also listed and defined the different kinds of chamchas or stooges among dalits, particularly in the Congress and the other mainstream parties, based on a sociopolitical break-up of oppressed communities. These dalit political activists and leaders held an extremely subordinate position in the mainstream parties even though they were instrumental in mobilizing the dalit vote for them. For Kanshiram this classification was useful for evolving his various political strategies. He termed the chamchas as follows: a) caste- and community-based chamchas; b) political stooges; c) ignorant stooges; d) enlightened or Ambedkarite stooges; e) stooges of the stooges; and f) stooges in foreign countries.

A. Caste- and community-based chamchas: The stooges based on caste and community can be divided into four types.

1. Scheduled Castes—Reluctant Stooges: The entire

struggle of the dalits during the twentieth century shows that they were trying to enter into a bright era but Gandhi and the Congress pushed them into the chamcha yug. Even today the dalits suffer pain and misery, and although they have not accepted the prevailing situation, they are unable to come out of it. That is why they could be classified as reluctant stooges.

2. Scheduled Tribes—Initiated Stooges: The Scheduled Tribes of India are not known for their struggle during the country's age of constitutional and modern development although they also started struggling to assert their identity and claim their rights after 1940, along with the Scheduled Castes. According to the Constitution, they, too, were granted all the rights given to the Scheduled Castes. However, they obtained all these rights as a result of the struggle of the Scheduled Castes. The Scheduled Tribes do not yet have any representation in the Central ministry but they appear to be satisfied with whatever they have obtained. The worst thing is that they still harbour the illusion that their oppressors and exploiters are their real well-wishers. That is why they can be given the name of initiated stooges because they have gained entry into the chamcha age.

3. Other Backward Castes—Aspiring Stooges: After a long struggle the Scheduled Castes and Scheduled Tribes were granted recognition and rights. As a result, some of them saw improved conditions beyond their means and power. This is evident in their education, acquisition of government jobs and in their political empowerment.

This development within the Scheduled Castes led to a rise in the aspirations of the Other Backward Castes but till then they had been unsuccessful in fulfilling them. In the recent past they knocked at every door but in vain. During the Haryana elections of June 1982, of a total of ninety seats they got only one ticket from the Congress and one from Lok Dal . . . Apart from a few places, especially in the south, they were seen to be struggling to get tickets, mostly unsuccessfully, like in Haryana. In fact, most of them aspired for the same benefits as those obtained by the SCs and STs, and their behaviour leads us to classify them as fast-moving, aspiring stooges.

4. Minority—Helpless Stooges: According to the 1971 census, the religious minorities in India comprised 17 per cent of the population. Before the British left India they had obtained their share based on their relative proportion, but after Independence they became dependent on the ruling religious group of the country. Frequent communal riots kept the Muslims standing on their toes, the Christians became vulnerable, the Sikhs were fighting hard for a respectable identity, while the Buddhists were not even able to stand upright. All this proved that the minorities of India were helpless and vulnerable stooges.

B. Political Stooges: Dr Ambedkar had described the helplessness of SC/ST legislators and MPs before 1945 in his book *What Have the Congress and Gandhi Done to the Untouchables?* and after that we witnessed their rapidly worsening condition. At that time there was only one political party of the upper castes which had created stooges

75

from among the Scheduled Castes. But today, at the national level there are seven parties and at the state level there are several parties which are creating stooges not just from the dalits but from all the exploited and oppressed communities of India. Today all the parties dominated by the upper castes are sucking up the juice and throwing out the pulp for the eighty-five exploited, miserable communities. These political stooges have worsened their condition and this aspect cannot be ignored by those who are keen to combat the major problem facing us.

C. Ignorant Stooges: All oppressed Indians, especially the dalits all over India, were struggling against injustice but most of the struggles were local and regional. In a country of India's size and population, these struggles were so scattered and isolated that they never seemed like being of a single community. The struggling people were aware only of their own struggles and not of those being carried out by their brothers in other places. From this fact about the inefficiency of the dalits, it could be understood that a major section of the dalits were ignorant of the lifelong struggle carried out by Dr Ambedkar for their welfare. Even today, nearly 50 per cent of the Scheduled Castes are unfamiliar with the life and work of Dr Ambedkar. This ignorance of the dalits has been fully exploited by the upper castes, enabling them to easily use them as stooges. These kinds of stooges can be classified as ignorant stooges.

D. Enlightened or Ambedkarite Stooges: Among all the stooges from the oppressed communities the most tragic condition is that of the enlightened or Ambedkarite stooges.

Dr Ambedkar had himself indicated how in the struggle of the dalits his own role vis-à-vis that of Gandhi's had led the ignorant dalits astray. One could understand the behaviour of the ignorant masses but what about the enlightened people, especially those made wise and knowledgeable by Dr Ambedkar himself? These enlightened individuals should definitely have known about the various roles played by Gandhi and Ambedkar.[11]

Kanshiram adds:

It was a matter of great surprise that nearly one year back [1981], on 24 September, a committee of these enlightened people had been formed in Poona to celebrate the golden jubilee of the Poona Pact. The initial committee included the secretary of the RPI, officials of the Dalit Panthers and some members of Dr Ambedkar's enlightened brotherhood. After learning about the roles of Dr Ambedkar and Gandhi, these enlightened people should not have even thought of celebrating the golden jubilee of the Poona Pact, but these Ambedkarite stooges not only did so but spent a year preparing for the celebration. The worst part was that those who had condemned the Poona Pact in 1946, under the leadership of Sri R.R. Bhole, on the suggestion of Dr Ambedkar, were themselves involved in the celebrations. Apart from this incident, because of their overall behaviour and attitude over many years and their consent to become stooges in exchange for a few benefits, they could be labelled as enlightened stooges or Ambedkarite stooges.

E. Stooges of the Stooges: The democratic structure of our country based on a mature electorate forced the ruling elite to create stooges from among the exploited and oppressed communities. We could see the emergence of plenty of stooges because of these political activities. The value of these political stooges could be understood from their standing in their own communities. The stooges, active on a large scale, were unable to get anything done on their own steam and so, because of their loyalty to the upper castes and to serve them properly, they were also forced to create their own stooges. Apart from this, the continuously rising number of educated and employed SCs and STs was a fertile ground for creating such stooges. The intelligent people from among these educated and employed people were always ready to become stooges of political stooges to obtain benefits from them. These stooges of the stooges increased in number with the passage of time.

F. Stooges in Foreign Countries: Although there had been no independent struggle by the exploited Indians, the number of stooges had declined in the past few years and touched a very low figure in the assembly and parliamentary elections of 1980. This small figure led some opportunistic untouchables living abroad to consider it to mean a shortage of stooges. In order to fill this vacuum, many selfish and opportunistic untouchables came to India and one gentleman came from America to Delhi to become a stooge of the ruling party and was seen hovering around the party members. After living in India for a long period, he became disillusioned and went back to New York to become a member of the Congress(I). All these selfish untouchables were forced to go back to their adopted countries after becoming disillusioned here.

I have mentioned these unsuccessful efforts so that it can be remembered that some stooges are also hidden in foreign countries and whenever an independent struggle is underway in India they will come out of hiding.[12]

Kanshiram's scathing attack on sycophants and stooges was an eye-opener for the dalit readers of the book. His deep understanding of stooge mentality among the dalits and other downtrodden sections made him strive to form an independent dalit political party, members of which would not be spokespersons of non-dalit political leaders who could decide the fate of dalit communities and provide them political space. The party which Kanshiram had envisioned and formed two years later strongly followed the dalit agenda and did not depend on any other party for ideological support, even though it entered into political alliances with various parties of differing ideologies to gain power. The theory that emerged in *The Chamcha Age* evolved into a praxis of dalit politics. The resolution of the issues raised by Kanshiram resulted in the real democratization of Indian politics.

There were four programmes that Kanshiram developed on the basis of his diagnosis in *The Chamcha Age*: 1) immediate measures, which entailed social action; 2) short-term measures, in which limited political action was involved; 3) long-term measures, which demanded total political action; and 4) permanent measures that required cultural transformation and cultural control. These steps were to be taken up and implemented within a time-bound programme. The immediate measures were to arouse consciousness among the marginalized at various levels. Awareness squads were set up and they organized the Ambedkar Mela on Wheels to disseminate Ambedkarite ideology, critiqued the Poona Pact and made plans for a 4200-kilometre cycle rally, to learn how to make use of small resources at an even larger level.[13] There was even talk of holding a people's parliament on 25 December 1982 in Delhi to deliberate specifically on the problems of the dalit community.[14] Political action would be necessary to end the chamcha age. The best means would be a political party formed by the dalits. Cultural transformation, from a culture of inequality to a more egalitarian one, would usher in a bright era. According to him, these four programmes needed to be internalized and deeply understood by the people. Only after that should they get involved in the activities of DS4.[15] This book and his other speeches revealed that Kanshiram had a deep understanding of the nature of the Indian state and of Indian politics post-Independence. The Indian state was essentially Brahmanical in which 15 per cent upper castes were ruling over 85 per cent bahujans. The parliamentary democracy that came after the British left did not represent the desires and aspirations of the majority of Indians. In our caste-ridden society, 4–5 per cent of people belonging to Brahman castes occupied more than 30 per cent seats in Parliament. The OBCs constituted 52 per cent, but their representation in Parliament was small. The reason for this misrepresentation, Kanshiram felt, was because the OBCs had stopped taking note of Mahatma Phule's teaching, to fight against Manuvad. Before the elections they could sometimes be seen raising anti-Brahman slogans, but when the elections came round they fell at the feet of the Brahmans for tickets. The SCs and STs entered Parliament through reserved seats but they were stooges of the Congress. Because of all this, Brahmanism dominated the politics, bureaucracy, economy, religion and culture of the country. He thus believed that freedom was actually freedom only for the rich and the influential, not for the deprived people. The capitalists, communalists and feudal landlords imposed their will on the dalits and other exploited communities. The poor and deprived sections could not even exercise their right to vote freely and were compelled to vote for people they did not like.[16]

The battle was then against Brahmanvad and Ambedkar would be his guiding light. He was, however, sceptical about Ambedkarites. Remembering his close association with them in Poona, he once said sardonically that 'he had learnt from Babasaheb Ambedkar how to run a movement, and from the miserable failure of the Mahars of Maharashtra in fulfilling Ambedkar's mission how *not* to run a movement, both of which he firmly believed held important lessons for his mission'.[17] He now sought to improvise on the teachings of Ambedkar in innovative ways, always keeping in mind his mentor's motto that political power was the master key for dalit liberation and that acquiring it should be the dalit war strategy.

Ambedkar's own life was a struggle for basic human rights as he was born (in 1891) in a poor Mahar family in Maharashtra. He bore the painful stigma of untouchability throughout his student life which began in a primary school in Satara. He faced numerous cruelties from caste Hindus, which left an indelible impression on his mind. The pressure of all manner of disabilities and maltreatment helped him understand the galling humiliation and abuse that his entire community had been suffering; it engendered in him a burning hatred for Hinduism.

Ambedkar returned to India after higher studies in the US in economics and law, but still had to struggle for employment because of his tag of being an untouchable. After several years, he joined the Appellate Side of the Bombay Bar to work as a barrister, which would provide him the opportunity, means and leisure to devote himself to the aim of his life—the upliftment of untouchables. He also ventured into social work and soon became the leader of the untouchables as he had sprung from amongst them, and thought as they thought and felt as they felt. His first organized attempt to achieve this was the Bahishkrit Hitakarini Sabha (Outcastes Welfare Association), which was intended to promote education and socio-economic improvement, as well as the welfare of outcastes, at the time referred to as 'depressed classes'. By 1927 Ambedkar decided to launch active movements against untouchability. He began with public movements and marches to open up and share public drinking water resources and for the right to enter Hindu temples. Ambedkar provided mobility to the dalit movement by opening educational institutions for the depressed classes, writing books and delivering public lectures. He established the Depressed Classes Education Society to organize the school education of his community on a sound basis and, later on, in 1956, set up the RPI.[18]

The characterization of caste and its role in society and politics were at the heart of Kanshiram's discussion of Ambedkar. Ambedkar expounded his theories about caste in Hindu society, the shastras and Brahmanism in his book *The Annihilation of Caste*.[19] Originally prepared as a lecture for the annual Lahore Jaat-Paat Todak Mandal sammelan in 1936, it was stopped from being presented by the welcome committee, fearing that the ideas in it would be intolerable to the gathering. The lecture was later published in book form, which sold 1500 copies in the first two months. It was also published in Gujarati, Marathi, Hindi, Punjabi, Tamil and Malayalam languages. There was so much demand for the English edition that it had to be reprinted twice.

About the evils of caste Ambedkar wrote that it had 'killed public spirit' and 'destroyed the sense of public charity'. He added: 'A Hindu's public is his caste. His responsibility is only to his caste . . . Virtue has become caste-ridden and morality has become caste-bound . . . There is charity, but it begins and ends with caste. There is sympathy, but not for men of other castes.'[20]

Explaining how caste is an agent of discrimination, Ambedkar said that because caste prevented common activity, the Hindus could not become a society with 'a unified life and a consciousness of its being'.[21] The higher castes, in fact, had deliberately not allowed lower castes within the pale of Hinduism to rise to a higher level, since caste was a 'closed corporation' and one had to be born into it.

Ambedkar attacked the Hindus' claim of being tolerant. He saw their so-called tolerance to insults or wrongs as an outcome of their indifference or weakness. It was reflected in their treatment of the oppressed in their own society as a result of the caste system, which ruled out cooperation even for a good cause. People would follow even a good man only if he were from their caste. 'It is not a case of standing by virtue and not standing by vice. It is a case of standing or not standing by the caste. Have not Hindus committed treason against their country in the interests of their caste?'[22]

Ambedkar then asked why people had tolerated these social evils.

There have been social revolutions in other countries of the world. Why have there not been social revolutions in India is a question which has incessantly troubled me. There is only one answer, which I can give and it is that the lower classes of Hindus have been completely disabled for direct action on account of this wretched system of Chaturvarnya. They could not bear arms and without arms they could not rebel. They were all ploughmen and they never were allowed to convert their ploughshares into swords. They had no bayonets and therefore everyone who chose could and did sit upon them. On account of the Chaturvarnya, they could receive no education. They could not think out or know the way to their salvation. They were condemned to be lowly and not knowing the way of escape, and not having the means of escape, they became reconciled to eternal servitude, which they accepted as their inescapable fate . . .

There cannot be a more degrading system of social organization than Chaturvarnya. It is the system which deadens, paralyses, and cripples the people [keeping them] from helpful activity. This is no exaggeration. History bears ample evidence. There is only one period in Indian history which is a period of freedom, greatness and glory. That is the period of the Mourya Empire. At all other times the country suffered from defeat and darkness. But the Mourya period was a period when Chaturvarnya was completely annihilated, when the Shudras, who constituted the mass of the people, came into their own and became the rulers of the country. The period of defeat and darkness is the period when Chaturvarnya flourished to the damnation of the greater part of the people of the country . . . The only question that remains to be considered is—How to bring about the reform of the Hindu social order? How to abolish Caste? This is a question of supreme importance.[23]

Ambedkar saw inter-dining and especially inter-marriage as ways of abolishing caste. Yet, because these ideas were repugnant to the beliefs and dogmas of the Hindus, this did not happen. As Ambedkar pointed out, 'Caste is a notion, it is a state of the mind. The destruction of Caste does not therefore mean the destruction of a physical barrier. It means a notional change.'[24] The culprit was not the observers of caste but the religion that inculcated this notion.

If this is correct, then obviously the enemy you must grapple with is not the people who observe Caste, but the Shastras which teach them this religion of Caste . . . The real remedy is to destroy the belief in the sanctity of the Shastras.[25]

Whether the relationship of guardian and ward was the real underlying conception on which Chaturvarnya was based, there is no doubt that in practice the relation was that of master and servant. The three classes, Brahmins, Kshatriyas, and Vaishyas, although not very happy in their mutual relationship, managed to work by compromise. The Brahmin flattered the Kshatriya, and both let the Vaishya live in order to be able to live upon him. But the three agreed to beat down the Shudra. He was not allowed to acquire wealth, lest he should be independent of the three Varnas. He was prohibited from acquiring knowledge, lest he should keep a steady vigil regarding his interests. He was prohibited from bearing arms, lest he should have the means to rebel against their authority. That this is how the Shudras were treated by the Tryavarnikas is evidenced by the *Laws of Manu*. There is no code of laws more infamous regarding social rights than the *Laws of Manu*. Any instance from anywhere of social injustice must pale before it.[26]

How do you expect to succeed, if you allow the Shastras to continue to mould the beliefs and opinions of the people? Not to question the authority of the Shastras—to permit the people to believe in their sanctity and their sanctions, to blame them and to criticise them for their acts as being irrational and inhuman—is an incongruous way of carrying on social reform. Reformers working for the removal of untouchability, including Mr. Gandhi, do not seem to realize that the acts of the people are merely the results of their beliefs inculcated upon their conduct until they cease to believe in the sanctity of the Shastras on which their conduct is founded.[27]

Ambedkar exhorted oppressed people to follow the paths of the Buddha and Guru Nanak, who denied the authority of the Hindu scriptures, and to gather courage to tell the Hindus what was wrong with their religion. He reminded people that the break-up of the caste system would adversely affect the Brahmans, who were synonymous with the intellectual class. 'The Hindus are taught that the Brahmins are Bhudevas (Gods on earth). The Hindus are taught that Brahmins alone can be their teachers. Manu says, "If it be asked how it should be with respect to points of the Dharma which have not been specially mentioned, the answer is, that which Brahmins who are Shishthas propound shall doubtless have legal force."'[28] It was futile to expect Brahmans to consent to lead a movement that would destroy their caste's power and prestige. Ambedkar saw no difference between the secular and priestly Brahmans. 'Both are kith and kin. They are two arms of the same body, and one is bound to fight for the existence of the other.'[29]

Brahmanvad was then the main foe. Earlier, this concept was used in the dalit movement to counter the dominance of the upper castes. Broad and abstract, it was unlike the term 'Manuvad' that Kanshiram coined subsequently. Manuvad explained how Manu's code led to the oppression and exploitation of the lower castes, by having chalked out punishments for the lower castes who dared to cross their limits. This term also gave space to the Brahmans and other upper castes, who disapproved of the *Manu Samhita* and were in favour of the dalit movement, to join his party. Kanshiram did not favour the annihilation of caste, which was Ambedkar's idea. His understanding of caste in politics stood quite apart from Ambedkar's, and he declared that just as the Brahmans had for long ruled on the basis of casteism, the dalits would now do the same, seeking to eradicate Brahmanism from society.[30]

Kanshiram understood that in spite of all the efforts made by various saints and gurus and leaders like Phule and Ambedkar, the caste system could not be eradicated and so he came up with the concept of politicizing the caste consciousness of marginalized communities. For this he firstly evoked the memories of the suffering of the dalits by the upper castes and dominant sections of society, and tried to mobilize the lower castes around these memories, and secondly he tried to raise the pride of the lower castes by culling out the caste histories and subversive interpretations of the cultures of each dalit caste, through which they could raise their confidence. He believed that for eradicating casteism like Ambedkar wanted, it was important first to make the lower castes politically influential, for which they had to acquire political power. By politicizing caste consciousness he tried to bring about social transformation and carve an egalitarian society. The BSP formed the government twice in UP with BJP support, though the latter's Hindutva ideology had the potential to strengthen Brahmanism. Ostensibly, raising caste consciousness was in the name of Ambedkar, but it was entirely Kanshiram's brainchild. Thus in UP, to strengthen Ambedkar's vision, Kanshiram and Mayawati transformed the slogan 'abolish caste system' into 'promote caste system' to mobilize dalits for the restoration of their caste identity and self-esteem. Kanshiram said:

In 1962–63, when I got the opportunity to read Ambedkar's book *Annihilation of Caste* I also felt that it was perhaps possible to eradicate casteism from society. But later, when I studied the caste system and its behaviour in depth, there was a gradual modification in my thoughts. I have not only gained knowledge about caste from the books but from my personal life as well. Those people who migrate in large numbers from their villages to big cities like Delhi, Mumbai and Kolkata take no possessions with them but their caste. They leave behind their small huts, land and cattle, etc. in the village and settle in slums, near sewers and railway tracks, with nothing else but their one and only possession—their caste. If people have so much affection for their caste then how can we think of annihilating it? That is why I have stopped thinking about the annihilation of caste.[31]

For Ambedkar, villages were the slaughterhouses of dalits since the Brahmanical forces that oppressed dalits were the strongest there. He has described villages in the following manner:

The Indian Hindu village is known as a republic and they are proud of its internal structure in which there is no democracy, no equality, no liberty, no fraternity. This is a republic of high castes for high castes. For untouchables, it is the imperialism of the Hindus. It is a colony for the exploitation of the untouchables where there are no rights for them. Service, with timeless patience and passivity, is the fate of the untouchables in this village. They have to either do or die. How polluted is this Hindu slaughter house. This is a fact that can't be challenged for this fact is its truth.[32]

That is why Ambedkar felt that migration of dalits to big cities would help liberate them from this kind of oppression. Kanshiram, on the other hand, believed that whether dalits migrated from villages or not, caste always remained with them. He believed that until a casteless society was formed, it was necessary for dalits to strategically use their caste as a tool for their own emancipation and to dethrone Brahmanism. The ultimate goal of both Ambedkar and Kanshiram was to form a casteless society. But while Ambedkar felt that inter-caste marriage was a pertinent strategy, Kanshiram felt that first the dalit castes had to acquire self-respect by using their own caste and identity resources which would help them attain status in society. Only then could other kinds of interactions like inter-dining and inter-caste marriages take place. According to Kanshiram, caste was a double-edged sword and he wanted to use it in a way that benefited the bahujans and at the same time destroyed Brahman hegemony.[33] In an interview published in the 2–8 April 1989 issue of *Chauthi Duniya*, a weekly newspaper from Delhi, in response to a claim that he was encouraging casteism, Kanshiram said:

> The people who want to maintain casteism say that we should not talk about caste. If there is any need to do so, they will do it on our behalf, meaning that we should continue to suffer indignities. We are consolidating people on the basis of their caste so that the caste system can be removed. So it is in the benefit of the people who suffered due to casteism that they come together. Here we are criticizing the oppressors less and the oppressed more. We want them to subvert this feeling of

inferiority complex linked with their caste due to Brahminism, and convert it into a matter of pride and in this process we are talking about caste. I tell them we will not tolerate oppression but break the audacity of the tormenters.[34]

In the same interview, the interviewer commented that this might lead to further tension in society. 'To this Kanshiram replied that when tension increases, a fire would be ignited and the upper castes will get burnt by it. When this would happen, they would be brought to their knees and this would lead to equality in society. This equality was their goal.'[35]

He also disagreed with Ambedkar's demand for a separate electorate for dalits even though both wanted dalits to attain respectability and glory in mainstream society.[36] Kanshiram's idea was to transform society into a *samta muluk* (egalitarian) society, with each caste seen as equal and having its own caste identity, and this was the philosophical underpinning of the BSP. He liked to explain his philosophy through the metaphor of a pen. According to him, Indian society was like a standing pen, with the Brahmans sitting at the top like the cap of the pen, while the other castes were the bahujans who formed the body of the pen, and came down gradually along it. The dalits and the untouchables were right at the bottom of the pen. If the pen was laid flat, however, it represented an equal society with all the castes at the same level. This was the kind of samta muluk society the BSP aspired for and to achieve which Kanshiram was ready to use any means, even take the risk of being dubbed opportunistic.[37] This explained why he agreed to ally with the BJP to form a government three times.

There were other aspects in which Kanshiram and Ambedkar differed. Having studied at Columbia University, where he had immersed himself in the traditions of Western knowledge, Ambedkar derived most of his ideological ingredients from his analysis of the dalits through history. Kanshiram's inspirations were more home-grown. Born in a village in Punjab and trained in Poona's dalit politics, his political arguments in favour of the dalits merged history and myth. One could call it mytho-history. Ambedkar, on the other hand, gave little importance to myth in his discourse. In fact, he tried to decode some of the ancient myths through history. Kanshiram believed that to empower the dalits a fruitful method was to link them with their genealogies, and caste myths were an important means of doing so.[38] The BSP selected myths that were popular in particular regions to mobilize the people of that region. The myths are not merely small anecdotes or incidents about lesser-known characters but long texts about persons who played significant roles in history and whose life stories could be used as inspiration to motivate and mobilize the communities concerned. The narratives selected were such that they facilitated the creation of visual texts and ignited the imagination of the viewers. The myths being used by the BSP for mobilizing dalit communities were influential because of the urge of the communities themselves to gain respect and relocate their place in the society.[39] (See chapter 4 for further details.)

Ambedkar, somewhat differently, drew parallels between ancient myths and history. He took examples from the tales, stories, psalms, quotations, proverbs, ancient texts like the Gita and the Mahabharata found in Indian literature to decode some of the ancient myths.[40] For example, he took the reference of the Mahabharata and pointed out how 'Kapot Panchi' got after 'Shayen Panchi', which sought refuge with Shiva to save its own life. Likewise, during the colonial period, dalits had sought refuge with the Britishers, when they got fed up of the atrocities of the upper-caste people.[41] Many of the untouchables sacrificed their lives for the protection of the Hindu religion. Just like the thumb of 'Eklavya', the heads of the untouchables in the battle of 'Kharde' were cut off.[42] Ambedkar also talked about the condition of women which was far better before the advent of Manu. He cited the example of the Buddha and went on to prove how women were liberated and emancipated when he gave them the status of *bhikshunni* (nuns) in the monasteries, wherein they got an opportunity of studying and learning.[43]

Ambedkar called the politics of emancipation of marginalized groups the 'Dalit movement' while Kanshiram preferred to term it the 'Bahujan movement', avoiding the use of the word 'dalit'. Kanshiram believed that the dalits had to become strong and emancipated—not by crying or begging but proactively liberating themselves from the vicious circle of 'dalitness'. He wanted them to now pass on this liberation to others rather than demand it for themselves.

Ambedkar tried to provide an ethical context to the politics of dalit liberation—for him, morality was more important in the attainment of political goals. Constitutional morality or 'abiding by the spirit of constitution and not just its legal provisions' was a part of such a larger morality in politics, crucial for a 'free ranging intellectual life and democratic political possibility rooted in democratic political struggle. Going beyond this

Dr. Ambedkar felt that "morality" in the sense of social ethics was indispensable for the realization of liberty and equality. In the absence of morality, there were only two alternatives: anarchy or the police.'[44]

By contrast, Kanshiram, in his political experiments, did not pay much heed to the means of establishing a political regime, emphasizing only the end—the attainment of political power. In this regard, Kanshiram was later upbraided by critics like Teltumbde who said:

The underlying value of the movement of Ambedkar was represented by liberty, equality and fraternity. Kanshiram does not seem to respect any value [other] than the political and money power. In Ambedkar, one cannot miss an overflowing concern for the oppressed and wrath against the perpetrators of oppression. Kanshiram's concern scarcely transcended his speeches in his electoral rallies. It was with this concern and commitment that Ambedkar kept on referring to Marx and Marxism till his end, something as a touchstone to test his alternatives. Kanshiram simply abhorred it. Ambedkar struggled to formulate the dalit problem. Kanshiram either took it for granted or did not care for it at all. He never tried to articulate the nature of his Bahujanas' ailment except for the rhetorical reference to their subordination by the minority upper caste Hindus. For Ambedkar certain values, moral code etc. were paramount; Kanshiram never seemed to be bothered by these issues. Ambedkar always foresaw plans and programmes, visualised appropriate structures for the downtrodden. Kanshiram expressed clear disdain for such things. For

Ambedkar political power was a means, to Kanshiram it appears to be the end. Notwithstanding these broad differences, he has succeeded in luring the dalit masses in certain pockets of the country by projecting an Ambedkar icon that sanctioned his unscrupulous pursuits of power.[45]

In practising his politics, Kanshiram made compromises for electoral gain many a time, which provided power to the dalits but somehow weakened their fight for emancipation. The BSP had to make an alliance with the BJP to run the government because of which it had to face criticism also. Many people joined the BSP not for the welfare of the bahujan society but for their self-interest.

The conversion of dalits to Buddhism remained problematic for Kanshiram and, indeed, for Mayawati. Ambedkar believed that dalit emancipation was not possible within the fold of Hinduism—a religion inherently based on casteism. He thought that as long as dalits remained within it, they would continue to face discrimination. On 14 October 1956, along with lakhs of dalits, Ambedkar converted to Buddhism at a conversion site in Nagpur. This was his commitment to the oath he had taken in 1935 in which he had asserted, 'I did not have any control on my birth and I was born in the Hindu religion. However, I will not die as a Hindu.'[46] In the same spirit, Kanshiram also announced at a mass gathering in Rambagh, Nagpur, on 30 March 2002, 'On the occasion of the fiftieth anniversary of Babasaheb's acceptance of Buddhism, Mayawati and I, along with two crore Chamar brothers, will also enter the fold of Buddhism.'[47] At other times, however, Kanshiram was critical of the Maharashtrian dalits' conversion to Buddhism, stating that they had brought casteism even into the Buddhist religion, which previously never had caste divisions.

Nevertheless, whenever Kanshiram spoke before Ambedkarites in Maharashtra or elsewhere he always vowed to convert to Buddhism—but he never did. Mayawati, too, has not converted to Buddhism. Their non-conversion could be out of the fear of offending and thereby losing the support of Chamar Hindus in UP villages, linked with Kabir Panth, Ravidasia sect, Shivnarayani sect and other Hindu sub-sects. Kanshiram, however, tried to explain this compulsion differently, by declaring at a Buddha Jayanti function in Bhopal in June 2001 that only the religion of the rulers moved ahead. 'He added that history had taught us that Ashoka and Harshvardhan could carry forward the Buddhist religion only because they were kings and so the dalits had to become rulers first. Kanshiram went on to say that he had brought up this issue on the occasion of Buddha Jayanti since religion was closely linked with politics.'[48] Mayawati, to prevent Kanshiram from being accused of marginalizing Ambedkar and his thought, added that dalits should remember that it was so in order to follow the Ambedkarite path and posit it against Manuvad and Gandhism. Defending Kanshiram, who did not give up Hinduism to embrace Buddhism, 'she said that in the present context conversion would not have been beneficial for the dalits . . .' She admitted that Kanshiram's last wish had been to embrace Buddhism. She qualified this, saying that as Kanshiram had advised, first the BSP should win an absolute majority in Parliament and rule the Centre. In other words, only when this happened 'would she convert to Buddhism along with crores of her followers'.[49]

Kanshiram, like Ambedkar, was a strong opponent of communism but with a difference. While Ambedkar only criticized the ideology of Marx, Kanshiram was critical of the Indian communists, who he thought had deviated from the revolutionary path, since they overemphasized class, ignoring the reality of caste in India. According to Kanshiram, the everyday existence of the marginalized was determined by their caste alone.

The differences between Ambedkar and Kanshiram also grew out of their distinct social base. Kanshiram used to call himself a rustic villager (*dehati*). He said: 'I am a rustic man, and like a rustic person churns curd to produce butter, I, too, am churning society.'[50] He also often commented that Ambedkar was a great scholar while he himself was a person with an ordinary education. Kanshiram reiterated that he had travelled up and down the country to grasp the problems of society.[51]

Kanshiram often asserted his own Chamar identity, saying, 'We are Chamars of Punjab. We are educated because of the Sikh religion. It is clear to me that I want to fight against the injustice perpetrated on the Chamars by the forward and upper castes.'[52] He went ahead with his strategic dalit/bahujan discourse by according the Chamars the primary position and trying to link the other lower castes with them. That this did not always work out and, furthermore, created problems between dalit castes is another matter. Nevertheless, Kanshiram did bring together eighteen kinds of Chamars under the umbrella of the BSP. His intention was 'to try to bring the viewpoint of the educated and employed members of the community to its illiterate and rural members'.[53] He was proud of saying that

UP was earlier known as 'Aryavarta' and he had converted it to 'Chamarvarta'.

Interestingly, Kanshiram was highly critical of the Mahars of Maharashtra, the backbone of Ambedkar's movement, and this was reflected in his speeches and interviews. In a speech delivered on 7 September 2003 at Chandrapur, Maharashtra, Kanshiram commented on the 'declining condition' of the Mahars and 'called them frauds who had been pulling down the name of Ambedkar for the last thirty-five years'.[54] He presented the Mahars as being badly fragmented and accused them for the failure of the dalit movement in Maharashtra. He even coined a term 'Maharki' for the tendency of the Mahars to remain divided, and said that whenever five, seven or ten Mahars got together they indulged in 'Maharki' by disparaging other Mahars and other dalit castes as well.[55] Kanshiram held this tendency responsible for the Mahars' inability to propel the dalit movement forward along with other castes like Matang and Kunbi and the OBCs. 'Kanshiram said that though Ambedkar's symbol was the elephant, the Mahars had themselves forgotten this, and it was the BSP that was making the lumbering elephant run fast in UP.'[56] He underlined how Ambedkar had remained confined to the Mahars of Maharashtra and not been able to enter the land of the Chamars, where the Congress had placed dalit leader Jagjivan Ram so that the Chamars there would not link themselves with Ambedkar; and he added how he had successfully linked the Chamars with bahujan politics, and that too on a big scale.[57]

Kanshiram also had a reply for the Ambedkarites of Maharashtra who had held that they respected Ambedkar's ideology but it was not possible to implement it due to practical problems. Delivering a speech at the Kasturchand Park in Nagpur, Kanshiram countered their claim, pointing to the example of cities and villages of UP, 'where 11,524 Ambedkar model villages had been created for dalits, with electricity, water and road networks'.[58]

Critiquing the demand of the Maharashtrians for a university named after Ambedkar, he observed that they should acquire state power and then set up such universities rather than beg the state currently in power. He pointed out that in UP, the BSP had formed a government and had then named nine universities after great dalits.[59]

About the use of reservation as a tool for acquiring equality and economic emancipation for dalits and the marginalized, Kanshiram differed strongly from Ambedkar. Ambedkar believed that reservations could help in liberating the lower castes from social and economic inequalities. While he critiqued Ambedkar, Kanshiram was practical enough to see that until society got rid of caste-based discrimination completely, the dalits would require reservation. According to him reservation was not so important for acquiring jobs but more importantly to ensure the participation of dalits in the society.[60] 'Reservation is a tool to provide space to the dalits in the present democratic structure.'[61]

However, in principle against reservation, Kanshiram felt that the dalits should convert themselves from reservation-claiming to reservation-giving communities. He believed that the entire struggle for reservation was for acquiring participation in bureaucracy and not in politics, whereas the struggle of the dalits would be strengthened only when they achieved participation and representation in politics. He felt that the main problem with the politics of the Indian state was the imbalance in the representation of the various communities. The conventional Ambedkarites felt that Kanshiram was taking a different stand from Ambedkar and was critiquing him, but Kanshiram had understood the limitations of reservations and was trying to develop the dalits as a confident and self-respecting community who did not require reservation.

Kanshiram was a pragmatic politician. This did not rule out his projecting a 'holistic vision' which would ensure the participation of the marginalized in the democratic processes. As part of his economic agenda, if his party came to power, he said 'it would aim to gradually acquire and nationalize the primary industries which would give sustainable wages to the labourers and create appropriate working conditions for them. Other industries would be allowed to be run by private companies, as he was not against industrialization in general.'[62]

Kanshiram suggested that natural resources should be under the control of the government and should not be given to the private companies. He also spelt out a land reform policy whereby vacant land should be taken over by the government and distributed among the poor and dalits.

Kanshiram was also very concerned that the share of dalits in economic activities should increase and they should emerge as an economically powerful and vibrant community. That is why in the initial phase of BAMCEF's mobilization he used to organize exhibitions during the conferences, highlighting the skills and economic activities of dalit communities. These exhibitions were organized during their national conferences.

The local units like Chandigarh and Solapur also organized them during seminars. These exhibitions tried to disseminate the message that the dalits should develop their own economic skills, diversify their economic activities and stand on their own feet rather than being totally dependent on the state that was dominated by parties run by Brahmanical groups.[63]

Here it needs to be said that though typically seen as the leader of the dalits, Kanshiram was also concerned about the role of other minority communities in nation building. He was strongly against communal mobilization and the riots that often ensued. Analysing the nature of communal riots, he warned the dalits that they were being used by communal forces, as was apparent in the riots that took place in Aligarh, Jamshedpur and Nadia in 1979. In Aligarh, the Muslims were poised against the Jatavs (Chamars). In Jamshedpur, the STs were openly incited against the Muslims, while in Nadia the goondas of the backward communities attacked the Muslims. This tendency was extremely dangerous for the dalits and backward communities. According to Kanshiram, the reason for this was that there was no political leadership among the SCs, STs and minorities who could check these tendencies and also promote brotherhood among all the dalit and backward communities in India.[64]

Kanshiram was also troubled about the lack of participation of Christians in the democratic process, who he felt were isolated and uninterested.[65] He constantly invited them to join the dalits in the process of nation building.[66] He also lamented the tribals' lack of political participation, despite their comprising 10 per cent of the population. Spread in various parts of the country like Chota Nagpur, Arunachal Pradesh, Dadra and Nagar Haveli, etc., their condition was extremely pathetic. He appealed to the tribals to join the struggle of emancipation of the marginalized by forming a common front.[67]

In conclusion, it can be said that Kanshiram expanded and modified Ambedkar's ideas, inverting or subverting them as the political needs arose with the changing times. Along with Ambedkar, he was also influenced by Phule, Shahuji Maharaj, Marx and the Buddha and his ideas emerged from combining the thought of all these leaders. In addition, he also generated debate and discussion about Ambedkar through his political actions. He was no blind follower of Ambedkar. Kanshiram would say, 'Ambedkar learnt from books but I have learnt from my own life and people,' and also, 'He used to gather books; I tried to collect people.'[68] In this way, he gave new meaning to Ambedkar's struggles.

Kanshiram was convinced that only a significant shift in the political structure of the country would allow dalits to change the existing power structure and subvert the dominance of the upper castes. His target group therefore comprised all communities that for centuries have been socially, educationally, economically and culturally marginalized. He wanted to bring in all the SCs, STs, OBCs, the so-called criminal tribes, nomadic tribes and other backward social groups, unlike Ambedkar who talked about other communities in his writings and speeches but himself focused on the Mahars for political mobilization.

Kanshiram saw caste more in terms of its sociological rather than its economic impact. He sought to remove the stigma attached to the concept of 'dalit', which for the lower castes symbolized change and revolution. Like Ambedkar, Kanshiram too rejected the term 'Harijan' coined by Mahatma Gandhi for the untouchables as being too patronizing and floated the concept of 'bahujan' as we have seen. It was a little different from the notion of 'majority' that the Buddha and Phule held, and was used by Kanshiram more to create an ideological basis for political empowerment.

Critics of contemporary dalit politics like Anand Teltumbde have been appreciative of this strategy. Teltumbde feels that purely in terms of electoral politics, which has somehow become a major obsession with all the dalit parties, the strategy has proved quite effective, though only in certain parts of the country. In Teltumbde's words:

> It may be said to his credit that he reflected the culmination of what [the] common place icon of Ambedkar stood for. Kanshiram shrewdly grasped the political efficacy of this icon that sanctioned the pursuit of power in the name of downtrodden castes. The religious minorities which potentially rears the sense of suffering marginalisation from the majority community could be easily added to it to make a formidable constituency in parliamentary parlance.[69]

Both Kanshiram and Ambedkar thought the dalits should organize themselves into such a strong political force that influential political groups fail to get an absolute majority. In such situations, the dalits, to whom they would come for support, could dictate terms. 'We do not have to form a strong government but a weak government. This sort of government will listen to the voice of the dalits and will work for their betterment.'[70] The differences with Ambedkar notwithstanding, Kanshiram worked hard to spread the Ambedkarite message across the country. Many scheduled castes did not fully know about Ambedkar and his ideas. Of these people, many believed that their battle had been fought by Gandhiji and the Congress and not by Ambedkar. Unlike others, he did not find this fact shocking. Before he left Punjab, he, too, had not known anything about Ambedkar. It was thus imperative to spread the message of Ambedkar among the lower castes all over the country.[71]

For the purpose of disseminating Ambedkar's ideas and also to strengthen the movement of bahujan communities, Kanshiram felt that it was important for them to have their own media. According to him, the Indian media was both Manuvadi and Brahmanvadi and misrepresented and distorted information about their mission.

The newspaper, he believed, was a powerful medium for arousing consciousness and had been used well in India as a weapon for struggle. In February 1981, in the newsmagazine *The Oppressed Indian*, edited by him, he presented a blueprint for developing a bahujan media within ten years. He promised to launch it on 14 April 1991 on the occasion of Ambedkar's birth anniversary. The plan would be implemented in five phases: beginning, regularizing, stabilizing, standardizing and making it permanent. He called it the Missionary Publishing Plan and under this plan he brought out a newspaper in Hindi called *Bahujan Sangathak*. Its price would depend on the cost incurred for publishing and also on affordability for the readers.[72]

Anand Rahate, a journalist working for the newspaper *Bahujan Nayak*, recalls an incident which brings out the politics behind Kanshiram's developing his own media. He says that on the first evening of a rally held in Kolkata, when the journalists went to Kanshiram, he said jokingly, 'Oh so the team of journalists has also arrived! Very good! There should be a good reporting of tomorrow's rally. The other newspapers will distort our news, and that is why I say we should have our own media.'[73]

Kanshiram's mission aimed at expanding the consciousness of dignity and emancipation among the dalits and the marginalized all over the country and also around the world. He did not consider the struggle of the dalits as a local or national one but as an international struggle of the oppressed. That is why he expanded his activities to all corners of the country. In the northeast he visited Manipur, Imphal, Siliguri, etc. At the international level he visited Japan to attend the first International Conference against Discrimination, a conference against inequality, organized by the Buraku Liberation Research Institute in December 1982 in Osaka. He described his experience thus: 'I contributed to making the conference a success in various ways throughout the week that I was there. While returning to India I was fully satisfied that this first international conference against discrimination would culminate in bringing equality all over the world. I want that the second conference be held in India.'[74] Kanshiram also visited England in 1985, and went to Birmingham, London and other cities, carrying the message of the ongoing struggle for the emancipation of dalits in India.[75]

Kanshiram's concerted efforts to popularize Ambedkar have borne fruit. In a poll conducted by the magazine *Outlook* in 2012,

B.R. Ambedkar was voted the greatest Indian after Gandhi. He is regarded to be relevant for all times because he gave millions of oppressed an identity of their own. Although he lived and worked in the first half of the twentieth century, his relevance—political, social, ideological, religious as well as economic—will remain so long as there are struggles for justice and equality.[76]

Kanshiram reinvented Ambedkar, in his own way, through bahujan politics, much to the dismay of Ambedkarites, who did not agree with him. Gradually but surely, before the 1980s, Ambedkar had been relegated to the margins of political discourse in independent India. But dalit discourse and dalit culture, with its own set of metaphors and symbols, introduced by Kanshiram, changed the pivot of Indian politics. They brought Ambedkar back into the consciousness of people. Once again in their political psyche he became a force to reckon with. The next chapter examines the discourse Kanshiram employed to bring marginalized groups together politically and culturally under the banner of bahujan, and thus the BSP.

4

The Elephant Rises

Kanshiram's Cultural Politics
and the Formation of the BSP

While working in Maharashtra, Kanshiram—who had begun to be addressed as 'Manyawar' or 'Sahib'—realized the need for expanding his movement in other parts of India. The office of BAMCEF was therefore shifted to New Delhi. Thereafter the DS4 was also launched from here. He sensed there was a strong impulse among the dalits mobilizing others in the community to move from under the banner of DS4 and create their own political party. Though Kanshiram was not happy with the limited political impact of DS4, he understood the need to change the weapons of battle with the passage of time. Heeding these signs, on 14 April 1984, Ambedkar's birth anniversary, Kanshiram announced the launch of a new political party called the Bahujan Samaj Party at the Boat Club in New Delhi.

At that time, there was widespread unrest due to the possible implementation of Mandal Commission's recommendations. The Mandal Commission had been established in India in

1979 by the Janata Party government under the then prime minister, Morarji Desai, with a mandate to 'identify the socially or educationally backward'. The commission was headed by Indian parliamentarian Bindheshwari Prasad Mandal to consider the question of reserving seats in government jobs and educational institutions and assigning quotas for the same to redress caste discrimination. The report used eleven social, economic and educational indicators to determine 'backwardness'. Submitted in 1980, the report acknowledged the need for affirmative action whereby a certain portion of seats were kept exclusively for members of other backward castes. It recommended fixing the quotas for OBCs at 27 per cent. The scheduled castes already had 15 per cent reservation and the scheduled tribes 7.5 per cent reservation mandated by the Constitution. The 27 per cent quota had been arrived at following a 1963 Supreme Court judgement whereby the total reservation, inclusive of the quantum for the SCs and the STs, couldn't exceed 50 per cent.[1]

The recommendations were sought to be implemented in 1989, nearly a decade after the commission gave its report, by the then prime minister V.P. Singh. In August 1990, based on the recommendations, he announced the reservations in respect of government jobs. The anti-reservationists were severely critical of this action. Protests rocked cities and towns across the country. A Delhi University student, Rajiv Goswami, immolated himself in protest. Some other college students, too, followed his example, leading to a formidable movement against job and educational reservations for the lower castes, especially the backwards. In this anti-reservation crisis, the dalits were forced to defend reservation per se, and to support the backwards or OBCs.

Before the recommendations were implemented and while the debate around them was still raging, Kanshiram decided to use this opportunity to bring the OBCs and dalits together to form the 'bahujan' group for launching his movement through the BSP. The BSP raised the slogan of 'Implement Mandal Commission recommendations or vacate the seat'. A 'jail bharo andolan' was launched by the party at the Boat Club in New Delhi from 1 to 14 August 1984 in which thousands of BSP activists, including women, courted arrest. Similar demonstrations and movements were also carried out in other states and district headquarters in the country. This was the first movement in support of the recommendations of the Mandal Commission. Other parties, too, like the Left Front, BJP, Rashtriya Janata Dal (RJD), Janata Dal United (JDU), Samajwadi Party and Congress were pro-Mandal.

Immediately after the BSP demonstration, from 15 August onward, a movement called 'All India Revolt against Political Slavery' was started, whose aim was to make the bahujan samaj, especially the OBCs, understand why they were still slaves even after thirty-seven years of Independence. In the same year, parliamentary elections were declared on 13 November 1984. The BSP had been in existence for only seven months till then, but it fielded candidates from nine states and three union territories. In this election the BSP won more than ten lakh votes. It got about six lakh votes in UP while in Punjab the number of votes was around two lakh. In the assembly elections held in 1984, too, the BSP fielded its candidates, and within a period of two months, the party registered an increase of more than three lakh votes in UP alone. This success made Kanshiram decide to focus his attention on UP.

～

The changes in the socio-economic contours of UP over time paved the way for Kanshiram to secure a foothold there. There were broadly three phases in UP politics, according to G.K. Lieten and Ravi Srivastava, which could be characterized on the basis of 'emergence of new economic classes' and the resultant 'shifting strategies of the dominant class'. The three periods were: from 1947 to 1967, climaxing with the Green Revolution led by the Congress; from 1967 to 1989, which marked the rise of the middle and rich peasants; from 1989 onwards, marked by the rise of the OBC and SC leadership and the 'accompanying attempts at Hindutva identity building'.[2]

Though the caste factor played a crucial role in elections since 1947, during the 1950s and until the late 1960s, the Gandhian and Nehruvian appeal of the Congress cut across all castes and classes. The Congress ideology could accommodate all within its umbrella, overriding any schisms. Until 1967, the Congress was dominant. Only after that was this position challenged, coming to a head in 1977, when in the elections following the Emergency, the Congress was defeated because of the excesses it had committed in the previous two years.[3]

It is noteworthy that the dalits and OBCs never combined in UP even for the sake of acquiring political power. Although Lohia raised the slogan of *'Pichhre payein sau mein saath'* (Backwards and dalits should get 60 per cent) in an attempt to bring together the dalits and the OBCs, at the ground level that alliance never happened. During the fifties, from 1952 to '57, the socialist parties—the Lohiaites, for example—took up the cause of the backward castes. Kanshiram in 1995 tried to make a government with the OBCs and dalits, to give shape to his bahujan politics, but this alliance could survive only for six months.

After the 1967 general elections, there was 'fragmentation of the electorate on class lines'. The emergence of the rich peasants in western UP saw the rise of Charan Singh. At his instance, there were large-scale defections from the Congress to the Bharatiya Kranti Dal (BKD), a party that he had just formed.[4] Dalits continued to tilt towards the Congress, and the OBCs were attracted towards non-Congress politics, from Lohia to Mulayam Singh Yadav. How did Kanshiram then make headway with his agenda of setting up a dalit party?

When Kanshiram entered UP politics with the BSP in 1984, the three major political streams there were the Congress, the BJP and the Samajwadi Party. The legacy of the anti-colonial nationalist movement and post-independence Nehruvian reconstruction of the nation was linked with the Congress. The BJP was active in Hindutva politics, while the SP was trying to mobilize the OBCs and also revive socialist politics in the state. The cultural fabric of Uttar Pradesh was rich and layered. It was the home of Brahmanical dominance and the epicentre of Puranic Aryavrat, the land of Puranic memory. At the same time, it was also at the centre of heterogeneous anti-Brahmanical religious reform movements because memories of the legends and places associated with the Buddha, whose *karmabhoomi* or field of action was the Gangetic plain, were still alive within the cultures of the marginalized. In addition, it had also been the hub of the Bhakti movement in the medieval period, which was led by saints like Kabir, Ravidas, Shiv Narayan, Daria Sahib and Jagjivan Das, who were very popular among the dalits. Several sects were formed based on the preaching of these saints. A large number of dalits were drawn to these sects, which provided a means to their religious and cultural empowerment, otherwise denied to them under the Brahmanical religious and ritualistic domains. Uttar Pradesh was thus a land of contradictions, marked by Brahmanical dominance, as well as anti-Brahmanical memories as a part of the everyday culture of the marginal groups. For all these reasons, UP was fertile ground for the rise of Kanshiram.

It is telling that Kanshiram was born and brought up in Punjab which has the largest dalit population in the country (29 per cent) but he could not build up as strong a base there as he did in UP. There were several reasons for this. Firstly, the dalits in Punjab did not face the kind of discrimination and humiliation which they did elsewhere in north India, especially UP. As mentioned earlier, Sikhism, which preached equality and universal brotherhood, attracted a chunk of lower castes, which led to their conversion. Besides, unlike UP, it was the Jats rather than the Brahmans who were dominant in Punjab. The ire of the dalits was less against Brahmanvad. That battle was left to the Arya Samaj. The coming of the Arya Samaj and other social reform movements, like Ad-Dharm and Ravidasis, helped create a more egalitarian society. The dalits in Punjab had also improved their economic situation through hard work, job diversification and emigration. They entered a number of professions which were traditionally considered to be the mainstay of the business and artisan castes.[5]

The dalits of Punjab thus constituted a motley group of castes, economic strata and religious identities. 'Divided into 37 sub-castes, many of them refused to be clubbed together in one group as dalits.'[6] Initially, Kanshiram had not only been holding political rallies to mobilize the dalits of Punjab but had also asked his party cadres to wage a war against casteism and fight for the rights of contractual farm labourers called 'Siri' in local parlance. After Kanshiram, other BSP leaders in Punjab failed to launch any such movement against casteism in the state. Perhaps Kanshiram himself realized how segmented the dalit community in Punjab was.

The results of the 2007 assembly elections are a good example of the range of dalits' political allegiances at present and amply demonstrate why even in the late eighties, despite their forming a significant proportion of the population, the dalits in Punjab were not enthused by the casteist card of the BSP. The absence of any tall BSP leader in Punjab, who could mobilize them across religious and regional divides, was also a factor. The intra-dalit cleavages thus hindered the BSP's emergence as a cohesive and major force to reckon with in Punjab. In the absence of a common platform, some of the dalits and their local elite sought to safeguard their interests through different political parties, including the Congress and the Shiromani Akali Dal.

The record of the Akali Dal, dominated by Jats, the Congress and the BJP is instructive. In 1969, 44 per cent of the scheduled caste legislators were from the Akali Dal. This percentage has been slowly rising: 48 per cent in 1977, 62 per cent in 1985 and 77 per cent in 1997. In contrast is the fluctuation in the number of Congress's SC legislators: 52 per cent in 1967, 61 per cent in 1972, 45 per cent in 1980, 63 per cent in 1992 and 48 per cent in 2002. The BJP, too, contributed a few SC legislators, 13 per cent in 1997. Ironically, there were no SC legislators from the BSP and Communist Party.

Likewise, dalit leaders are to be found across party lines. From the Akali Dal there have been Dhanna Singh Gulshan, Gurdev Singh Badal, Charanjit Singh Atwal, Satwant Kaur Sandhu, Basant Singh Khalsa, Gulzar Singh Ranike, Mahinder Kaur Josh, Des Raj Dhugga, Sarwan Singh Phillaur, Gobind Singh Kanjhla, Shetal Singh and Dr Dalbir Singh Verka. Dhanna Singh Gulshan and Charanjit Singh Atwal became minister of state in the Central government and Deputy Speaker of the Lok Sabha respectively. Among the prominent stalwart dalit Congress leaders were the Central minister Buta Singh, Master Gurbanta Singh, Joginder Singh Maan, Darshan Singh K.P., Chaudhry Jagjit Singh, Mahinder Singh K.P., Shamsher Singh Doolon, Chaudhry Santokh Singh, Aruna Chaudhry, Chaudhry Sunder Singh, Chaudhry Ram Lubhaya, Santosh Chaudhry; Shamsher Singh Doolon and Mahinder Singh K.P. were made party chiefs at the state level.

The spread of dalit legislators across these various parties and the lack of the BSP's presence are explained by Brahman and Baniya vote banks being connected to the Congress and the Jats to the Akali Dal. 'They are [the major contenders to power]. All other political parties, namely the BJP, BSP and

CPI are minor players and become effective only if they fight elections by forging an alliance with any of these two parties.[7]

Unable to create a space for the BSP in Punjab, given this political configuration, Kanshiram concentrated his efforts on establishing the party in UP instead. The presence of the Chamars, numerically the largest and most politically aware dalit caste in UP, favoured his emergence there. A section of the Chamars had become educated prior to Independence and, consequently, more politically conscious than other lower castes. The Chamars were traditionally engaged in skinning dead animals, tanning leather and manufacturing leather goods while their womenfolk helped in childbirth, severing the umbilical cords of newborn babies of upper-caste households. The upliftment of the Chamars began during the colonial period when a section among them, oppressed in their villages, migrated to big cities to better their economic conditions. Some Chamars came in contact with Western influences, picked up a working knowledge of English and other European languages and also acquired education through mission schools. The educational institutions set up by Arya Samaj played an important role, particularly in western UP, in educating the Jatavs, a sub-caste of the Chamars.[8] Swami Achhutanand, a social reformer belonging to the Chamar caste, also carried out a movement in this region during the colonial period to motivate the dalits to educate their children.

After Independence, during the 1950s, the Chamars who were still engaged in their caste-based profession launched the Nara-Maveshi Movement, which was an attempt to free themselves from this despised profession and exercise their basic right to choose the profession they desired. This movement, as described earlier, had a significant impact on the life of Chamars, and attaining freedom from menial jobs helped them gain social respectability. This movement spread through much of the rural areas of Bihar and UP throughout the decade of the 1950s. The educated 'sahibs' (schoolteachers and government employees among the dalits), who had migrated to places like Kolkata and Mumbai, returned to the villages and played a crucial role in propagating this movement. Most of them were inspired by Ambedkarite thought and they motivated the people to educate their children.[9]

Arya Samaj through its campaigns also aroused consciousness among the Chamars to resist nara-maveshi work. The movement in 1954 to establish the Republican Party of India, which ultimately took off in 1956, played a pivotal role in propagating this consciousness through its workers and the newspaper they brought out. The message that went out to people was to quit this profession and educate their children.

The UP branch of the RPI was formed in Agra in 1958.[10] Like the Mahars of Maharashtra, the Jatavs, followers of Ambedkar as well, expected that the RPI would articulate and realize their interests better.[11] It marked the culmination of the Jatavs' or leather workers' political mobilization from the 1930s onwards, when they participated in the Civil Disobedience movement, agitated against the Poona Pact, participated in formation of the Scheduled Castes Federation in Agra in 1944–45 and even contested the reserved seats in the 1946 legislative assembly election.[12] The RPI workers and educated dalit groups pressurized the government to prevent the suppression of dalits participating in the movement.

In the initial phase of the movement in UP, Kanshiram, himself a Ravidasia Chamar, followed the strategy of consolidating the Chamars spreading from Delhi to Ranchi. Kanshiram wanted that the party cadres should at least be graduates. 'He believed that if there was any community after the Brahmins who were the most educated in the country, it was the Chamars.'[13] He opined that while the other dalit communities would also be linked with the BSP, the nucleus of the BSP, from Punjab to Bihar, would be formed by the Chamars. On another occasion he also declared that he would transform the land between Ganga and Yamuna from 'Aryavrat' to 'Chamarvrat'. In this way, he broke the dependence of this large and politically potent social group on political parties led by the leaders of the forward and backward castes. In the Chamar activists of the NMM, he found a ready-made cadre for the BSP.

The socialist movement in UP also prepared the ground for Kanshiram's politics there. We have already seen how socialist stalwart and leader Ram Manohar Lohia raised the slogan that the backward castes and dalits should get 60 per cent of the share in state legislature. Kanshiram too followed a similar logic by coining the slogan *Jiski jitni sankhya bhari uski utni hissedari'*. Both Lohia and Kanshiram thus highlighted the importance of numbers in democracy to claim the major share for dalits and the backward castes. Another socialist group inspired by Lohia was the Arjak Sangh, active in UP during the 1970s, which helped empower the dalits, especially the Chamars, and also attempted to bring the backward castes together with the dalits. It was established by Ramswaroop Verma on 1 June 1968, and the *Arjak Saptahik*, a weekly, started appearing from 1 June 1969.

The main motive of Arjak Sangh was to obliterate Brahmanism and form an egalitarian society.

Ramswaroop Verma was a companion of Ram Manohar Lohia and was active in the Arjak Sangh. In the assembly elections of 1952, Vermaji contested on a ticket from the Socialist Party for a seat in the Rajpur assembly, Kanpur district, but lost by 100 votes. In 1956, he won the election against Ram Swaroop Gupta and became the MLA. He lost again, in 1962, but gained success in 1967, becoming the finance minister in the government led by Chaudhary Charan Singh.[14] The Arjak Sangh carried out a campaign for dalit emancipation in various parts of UP. In this campaign they supported the NMM and the Chamars. Wherever the NMM was on, the people of Arjak Sangh became active. Ramswaroop Verma himself went to Bihra and Katka after the subjugation of the Chamars in a series of incidents there. Arjak Sangh articles based their discussion on the condition of untouchables and were published as booklets like *Achooton Ki Samasyayein Aur Samadhan* (The Problems of Untouchables and Their Solutions), *Niradar Kaise Mite* (How to Eradicate Humiliation), and so on. It was a determined effort to arouse the consciousness of resistance among the dalits and backward castes through scholarly articles. However, like Ram Manohar Lohia, the efforts of the Arjak Sangh to bring together the dalits and backward castes failed.

To signify that the party represented the dalits and other downtrodden sections, which together constituted 85 per cent of India's population, Kanshiram chose the name 'bahujan' (majority) for the BSP. The remaining 15 per cent were Brahmans, Kshatriyas and Vaishyas, who together made up the 'alpajan', or 'minority'. The negation of Brahmanism, as we have seen in chapter 3, was the basis of the BSP's philosophy. Acquiring political power was the priority, but the aims of the BSP were not limited to this. It also sought to bring about social change. In this sense, it was a movement and a mission and not just a party. Kanshiram and his workers addressed the BSP along these lines, emphasizing that his mission was his message. He exhorted the dalits to 'Rebel against Brahminism, surrender yourself, become martyrs, create fraternity amongst yourselves, liberate yourself from the fear of destiny and God, and try to create a society in which there is freedom, equality and brotherhood, by organizing yourself and acquiring power over politics. This is the path for your liberation. Walk along Babasaheb's path—be educated, organize yourself, and fight.'[15] He made it clear to his supporters that the struggle, which began with Mahatma Phule, Shahuji Maharaj and Babasaheb, was now on their shoulders and they had to take their mission to its logical end.

The election symbol Kanshiram selected and demanded from the Election Commission was the elephant, an important cultural symbol of the earliest settlers in the region, comprising the subaltern communities. On the head of this huge elephant-like society sat the minority upper-caste Manuvadis, like the mahout, prodding the poor majority (elephant) with rods of injustice, exploitation and oppression till it bled, and forcing it into back-breaking work all day. The elephant was also the symbol of hard labour. Elephants tirelessly carried heavy tree trunks from the forests and loaded them on to trucks, while surviving only on leaves and branches. Similar was the fate of the poor majority of Indians who also toiled daily and survived on a frugal fare of vegetables and chapattis, unlike the rich upper castes who gorged on costly and nourishing food and drink.'[16]

In addition to the symbolic meaning, the elephant for dalits was related to Buddhism, the religion adopted by a number of them. There are many stories of elephants in the Jataka tales and in Buddhist literature in general. One tale describes how Mahamaya, the mother of Lord Buddha, dreamt of a white elephant, its trunk raised and bearing a lotus flower, directly entering her womb. When Mahamaya described this dream to Maharaj Suddhodana, the savant predicted the birth of a boy who would become a universal monarch, following a *grihastha* (householder's) life at first but becoming a *parivrajak* later by leading an austere life, and work for the emancipation of the deprived people.[17]

The elephant also had a third significance, associated with Dr Ambedkar, who had made it the symbol of the RPI. Since the BSP acquired Ambedkar's political mantle, it chose the elephant as its electoral symbol. This helped the RPI supporters and Ambedkarites to relate to the new party. Additionally, the elephant was considered the vehicle of the deities worshipped by dalits across India, in Himachal Pradesh, Punjab, Bihar, and so on.[18] Kanshiram thus showed great foresight by selecting this symbol. The flag chosen by the BSP had an elephant on a blue background.

He now tried to inculcate self-respect among the dalits by building up a cultural politics. One method was to give importance to the saints, gurus and heroes of each dalit and backward caste. Each lower caste had its own heroes who were revered in its oral tradition, through ballads and narratives, but without any visual form. Kanshiram adopted the strategy of converting these heroes into political resources. The BSP created images of them which the illiterate and semi-literate dalits at the grass-roots level could internalize as symbols of their identity.

Kanshiram formed committees of local cadres and intellectuals at the block level, comprising mainly schoolteachers and dalit activists, who were interested in folklore and history. They were instructed to collect information from the various castes about their caste history, caste heroes and their sect (*panthi*) gurus like Sant Ravidas, Sant Kabir and Swami Shiv Narayan.[19]

Dalit Guru Ravidas, like the other two gurus, was born in medieval times, when casteism, social hierarchy, untouchability and religious orthodoxy and obscurantism were reigning supreme. The Brahmanical cultural code laid down in the *Manu Samhita* was being openly practised everywhere, without any protest being raised against the wrongdoings. In addition, the Mughal rulers were frantically converting the lower castes to Islam through various allurements and temptations in order to expand their numbers and consolidate their position in India. Sant Ravidas, through his preaching, tried to reform Hindu society so that the lower castes were not tempted to convert to Islam and the Varna system was maintained.[20] He was an extremely revered dalit saint, and the Ravidasia sect, comprising mostly Chamars, is named after him.

All these gurus fought against Brahmanical norms and social inequality while exhorting dalits to fight for their rights. Later, *panth*s or sects like Kabir Panthi and Shivnarayani developed and became highly popular among dalits and OBCs. Popular booklets containing the life stories of these dalit caste heroes, saints and other such figures were put to use for political mobilization. About fifty to sixty pages long, these booklets were printed on cheap newsprint. They were sold or distributed in large numbers at political meetings, fairs and Chetna Mandaps (small bookstalls run by dalit writers in cities and towns of UP like Ballia, Bahraich, Etah, Etawah, etc.). Educated and politically conscious, the writers and publishers of these booklets were mostly dalits and belonged to the middle or upper-middle class.[21]

The next job was to give a face to these heroes. Sometimes the narrative itself had a description of the hero, but often they needed to create an image that would fit into the general narrative, when no other visual source was available. Kanshiram and other BSP leaders actually sat down with artists and developed sketches of these heroes. Statues of dalit local heroes too came up across UP. Pictures, in the form of posters or calendars, of heroes like Ambedkar, Kabir and Ravidas, besides the folk heroes, were put up on the walls of dalit houses. In the homes of some Hindu dalits these posters were hung alongside pictures of Hindu gods like Ganesha, Hanuman, Durga, etc., while Buddhist dalits had pictures or idols of Buddha in their houses. It is noteworthy that these calendars and posters of revered dalit icons like Ambedkar, Phule, Shahuji Maharaj, and so on, are to be found mainly in the homes of people in cities or small towns. In villages, on the other hand, pictures of local dalit heroes and saints like Ravidas, etc., are distributed free of cost during political rallies in the form of leaflets, pamphlets and handbills, in order to popularize them there.

All these things helped create myths and a shared memory. Through dissemination, these now became part of the dalits'

Plate 1. Kanshiram's birthplace in Bunga Sahib village, Ropar district.
Courtesy: Brijendra Kumar Gautam

Plate 2. Paternal house of Kanshiram in Khawaspur village, Ropar district.
Courtesy: Brijendra Kumar Gautam

Plate 3. Kanshiram's mother, Bishan Kaur.
Courtesy: Brijendra Kumar Gautam

Plate 4. Kanshiram's sister Sabran Kaur. Courtesy: Brijendra Kumar Gautam

Plate 5. Kanshiram's brother Dalbara Singh. Courtesy: Brijendra Kumar Gautam

Plate 6. Kanshiram addressing a political rally. Courtesy: Brijendra Kumar Gautam

ब॰ स॰ पा॰

चुनाव चिन्ह हाथी

हाथी पर मोहर लगायें

बहुजन समाज पार्टी

Plate 7. Election symbol of the BSP. Courtesy: Nivedita

मा. कांशीराम जी द्वारा डा. देवी सिंह 'अशोक' को लिखा गया पत्र

BAMCEF

ALL INDIA BACKWARD S.T., O.R.C.) AND ORITY COMMUNITIES OYEES FEDERATION - DELHI H.Q. - DELHI

Address:
BAMCEF CENTRAL UNIT
10912, GALI NO. 2 (A)
SATNAGAR, KAROL BAGH,
NEW DELHI - 110005.

No. BAMCEF/Seminar/77.

Dated 4th August, 1977.

Dear Mr *Ashok*,

Please refer to my earlier letter for inviting you to participate in the Seminar on the subject," Significane of first 3 decades of Independence to the oppressed and minority Communities of India and future outlook for them." To give further details of the programme regarding place and time etc. please note the following :

Place : Community Hall, Panchkulan Road, Paharganj, New Delhi.

Time : 11th August, 1977, 11.00 A.M. to 6.00 P.M. 3 Sessions with tea and lunch breaks.

12th August, 1977, 9.00 A.M. to 6.00 P.M. 4 Sessions with tea andlunch breaks.

Hoping to meet you to on 11th August, 77 when our programme starts.

With best wishes and kind regards,

Yours sincerely,
(Kanshi Ram)
Convenor.

N.B :- We want you at Delhi on 11th. and 12th. Aug. 1977. for the Seminar. Time & Place are mentioned in the letter. Rest. then we do meet at Delhi

Kanshi Ram

Plate 8. Letter (handwritten) from Kanshiram to Dr Devi Singh 'Ashok'.
Courtesy: Dalbara Singh

Plate 9. Party badges worn by the BSP supporters during the election period for campaigning. Courtesy: Nivedita

Plate 10. Mayawati addressing a political rally in Allahabad. Courtesy: Nivedita

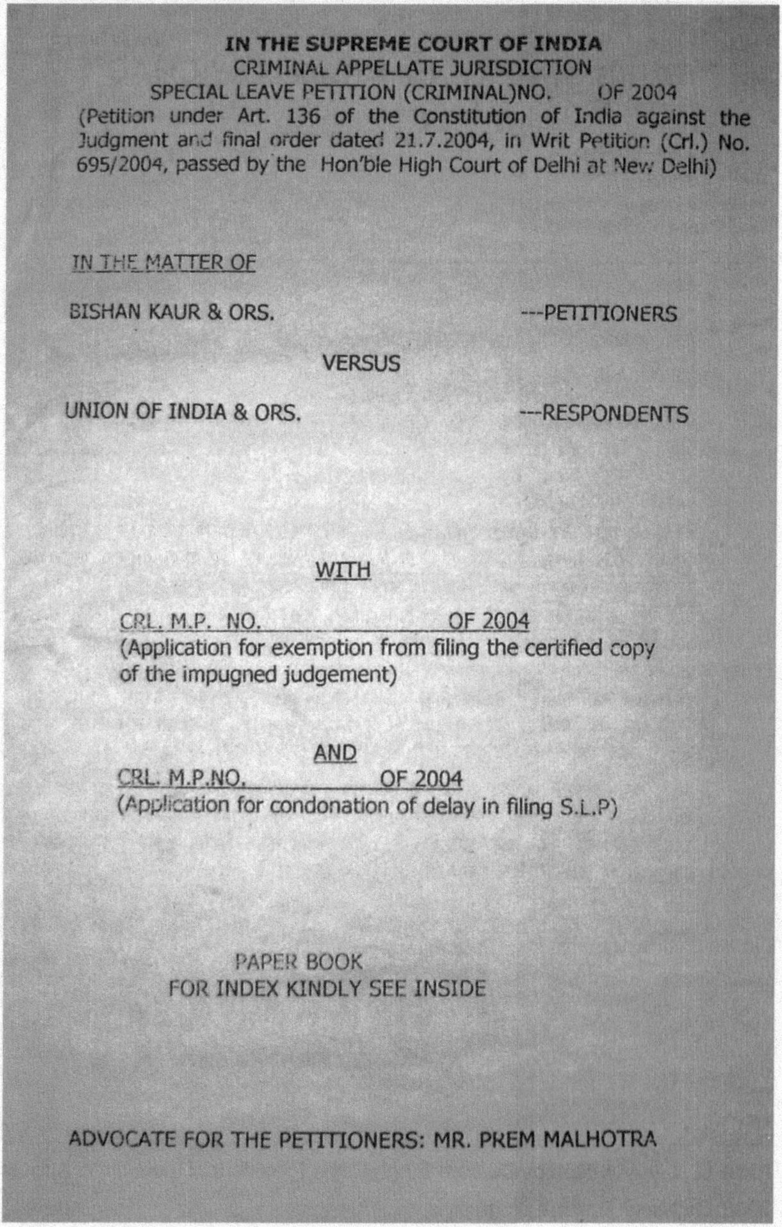

IN THE SUPREME COURT OF INDIA
CRIMINAL APPELLATE JURISDICTION
SPECIAL LEAVE PETITION (CRIMINAL)NO.   OF 2004
(Petition under Art. 136 of the Constitution of India against the Judgment and final order dated 21.7.2004, in Writ Petition (Crl.) No. 695/2004, passed by the Hon'ble High Court of Delhi at New Delhi)

IN THE MATTER OF

BISHAN KAUR & ORS. ---PETITIONERS

VERSUS

UNION OF INDIA & ORS. ---RESPONDENTS

WITH

CRL. M.P. NO.   OF 2004
(Application for exemption from filing the certified copy of the impugned judgement)

AND

CRL. M.P.NO.   OF 2004
(Application for condonation of delay in filing S.L.P)

PAPER BOOK
FOR INDEX KINDLY SEE INSIDE

ADVOCATE FOR THE PETITIONERS: MR. PREM MALHOTRA

Plate 11. Petition filed by Kanshiram's mother, Bishan Kaur, and others over Kanshiram's custody. Courtesy: Dalbara Singh

SAHIB SHRI KANSHI RAM JI BACHAO
SANGHARSH COMMITTEE

DALWARA SINGH
National Chairman
Village-Khawaspur, P.O. Mallakpur,
Distt. Ropad, Punjab.
Tel: 01881-242241, Mob: 9814465229

HIRA LAL JAWADDI
National General Secretary
BRS Nagar, Ludhiana, Punjab.
Tel: 9316948370

सेवा में,
महामहिम राष्ट्रपति मृहोदय
भारत गणतंत्र
नई दिल्ली।

विषयः मा0 कांशीराम साहिब को कु0 मायावती की निजी कैद से मुक्त कराने हेतु।

<u>ज्ञापन</u>

आदरणीय महामहिम जी,

आपको सादर अवगत कराना है कि मा0 कांशीराम साहिब संघर्ष कमेटी (भारत) के द्वारा 10 मई 2006 से कु0 मायावती की निजी कैद से मा0 कांशीराम साहिब को आजाद कराने हेतु जंतर-मंतर पर अनवरत धरना दिया जा रहा है और लगातार मांग की जाती रही है कि शासन और प्रशासन हस्तक्षेप कर यदि मा0 कांशीराम साहिब बीमार हैं तो उन्हें अस्पताल में होना चाहिए और यदि स्वस्थ हैं तो उन्हें बहुजन समाज के बीच होना चाहिए। पर खेद है कि राष्ट्रीय मान्यता प्राप्त राजनैतिक दल 'बहुजन समाज पार्टी' के संस्थापक/ अध्यक्ष एवं लोकसभा व राज्यसभा के पूर्व सदस्य मा0 कांशीराम साहिब जिन्हें कु0 मायावती ने अपने सरकारी आवास सी 1/ 11, हुमायूं रोड, नई दिल्ली में कैद कर रखा है को आजाद कराने हेतु न ही लोकसभा सभा अध्यक्ष और न ही राज्यसभा सभापति और न ही सरकार द्वारा कोई कार्यवाही की गई है।

अतः आप से जनहित में मांग है कि मा0 कांशीराम साहिब को कु0 मायावती की निजी कैद से मुक्त करा कर एवं अस्पताल में भर्ती कराकर उनके स्वास्थ्य का मेडीकल बुलेटिन जारी करवाने का आदेश प्रदान करें ताकि देश के करोड़ों करोड़ मा0 कांशीराम साहिब के समर्थकों को सही तथ्यों की जानकारी मिल सके। इसी आशा और विश्वास के साथ।

आपका

दिनांकः 11.08.2006

D. Singh
(दलबारा सिंह)
अध्यक्ष
मा0 कांशीराम बचाओ संघर्ष कमेटी (भारत)

Plate 12. Letter written by Dalbara Singh to the President of India on 11 August 2006. Courtesy: Dalbara Singh

everyday existence, in new forms and interpretations. The BSP fully exploited the powerful visual medium to make a greater impact. It succeeded in creating a cyclical relationship between myths, memories and visual images to arouse the sense of caste pride and glory among the dalits of UP.

Local heroes from different places in UP were popularized as symbols of dalit identity. In the Bundelkhand region of Jhansi, Hamirpur, Lalitpur and Banda, among the Kori caste, it was Jhalkaribai; in Lucknow, Bahraich, Barabanki, Jaunpur and Allahabad, it was Bijli Maharaj among the Pasi caste. In the area of Raebareli, Jaunpur and Allahabad, Daldev Maharaj was popularized among the Pasis, while among the Pasis of Purvanchal and Awadh, it was Baaledeen. Among the Pasis of the Awadh region of Pratapgarh, Sultanpur and Allahabad, Veera Pasi was also popularized, while among the Pasis of Allahabad, Pratapgarh and Sultanpur, it was Udadevi. Among the Buddhists of the Purvanchal region of Varanasi, Ghazipur, Ballia, Basti and Deoria, Mahamaya was popularized, while among the Chamars of Varanasi, Jaunpur, Allahabad and Azamgarh, it was Sant Ravidas.[22]

In addition to the mythological heroes, the unsung dalit heroes of the Revolt of 1857 were the richest historical resource for the BSP. The heroes of this movement claimed by the dalits were Ballu Mehtar, Udaiya Pasi, Chetram Jatav, Banke Chamar, Ganga Baksh, Veera Pasi, Makka Pasi, Matadin Bhangi and women heroes like Jhalkaribai, Udadevi, Avantibai, Pannadhai and Mahaviridevi.[23] These heroes formed the key base of the BSP's cultural resource. It is noteworthy that the BSP did not find the heroes of the other phases of the Indian freedom movement—like the Kisan Andolan that took place in UP in 1914, under the leadership of a dalit called Madari Pasi,[24] or the Chauri Chaura incident in which many dalits became martyrs[25]—significant enough to be developed as icons.

Among the myths Kanshiram selected were the immensely popular tale of Chhaur of the Yadav caste in the Rewa and Satna districts of Bundelkhand region, where Chhaur, a cowherd, fought against the local king; the life story of Chuharmal, a Dusadh chivalrous hero; the legend of Jhalkaribai of the Kori caste in the districts of Jhansi, Hamirpur, Lalitpur and Banda in the Bundelkhand region; and the story of Udadevi of the Pasi caste in the districts of Allahabad, Pratapgarh and Lucknow in Awadh and central UP. He used them as sources of inspiration and motivation.

The story of Chuharmal and Rani Reshma, the beautiful daughter of a local raja of Bhumihar caste, is a legend in the region. Chuharmal and Ajab Singh, Reshma's brother, were schoolmates and became fast friends. Once when Ajab Singh fell ill, Chuharmal went to see him at his house. There Reshma saw Chuharmal and was so fascinated by him that she wanted to marry him. Reshma later sent a message for Chuharmal to meet her at an isolated place. Chuharmal was a brave and handsome youth but also deeply religious. He refused Reshma's offer. Reshma felt insulted and wanted to take revenge. Consequently, there was a fight between the army of her zamindar father and Chuharmal. The zamindar's army was defeated. Reshma, determined to take her revenge, now sought the help of a tantric to defeat Chuharmal but to no avail. The rest of the tale describes a fierce struggle between the army of Reshma's father and Chuharmal. But Chuharmal was so powerful that he could not be defeated. According to this narrative, he is still alive. With the blessings of Goddess Durga he has become immortal.

The myth of Jhalkaribai, as told by the dalits of Jhansi, Hamirpur, etc., lies within the ambit of the narrative of the Revolt of 1857, also known as the first war of Indian independence.

> There was a *dasi* [maidservant] named Jhalkaribai in the palace of Rani Laxmibai of Jhansi. She was a low-caste woman. When the British besieged the fort of Jhansi and started firing from all sides, Jhalkaribai suggested that the Rani should leave the place after securing her child [who was the heir apparent] to her back. She, on her part, would hoodwink the British by assuming the appearance of the Rani. The Rani accepted this advice and made good her escape with the child. The ruse worked and for a long time the British were uncertain about the true identity of Jhalkaribai . . . It was much later that they learnt that the 'Rani' was in fact the maid Jhalkaribai. But by then it was too late and the Rani had already covered a considerable distance.[26]

The story of Udadevi, the personal aide of the Lucknow Nawab's wife, Begum Hazrat Mahal, which is narrated by the Pasis of the Awadh region, is also related to 1857. The incident, they believe, took place on 16 November 1857.

> There was a peepal tree, heavy and thick, in the middle of the inner portion of Sikander Bagh of Lucknow. Under it were kept earthen vessels, mostly filled with cold water. When the bloodshed ceased, many soldiers came there to quench their

thirst and enjoy the cool shade and to rest. They found there the bodies of British soldiers, belonging to the 53rd and 59th regiments of the British army. From the wounds on the bodies Dawson (Captain of the British troops) noted, it was evident that the soldiers had been hit by bullets fired from above. Leaving the shade, he called for Wallace, as he wanted to check whether there was someone on the tree . . . Wallace had his loaded gun with him. Cautiously, moving back, he pointed his gun at the tree searchingly. He spotted a person and immediately called Dawson. Lifting his gun, he declared that he would fulfil his promise before God. A body fell to the ground when he fired. The person was wearing a red jacket and tight rose-coloured trousers. When the jacket was removed, they found it was a lady. She had two pistols of an old model. One pistol was full of cartridges and the other was exhausted. She had in her pocket live cartridges, which had been manufactured with extreme care. Wallace wept when he saw whom he had killed. 'Had I known that she was a woman I would have died a thousand times but never harmed her,' he moaned. The lady was none other than Udadevi.[27]

The heroes picked by BSP were initially used to mobilize the caste groups to which they belonged but gradually they grew into icons for the dalit community as a whole. For example, when Jhalkaribai was being used for mobilizing the Kori caste to which she belonged, she was referred to as Jhalkaribai Kori. Later, when her myth was used for building up the image of Mayawati, she came to be known only as Jhalkaribai. Similarly, Udadevi 'Pasi', Mahaviridevi 'Bhangi', Avantibai 'Lodhi' and

Pannadhai 'Dhanuk' were mentioned only by their first names when their stories were linked with Mayawati's. This, however, did not mean that the individual caste identities of the different dalit sub-castes were being diluted. Rather, their caste identities were being strengthened through the stories of their caste heroes, even though they linked themselves with the broader dalit identity and were brought under one political umbrella through mobilization by the BSP.

The narratives of the 1857 Revolt helped them to not only establish their own heroes but also served the purpose of dethroning the existing high-caste heroes from the mainstream narratives. The high castes were presented as traitors, conspirators and communities that had been unfaithful to their motherland. The dalits wanted to prove that, though traitors, the high castes had managed to project themselves as the greatest nationalists simply by capturing historical narratives.

As part of the BSP's political strategy, statues of Jhalkaribai, Udadevi, Suhaldev and Bijli Pasi were installed at roadside crossings all over UP in the first phase between 1985 and 2005.[28] Jhalkaribai's statues were also installed in Jhansi and Bundelkhand region where her myth is popular. Udadevi's statues were installed especially in the Awadh region because of her connection with Lucknow.

The story of Maharaja Bijli Pasi, a Pasi king, was particularly significant as a symbol of caste glory for the dalits, as it proved that some of the lower castes were also kings. An able leader of the Pasis—a fiercely independent people indigenous to the Awadh region—he is supposed to have consolidated his position and reigned over large tracts of land in the medieval period.

He was a contemporary of Prithviraj Chauhan and is credited with founding Bijnor, now a small town near Lucknow. He constructed twelve forts, an indication of the prosperity of his kingdom as well as of the power he wielded. The ruins of the fort from where he ruled still remain in Lucknow and have been converted into a memorial by the BSP. A statue of Bijli Pasi, in the image of a medieval warrior holding a bow and arrow, has been installed there.

Maharaja Bijli Pasi was a celebrated figure in the early twentieth century, even before the BSP adopted him. The then Government of India issued a stamp in memory of Maharaja Bijli Pasi to draw the attention of the people towards this legendary ruler and his tales of bravery. There had also been other lower-caste kings before him. Suhaldev was the eldest son of the king of Sravasti, Raja Mordhwaj. It is popularly believed that he was the king of the Bhar community, from which the Pasi community emerged. But some people of the forward castes of Bahraich project him as a Vais Kshatriya (Suryavanshi Kshatriya), although there are no historical records to substantiate it.[29]

The party developed a pyramid of heroes and saints. At the base of the pyramid were the local heroes and *virangana*s of the 1857 Revolt like Jhalkaribai and Udadevi. The second level comprised local kings like Baldev, Daldev, Bijli Pasi, and so on. At the third level were dissenting Puranic and mythological heroes like Eklavya from the Mahabharata and Shambook from the Ramayana, who were projected as a counter-narrative to subvert Brahmanical dominance. Above them were the saints like Kabir, Ravidas and the Buddha, and at the top were Ambedkar, Periyar and Shahuji Maharaj. In front of the pyramid were Kanshiram and Mayawati. The idea was to show how symbolic power accumulated from each level of the pyramid, beginning from the memory of local heroes up to Ambedkar, from where it reached Kanshiram and Mayawati and was used for their image building.

The strategy developed by Kanshiram was to tell and retell the stories of the heroes of a particular region, build memorials and organize celebrations around their stories in order to create a collective memory in the minds of the dalits. The stories were narrated in such a manner that dalits could imagine the making of the nation and the significant role they had played in it. The contributions made by their ancestors were reinforced by stating that, despite their sacrifices, the desires, dreams and aspirations of millions of dalits were yet to be fulfilled. These narratives helped dalits claim a respectable place in the story of nation building and a considerable share in state-sponsored development projects and other democratic benefits. They put forward a moral logic in favour of reservations and social justice for themselves. 'They contended that though they had shed their blood and sweat for the building of this nation, the state had not helped them recover from their social, cultural and economic losses; that their role in the history of nation-making had not been sufficiently acknowledged and their contribution in the freedom struggle had been ignored.'[30] Using these narratives, Kanshiram recreated the meaning, social and historical, of the past of the marginalized castes, which would help arouse their pride in their caste glory and, in the process, enhance their dignity and self-respect.

In addition to creating images of dalit heroes, Kanshiram also tried to popularize Ambedkar among the UP dalits. The groundwork for popularizing Ambedkar in the state had already been done by Swami Achhutanand while he was involved in the Adi-Hindu movement with which Ambedkar had a close association. The Poona Pact of 1932 further consolidated their friendship, since Swami Achhutanand was one of the signatories of the pact. Ambedkar was also a close associate of Hari Prasad Tamta, the first editor of *Samta*, a newspaper published from Almora during the colonial period. Ambedkar's fame thus spread in this region by word of mouth, with Tamta talking about him to his friends, and in print via the newspaper *Samta*, which regularly published Ambedkar's writings. Also, the educated dalits of north India had read about Ambedkar's role in the Poona Pact in the newspapers. These people started subscribing to dalit newspapers published from Maharashtra, which contained the writings of Ambedkar. In this manner they became aware of his opinions and writings and he gained repute in UP.[31]

After Independence, from 1958 onwards, the RPI expanded in UP. With the spread of its political discourse, Ambedkar became a part of the people's collective psyche. The image carved in the mind of the common dalit was that of a super human (*maha manav*), the messiah of the dalits, and one who would lead them towards enlightenment through education and development. The RPI's political spread began from western UP and extended towards Kanpur and its adjoining regions. Agra had started emerging as a hub of dalit politics. Ambedkar addressed a rally there on 18 March 1956, which lakhs of educated dalits attended. Through such meetings, Ambedkar's fame spread further in the region. Earlier, his picture was popularized through posters and pamphlets published and distributed by the RPI for disseminating information about forthcoming meetings. The image was that of a suited and booted, westernized gentleman holding a copy of the Constitution in one hand. This image appeared to the common dalits as a symbol of the awareness to be achieved through education and their fight for a better future. It also helped deconstruct the stereotype notion of dalits as being oppressed, suppressed and illiterate.

After Ambedkar's death his photographs were published in calendars and posters and his statues began to be erected. His photographs were also published on the covers of dalits' magazines, newspapers and booklets. This image reached the common and illiterate dalits; with this when they heard the mythical and eulogizing narratives of him in everyday political talk and occasional speeches, his image as a saviour and the architect of Indian democracy became ingrained in their minds. In some places he was referred to as an incarnation of the Buddha while in others he was hailed as being more knowledgeable than the upper castes.

When the BSP jumped into the political fray in UP in the mid 1980s, Kanshiram found that there were very few statues of Ambedkar in the state. The only ones there had been installed by the government, semi-political and social organizations. After the launching of the BSP and its strategy of aggressively asserting its identity, statues of Ambedkar began to be installed by dalit politicians and activists in various places. Through them his image was brought to the dalits at the grass roots in the region where people knew little about him, unlike in Maharashtra where he was a household name.

In the first phase, before the BSP understood the peculiar society and culture of UP, in which saints, seers, epic heroes and local heroes occupied an important space in people's minds, both upper and lower caste, it tried to mobilize dalits using the Ambedkarite narrative, dominated by social and economic aspects.[32] In the later phase, once the BSP had grasped the pulse of the people, it had to change its political language from that of the Maharashtrian dalit movement, with its dominance of the myth of Ambedkar, to one that was interspersed with the cultural symbols of the people of this region. As we have seen, Ambedkar and the local cultural heroes were now projected as being complementary, part of one pyramid, rather than opposed to each other.

As an architect of the cultural politics of the BSP, Kanshiram formed a separate wing of the party which was called the Jagriti Jatha. Formed during the time of BAMCEF, it continued as an important instrument of mobilization for the BSP also. The wing comprised artists, singers, performing artistes, littérateurs and intellectuals. Kanshiram believed that this wing served two purposes. Firstly, it would be used to spread the political message among the masses and, secondly, creative people from among the dalits would be discovered and nurtured. He said that 'through this process we have identified numerous artistes from among the dalit community, which includes both men and women. After training them a new cultural consciousness will spread among the dalits. Through this process we are in contact with many cultural activists, cultural leaders and writers who have become involved in our mission.'[33]

During the second BAMCEF conference held at Ramlila Maidan in Delhi in 1981, Kanshiram described the importance of the Jagriti Jatha by saying that among all the activities organized as a part of the conference the most splendid were the ones put up by the Jagriti Jatha. The huge murals that were part of the exhibition prepared by the wing under the supervision of the artist Mr Patil were admired by each and every one. The dances, drama and the other performing arts presented on all the five nights, which went on from nine till one in the night, and which were watched by a huge crowd, showed how strong the wing has become. The members of the wing also made films on all the activities which will be a legacy for the coming generations.[34]

The programme, Ambedkar Mela on Wheels, was a part of this politics, in which painters and artists of the Jagriti Jatha painted pictures and posters to disseminate the message of social equality. Kanshiram also appealed to writers and intellectuals, who knew about the inequalities in society, to give him ideas to strengthen the dalit and bahujan movement. Kanshiram said that 'in short, if we look at the balance sheet of the results of these small efforts, we can say that there is a huge benefit from them'.[35]

Kanshiram also tried to use the traditional dalit melas as a political space. He used to visit such fairs where the dalits gathered in huge numbers and deliver his political message. He tried to provide a political meaning to the undercurrents of dissent in the traditional dalit memories and the narratives, tales and messages associated with these fairs. 'Kanshiram was once invited to such a fair, the Ramnami mela held in Chhattisgarh. This fair provided an opportunity to Kanshiram to understand the land and people living there.'[36]

These various strategies of cultural politics helped Kanshiram mobilize the dalits, especially in UP, and created the ground for the progress of the BSP.

∼

Kanshiram decided to set up the headquarters of the party in a densely populated dalit colony in Delhi called Raigarpura. He wanted a place that was cheap and centrally located and Raigarpura was ideal. The office was a single, spartan room. Some of the key people who joined Kanshiram at this point were Rajaram Fauji, Bhudev Prasad Gautam, Pratap Singh Suman, Omprakash Gautam, Salim Siddiqui, Salim Varisi, Hari Singh Baghel, Rajaram Anand, K.P. Rana, Ramprasad Swami, Dhaniram Foreman, Ram Charan Lal, R.P. Mehra, Hari Mohan Chintak, Hoti Lal Sewak, Munshi Lal Gautam, Hari Om Sharan, Dr Ramswaroop Mahaur, Kunwarpal Singh, Raghuveer Singh Gautam, Beni Ram.[37] All these people were eventually marginalized once Mayawati took over the reins of the party. Among those who are still alive, none occupy important positions in the party today.

In the initial phase of the BSP, the party was run by workers of both BAMCEF and the BSP, but the members of BAMCEF were not compelled to vote for the BSP, since BAMCEF was not politically affiliated to any party. As government employees, these people could also not be members of any political party. However, the members of BAMCEF usually voted for the BSP and at the time of elections, they looked after the running of the election office.

The contribution of BAMCEF in the development of the BSP was immense. Indeed, the manifesto of the BSP was prepared by BAMCEF since their members were more educated. The head of the election office of the BSP was also usually a member of BAMCEF. All accounts of the money spent during elections were maintained by BAMCEF, since it raised most of the funds and wished to keep a check on them. The BAMCEF members also planned out the electoral strategies of the BSP.

The closeness between these two bodies created its own problems. Many workers of the BSP were not convinced about BAMCEF's control over their party. Being educated and working in government offices, BAMCEF members, they believed, were unfamiliar with the ground realities of UP society. Moreover, they often ignored the BSP workers' ground reports and went ahead and planned everything their own way. Many BSP workers also believed the BAMCEF members tried to misguide Kanshiram by feeding him with wrong information from the grass-roots level.[38]

Ultimately, the responsibility rested on Kanshiram's shoulders. The entire election strategy was chalked out by him. He regularly interacted with people through his campaign tours. He also organized the BSP according to the functional needs of the party rather than with any pre-planned strategy in mind. His belief was that the party would grow as the bahujan samaj did and new dimensions would get added as the need arose. Kanshiram had thus conceived the BSP as a constantly evolving entity.

'For organizational purposes, the country was divided into 100 zones and more than 3,500 party offices were set up all over. The headquarters remained in Delhi and Kanshiram remained its

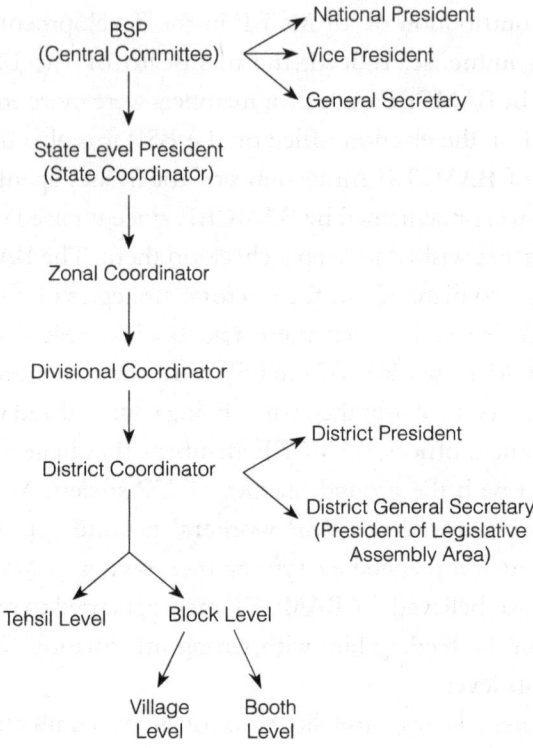

ORGANIZATIONAL STRUCTURE OF THE BSP

undisputed head. In the beginning there were no office bearers like vice president, secretary, etc. Everyone was a party worker. Although technically Kanshiram was the head, he preferred to call himself a worker. At the local and state levels the heads were known as coordinators and they were all handpicked by Kanshiram.'[39] Initially, there were no state-level offices but later offices were opened in UP and a few other states. There used to be no internal elections and neither were manifestos released until 2004. Even now there are no internal elections in the BSP and the speeches of Kanshiram, his written statements and the 'new declarations made by him at election rallies' are employed more than the manifesto.[40]

At the state or local level, the coordinator of the party was unofficially referred to as 'president' while Kanshiram was referred to as 'national president'. Each regional president was selected by Kanshiram. Each block also had a division head, chosen by Kanshiram himself. In the initial stages the division head of the BSP functioned with the help of BAMCEF members but was directly accountable to Kanshiram. He usually acted as the mediator between Kanshiram and the district head—also appointed by Kanshiram and accountable to him. All the heads were selected using the same criteria, with most weight for dedication, efficiency, honesty, availability of time and the caste factor. The functions of the heads ranged from recruiting new members to giving momentum to the movement. The new members were usually government employees and belonged to the dalit and backward castes. The work of the members was to inspire more people to join hands in the fight for dalit emancipation. They also inspired people to legally and financially help dalits who were victims of atrocities. These new members worked as cadres for dalit mobilization. These members were in addition to those of BAMCEF, who went from house to house and appealed to the people to join BAMCEF. Not only dalits but also the Muslims and backward-caste people gave monetary contributions to BAMCEF, who then issued them receipts. The collected amount reached their head office via the coordinators.

After a few years, as the BSP gained in strength, BAMCEF started losing its importance and was later completely dissolved.[41]

In Uttar Pradesh, there were fourteen zones and the head of each zone was called 'zonal coordinator'. These zonal coordinators used to select district coordinators and the district coordinators in turn chose booth-level workers, of course with the approval of Kanshiram. The BSP made full preparations for controlling the various assembly election booths. The booth committee comprised ten members who belonged to different castes, representing the voters belonging to them in the village. The information about the activities and functioning of each village was passed on to the district coordinators. At cadre camps, block-level coordinators were instructed how to send the information up, a year before the elections. Organized in each assembly constituency, the training in these camps was imparted by BSP state-level coordinators. All the instructions were given on behalf of Mayawati, whose words carried the most weight in the party after Kanshiram's. The responsibility for increasing vote percentage of the party was with the cadres or coordinators at each level. For this, electoral strategies were chalked out by the BSP high command, which were passed on to the booth-level workers and other party workers. The district coordinators used to look after the management of these training camps.[42] The BSP was a centralized party and the deciding force were Kanshiram and Mayawati. They sought information from the grass roots and the local coordinators but the ultimate decision was taken by them.

The political activists of the BSP were divided into two categories: worker and cadre. While the cadres comprised dalits who were educated, employed, had migrated or had become a part of the mobile dalit community in urban slums, the workers were full-time and part-time activists; while the full-time workers devoted all their time to the activities of the mission, the part-time workers spent only a few hours for the party activities. The workers mostly comprised people from the urban slums. Most of them were unemployed youths. Some of them were also engaged in small businesses or held jobs in cities. There were field labourers and vendors as well. It was a mix of literate, semi-literate and illiterate members.

The cadres were basically the think tanks of the BSP and the focal point around which the workers revolved. They supervised the workers and educated and mobilized them. The full-time workers were selected very carefully and were usually those who did not have heavy family responsibilities or too many social obligations. They also had to be committed to the cause of the party. Their chief responsibilities were to spread dalit consciousness, help needy dalits by agitating on their behalf, take out rallies, and so on. The part-time workers also worked full-time for the party during elections, rallies, etc. They were usually selected by the local heads. Activists wore white shirts and blue pants, which were the party colours. They greeted each other with 'Jai Bhim'—distinct from the Brahmanical castes' salutation of 'Jai Sri Ram'—as a mark of respect to Bhimrao Ambedkar and all that he had fought for. Meaning 'Hail equality, hail freedom, hail fraternity and hail justice', 'Jai Bhim' was not merely a salute to a single individual but to an entire ideology.

In order to become a member of the BSP one had to first work for dalit society; only when a person's dedication

Kanshiram

was proven was he or she allowed to become a member. The person had to be nominated by an existing BSP member and pay a membership or registration fee of three rupees and after becoming a member, an annual fee of twelve rupees. Kanshiram had made graduation an essential qualification for all full-fledged party cadres as it would be easy to politicize them. He visualized this educated class as agents of social mobility and political socialization for oppressed dalits. This educated class of party workers became the backbone of Kanshiram's bahujan movement, mediating between Kanshiram and the dalit community and disseminating his thoughts among them.[43] About twenty lakh educated SC and ST government employees, who were intelligent and had the skills and the capital, were trained and harnessed as cadres, to arouse political consciousness among the common and illiterate dalits.

Although no castes were excluded from membership of the BSP, upper-caste people generally did not join.* The BSP members were also instructed to maintain their distance from upper-caste people and not to share with them their secrets and strategies. In principle, they could become members but not leaders. As Kanshiram said, 'Upper castes can join the party but the leadership will remain in the hands of the dalits.'[44] Kanshiram believed that the upper castes were status quoists. He said, 'The upper castes ask us why we don't take them in the party but I tell them that you are leading all the other parties. If

*In the initial phase, upper-caste people did not join the BSP. But after Mayawati acquired power, her social engineering strategy and the notion of 'sarvajan' enabled the upper-caste people of Brahman and Vaishya communities to join the party.

you join our party you will prevent change. I am scared to take upper castes in the party. They are status quoists and always try to seize leadership. This will thwart the process of changing the system. Only when I will be rid of my fear will I allow them to join the party.'[45]

In keeping with his dream for the BSP, Kanshiram sought to develop its intellectual base by forming a research wing which comprised the party's intellectuals and ideologues. This wing was like a committee and the members were selected directly by Kanshiram. Some people were appointed for a short time and some for a longer period. The selection of the members was done on the basis of the assignment to be accomplished. This was before Mayawati joined the party. The committee had no office bearers; all the members were equal in status. The committee took policy decisions about the party and alongside also dug out caste histories, created myths and produced literature on the basis of which dalit castes were mobilized. There were also research wings at the district and block levels, which functioned like the national research wing; the members of these wings were chosen by the district head.[46]

Kanshiram laid great emphasis on creating party literature for disseminating his ideas. As already stated, he used to bring out an English newsmagazine called the *Oppressed Indian* and later he started publishing a weekly newspaper called *Bahujan Sangathak*, which was published in both Hindi and English. The publication unit was an important unit of the BSP and its headquarters were in Delhi from where the English and Hindi publications were brought out. The responsibility of bringing out publications in other languages lay with the respective states.[47]

'The BSP also had a secret service which collected information from several sources and passed it on to Kanshiram. Most members of this wing belonged to BAMCEF and Kanshiram claimed that through informers in every department, within twenty-four hours, he received information about what the other parties were doing or what the government was planning.'[48] In addition, rather than depending on the police during rallies, the party had its own security guards. If the police entered the premises during a rally or meeting, they were politely requested by the party's guards to leave, with the assurance that no disorder would be caused. There was also a psychological reason for not accepting police help; as a senior BSP activist explained, the senior workers of the party wanted to prove to the ordinary members attending the rally that they had the courage to look after their own security. By doing this, they also instilled a sense of security in the members, inspiring them to shed their feelings of helplessness and vulnerability and to ensure their own safety without depending on others, especially upper-caste policemen.[49]

The party's establishment of its own security force also sent out a stern message about the violence commonly inflicted by the upper castes on the lower castes. The BSP security personnel were told at the time of recruitment that they should give a fitting reply to violence perpetrated by the upper castes on any of their caste members. Although there was no specific criteria for recruitment to be a security guard in the BSP, well-built individuals were usually selected and the selection was done by the block or district head. The security force also had its own head. The security guards wore blue trousers and white shirts and carried only sticks as weapons. No revolvers or rifles were allowed. At the time of a rally or meeting the guards used to spread out all over the ground, especially around the dais. When Kanshiram entered or left the meeting venue, the guards would stand in two rows from the gate till the dais, forming a passage for him to walk through.[50]

Soon after the formation of the BSP, Kanshiram embarked on an expedition to mobilize dalits and other oppressed and downtrodden castes and bring them together under the BSP banner. While explaining this strategy Kanshiram said:

> According to the Mandal Commission report, 1500 castes fall in the SC category, 100 in the ST category and 3743 in the OBC category. Overall, these castes are over 5000 in number. We have started forming a bahujan society by giving birth to fraternal feelings among these castes. In the last five years, we have been able to associate with only 600 castes, which accounts for nearly 10 per cent of the total castes. Thus, we see that just by associating with 600 castes our party has become the fourth largest party in the country. If we associate with 400 castes more then this value will reach to 1000 and the bahujan society will occupy the first position in the country.[51]

For strengthening the mass base of the BSP, Kanshiram launched several social programmes. By 15 August 1988, he had already undertaken activities against wrongs like untouchability, injustice and inequality. After that, for a year he ran an all-India movement for social change and economic empowerment. Under the social change programme he began five movements, which were for self-respect, liberty, equality, breaking caste barriers and consolidating the scattered dalit groups, and finally for wiping out untouchability, injustice, oppression and fear. In the same way, under the economic empowerment programme he started five movements, namely the farmer–peasant movement, the sweeper movement, the artisan movement, the refugee movement and the participation movement.[52]

Kanshiram believed that previous peasant movements had worked in favour of the landed farmers and not the small and marginal farmers. So the peasant movement he embarked upon through the BSP was different; he divided farmers into categories depending upon the amount of land they owned. Marginal farmers comprised 26 per cent, agricultural or khetihar farmers 22 per cent and large land owners 18 per cent. Together they made nearly 66 per cent of the farming community. 34 per cent were the landless farmers. According to him the peasant movements that had been run by the Congress and other leaders like Mahendra Singh Tikait and Sharad Joshi in recent times had talked about raising the price of production but not about the agricultural labourers who were linked with production. A rise in price would benefit the land owners, 90 per cent of whom were upper castes, which was what Kanshiram was against. The BSP movement for the agricultural labourers was a reflection of the movement launched by Ambedkar in 1927 for the Mahar community and the peasants who were victims of the Khoti system.[53]

The refugee movement launched by the BSP was concerned with the welfare of dalit rural migrants. According to Kanshiram, at the time of Partition the Central government had established a rehabilitation ministry to rehabilitate the nearly fifty lakh refugees from Pakistan. While the government spent nearly 5.30 crore rupees in 1978 to rehabilitate the 5000 families who fled Punjab in the wake of terrorism in the state, it had not spent a single penny for the welfare of 10 crore rural migrants, nor had it set up a ministry to look after their needs. Most of these migrants belonged to SC/ST communities. Kanshiram felt that this condition would change only when the government reformed its agricultural policy and provided alternative job opportunities in villages.[54]

Kanshiram's social change and economic empowerment programmes acted as magnets, serving to attract to the BSP all those dalits who had been seeking self-respect and economic betterment. These organizational strategies and methods certainly swelled the numbers of the BSP supporters in UP, as the party took shape there. The electoral politics of the BSP, as it grew in stature over the years, as well as the politics and internal differences that developed within the party need to be understood for appreciating its role in the rising power of the dalits.

5

The Bid for Power
Electoral Politics of the BSP

The BSP registered its political presence by contesting elections in the very year of its formation. Through the electoral strategies devised by Kanshiram, the BSP gradually worked its way up to become a formidable party and in this Mayawati played a significant role. In these elections to the Lok Sabha, the BSP got 10.05 lakh votes from across the country.[1] Both Mayawati and Kanshiram were candidates. While Mayawati sought election to the Kairana (Muzaffarnagar district, western UP) seat, Kanshiram contested the election from the Janjgir constituency (then in Madhya Pradesh, it later became a part of Chhattisgarh). Since the BSP had not yet been recognized by the Election Commission and had not been allotted a symbol, they contested as independent candidates supported by the party. Although both of them lost, they put up creditable performances with Mayawati coming in third with 44,445 votes, after being beaten by the Congress and Lok Dal candidates, and Kanshiram receiving around 9 per cent of the votes.[2]

In 1985, the BSP contested the Punjab assembly elections. The state was reeling under terrorism at the time and circumstances were unfavourable for the BSP. The main support of the Sikh terrorists came from the powerful Jat peasants while that for Kanshiram was from the religious, or Ramdasia, Sikhs, the community to which he belonged. The latter were relatively poor, unlike the Jats, who owned agricultural land. Under pressure because of Punjab's difficult socio-economic condition at that time, the religious Sikhs were not in a position to protest against the Jat Sikhs.

The support base of the Congress in Punjab was the dalits, peasants and businessmen. Kanshiram could kill two birds with one stone by contesting elections here. Firstly, he could emancipate the religious Sikhs from the domination of the Jat Sikhs and secondly, he could stop their votes from going to the Congress party. Kanshiram campaigned vigorously in spite of the repeated threats from the Akali Dal and the Sikh terrorists. On the day of the election, the Jat Sikhs did not come out to cast their votes and the Hindus mainly voted for the Congress. The BSP thus cornered the votes of the religious Sikhs.[3]

Although this time, too, the BSP lost, it succeeded in making a dent in the Congress vote bank in Punjab, which lost 24 per cent votes to it. The party had fought in thirty constituencies in the state and it won in nine of them. In Jalandhar, Hoshiarpur and Kapurthala, which lie in the region between the rivers Sutlej and Beas, it beat the Congress and won. In the same year, during the by-elections in UP for the Bijnor parliamentary seat after the death of Congress MP Girdharilal, Mayawati—this time as an independent candidate backed by the BSP—stood for the election opposite Meira Kumar, the daughter of Babu Jagjivan Ram, who was a member of the Congress, and Ram Vilas Paswan of the Lok Dal. The Congress party used all the resources at its disposal for the campaigning of Meira Kumar while the BSP and Mayawati had neither the political experience nor the resources. When the results were declared, Meira Kumar had won with 1,28,086 votes, Ram Vilas Paswan had obtained 1,22,747 votes and Mayawati was far behind with 61,504 votes.[4]

In 1987, when the Haridwar by-elections were held, Mayawati once again contested elections against the Congress party candidate and Ram Vilas Paswan of the Lok Dal. By then the party had been recognized by the Election Commission and she contested on her party symbol of the elephant. This time, the Congress candidate got 1,49,399 votes, while Mayawati was close, obtaining 1,35,399 votes. Ram Vilas Paswan was far behind, with 34,255 votes. He lost his deposit and decided never to stand for elections from UP again.[5] The years 1988, 1989 and 1990 were extremely significant for the BSP, since the party built an extensive base and gained mass support, and also garnered national and international attention. Between 1988 and 1989 the ideology of the BSP spread far and wide due to Kanshiram's unique creative ideas for disseminating the party's philosophy.

As mentioned in the previous chapter, Kanshiram had 'a five-point agenda: struggling for self-respect, struggling for liberty, struggling for equality, fighting caste discrimination and establishing harmony by fighting against untouchability, injustice, violence and terror'.[6] Earlier, as we have seen, in 1984 Kanshiram's DS4 workers undertook a massive cycle rally to spread his message. Starting from five points across the country, they had converged on Delhi.

In the same way, Kanshiram now organized six conferences in different parts of the country. The first conference in Moradabad on 10 September 1989 was a gathering of Muslims. On 13 September there was a conference in Delhi for the scheduled castes. On 1 October, a conference for the backward castes was held in Kanpur. On 8 October a conference for Sikhs was held in Ludhiana while on 15 October a conference for scheduled tribes was held in Bilaspur. The last one was held in Bangalore for Christians. Through these conferences he wanted to spread the message that Muslims, dalits, Sikhs, backward castes, Christians and tribals should link themselves with the BSP for their own security and upliftment.[7]

In 1989 Mayawati again stood for the parliamentary election from Bijnor, which she won with a tally of 1,83,189 votes. Though Kanshiram was personally not interested in acquiring political power—only in using it to empower dalits—he contested the Allahabad parliamentary by-election in 1989 for the seat that fell vacant after Amitabh Bachchan's resignation. The election was a triangular one and was of great interest to people even beyond India since he was contesting against V.P. Singh, who stood as an independent candidate, and against Sunil Shastri of the Congress party. Unlike the BSP, with its limited resources, the Congress party and V.P. Singh had huge funds at their disposal for their pre-election campaigns.

V.P. Singh used a motorcycle for his campaign. He would come out of his house at nine every morning, dressed in a white kurta–pyjama and sit there for some time, winnowing rice grains like a farmer, because that was what his election symbol was. He would then leave on his motorcycle for campaigning which went on until late in the evening. Sunil Shastri was provided a cavalcade of cars by the Congress party as he went all over the city campaigning. Kanshiram's electioneering on the other hand was unique, because he used only wall writing to campaign, while the BSP activists rode around the countryside on cycles fitted with mikes propagating the party's philosophy. V.P. Singh won the elections with 2,35,167 votes while Sunil Shastri came a poor second with 92,221 votes. Kanshiram on the other hand obtained only 68,836 votes.[8]

Nonetheless, Kanshiram succeeded in establishing his party as a representative of the dalits in the public eye.

Kanshiram also contested the 1989 parliamentary elections against Rajiv Gandhi from Amethi constituency. The other contestant was Mahatma Gandhi's grandson Rajmohan Gandhi, who was the candidate of the united group opposing the Congress party. This election was a tremendous test of ability for Kanshiram since he was pitted against two world-renowned figures; it also brought him under the spotlight of the international media. Kanshiram used this opportunity to project the BSP to the world as the party of the oppressed and the exploited.

Despite his vigorous campaigning, predictably, Kanshiram lost, but the BSP became firmly entrenched on the national plane, besides getting international exposure.[9] This general election was also a litmus test for the efforts Kanshiram and

Mayawati (who had become his right-hand support by then) had made in the preceding years, to mobilize the different communities of the bahujan samaj. The demolition of Rajiv Gandhi and the Congress party and the formation of the V.P. Singh–led minority Janata Dal supported by the Left and the BJP was the big story of that election. But the BSP's entry into Parliament also made headlines.

The BSP contested 245 seats and to their delight won 2.07 per cent of the national votes, with three parliamentary seats, including the Bijnor (reserved) constituency in UP from where Mayawati won, defeating her nearest Janata Dal rival by a margin of nearly 10,000 votes. The BSP also won from Azamgarh in UP and from Phillaur in Punjab where Ramkrishna Yadav and Harbhajan Singh Lakha respectively put up impressive performances. Overall, the party had got three MPs and was second in thirty-one constituencies.[10]

In addition to their success in the parliamentary elections, the BSP also won thirteen seats in the state assembly elections in UP, held along with the parliamentary elections.[11] The encouraging results from UP and Mayawati's entry into Parliament were the fulfilment of Kanshiram's long-cherished dream of entering mainstream politics through the BSP and obtaining the master key Ambedkar had always desired for the dalits.

After this victory, Kanshiram embarked on a 130-day countrywide tour to consolidate the alliance of all the bahujan samaj castes against the upper castes and also to celebrate Ambedkar's birth anniversary, leaving Mayawati to monitor the alliance in UP.[12] His journey began from Kanyakumari on 6 December 1990. He covered thirteen states in three months, in his 'Social Transformation Vehicle'. The tour terminated at the Boat Club lawns in New Delhi, with a historic rally on 15 March 1991. The places covered included Tamil Nadu, Kerala, Karnataka, Andhra Pradesh, Punjab, Himachal Pradesh, Jammu and Kashmir, and Chandigarh as well as Mahu in Indore, Madhya Pradesh (Ambedkar's birthplace).[13] 'Kanshiram's vehicle had a reception room, a resting room, a bathroom and a washroom. It was fitted with a generator, a lighting system and a microphone.'[14] The rally, however, ended on a sour note in New Delhi when a few excited BSP workers went to Rajghat from the Boat Club shouting 'Ambedkar Zindabad' and anti-Gandhi slogans. There was a huge ruckus as they went on a rampage, climbing on to the Gandhi Samadhi with their shoes on. This incident invited strong criticism from the Congress and other parties. Kanshiram tried to counter it, but his statement was released much later. Incidentally, in the same campaign tour, Kanshiram met his mother and other family members when the rally passed through Punjab. He also visited the Golden Temple and Anandpur Sahib Gurudwara in Amritsar where people gave him a warm welcome.[15]

The two big rallies Kanshiram organized in Maharashtra to garner support for the BSP there did not meet with much success because the dalit and the backward castes that were supporting the Shiv Sena did not join hands with him.[16] Apart from Maharashtra, Kanshiram also organized a rally of nearly one lakh people in Hyderabad.[17] After Hyderabad, Kanshiram turned his attention towards other places in Andhra Pradesh. He organized big rallies in Visakhapatnam and Nalgonda which helped increase the party's popularity.[18] Kanshiram tried to popularize the BSP in Gujarat too but with little success. His first rally was a failure there.

Mayawati's first stint in Parliament was short-lived. The V.P. Singh–led government fell within a year. It was replaced by a minority ministry led by the Janata Dal rebel leader Chandra Shekhar and supported by the Congress. Soon this ministry, too, fell, forcing mid-term polls.

This was a period of great political and social turmoil: on the one hand, V.P. Singh's sudden decision to implement the *Mandal Commission Report*, granting reservations to lower castes and OBCs in jobs and education, led to violent agitations by the upper castes across north India, and, on the other hand, BJP leader L.K. Advani, set off on a *rath yatra*, or chariot tour, to gather support for the construction of a Ram temple at the Ram Janmabhoomi site and for the demolition of the Babri Masjid standing there. In reality, this move was aimed at mobilizing the support of the lower castes, who had begun feeling alienated from the upper castes after their hostile reactions to the Mandal report. It was a clever and successful move since many among the backward castes, including OBCs and dalits, were converted to the BJP's cause and volunteered to help in the construction of the temple.

The assassination of Rajiv Gandhi while he was campaigning in the run-up to the elections added to the churning. The sympathy wave for the Congress that followed helped it win back power at the Centre with the support of some parties and groups of dalits and poor backward castes from UP.[19]

These factors coalesced to pull the BSP down, and its performance in the 1991 elections was disappointing. Mayawati lost her seat in Parliament and her party's vote percentage in UP came down from 10 to 8.4 per cent. The only gain was Kanshiram's victory from Etawah; he was the lone BSP winner from UP. This was the period when the BJP's popularity was at an all-time high, precipitated by the Ram Janmabhoomi movement. Its position was particularly strong in UP, where it formed a stable government with Kalyan Singh (a member of a backward caste) as the chief minister. His selection was another strategy of the party to win over the lower castes of the state who had already been mobilized as volunteers in the Ram Janmabhoomi movement. However, the BJP dug its own grave when it allowed a frenzied mob of Hindu fanatics to demolish the Babri Masjid in 1992, despite having promised (in response to a Supreme Court order) that it would not harm the mosque. The incident, which drew flak worldwide, pulled down the BJP in one stroke, and the first casualty was its government in UP—Kalyan Singh resigned before he could be sacked by the headquarters.[20]

All political parties shunning the BJP after the incident enabled the BSP to come to power in UP following the mid-term state assembly polls held in 1993. Kanshiram joined Mulayam Singh, leader of the SP—the party of the backward castes and Muslims, the bête noire of the BJP. The BSP and the SP went in for seat-sharing and together formed a coalition government supported by the Congress, smaller parties and independents even though BJP was the single largest party. In Mulayam Singh's cabinet of twenty-seven, the BSP had eleven ministers. In less than a decade since its formation, Kanshiram's party had partly fulfilled his dream of seizing the master key.[21]

Unfortunately, the alliance was doomed from the very beginning. It was Kanshiram's dream to bring together the backward castes, Muslims and dalits on one platform, but Mulayam Singh cared little for this ideological vision and had agreed to the alliance purely out of political expediency.

Initially, everything seemed to be going smoothly, but rifts soon began to appear in the alliance. There were several reasons for this, including Mayawati's strong attempts at controlling the alliance, which Mulayam Singh resented. The main stumbling block, however, was the ideological gulf between the two party leaders. This was compounded by the growing atrocities on dalits in UP, especially in western UP, where most dalits were landless farmers working on land owned by rich, upwardly mobile backward castes. From the very beginning of the alliance, Mulayam Singh had been trying to lure BSP legislators to his side and to break the BSP. Unknown to him, Kanshiram had likewise been secretly approaching leaders of the opposition parties, particularly A.B. Vajpayee, leader of the BJP, to jointly unseat Mulayam Singh as chief minister. The earlier antipathy to the BJP was conveniently forgotten. All opposition parties, including the Congress and the Janata Dal, hatched a conspiracy to oust Mulayam Singh and replace him with Kanshiram. Their efforts were thwarted by Kanshiram's falling seriously ill in mid 1995, when the strains between the BSP and the SP were already out in the open. At the end of May, news reached Kanshiram that Mulayam Singh was trying to create a split in the BSP. Not being well enough to take on the responsibility of chief minister himself, he asked Mayawati to meet the Governor to inform him of the BSP's withdrawal of support from the government, and for staking her claim to form a government supported by the BJP. Mayawati met the Governor on 1 June 1995 and was sworn in as the chief minister on 3 June.[22]

Even though the BSP knew very well that it was only a matter of time before the BJP withdrew its support, it took this opportunity of being in power to aggressively push the dalit agenda. Crores were spent on building memorials of dalit icons; various institutions were renamed after saints from the dalit pantheon, Ambedkar statues were installed all over the state, dalits were placed in a number of top positions and festivals like the one to honour the early twentieth-century reformer Periyar were held. Periyar had proffered a controversial, alternative reading of the Ramayana in *The Ramayana: A True Reading*, openly depicting Ram and Sita in an irreverent manner. These gestures won the hearts of the dalits, but were widely seen as deliberate attempts to provoke the upper-caste alliance partners. On 18 October 1995, after 136 days in power, Mayawati lost BJP's support and President's Rule was imposed.[23] Unfortunately, in the assembly polls held in UP at the end of September 1996, the BSP did not win a majority even though this time it had the Congress's support. This was surprising as the BSP had fared reasonably well in the parliamentary elections held earlier that year. Since no party managed to attain a clear majority, President's Rule was once again imposed on the state.

On 20 March 1997, Mayawati was once more sworn in as chief minister after another deal Kanshiram made with the BJP. This deal was a formal one—quite different from the informal arrangement in her earlier stint. It was in the form of a memorandum of understanding announced to the media at a joint press conference. According to the memorandum, the chief ministership would be shared on a six-monthly rotational basis by the two parties with Mayawati getting the first term. After the completion of one year the two parties would review the coalition experiment and if satisfied would continue it on the same terms.

This time, too, Mayawati and the BSP went on a spree, renaming or creating a large number of monuments, parks, institutions and districts after dalit heroes, ignoring the feelings of their coalition partner. At great expense, they installed nearly 15,000 statues of Ambedkar across UP. They also launched several welfare schemes for the dalits. In addition, more than 2,50,000 dalits were granted lease on agricultural land. The Scheduled Castes and Scheduled Tribes (Prevention of Atrocities) Act was strictly enforced, instilling a sense of security among the dalits.[24]

After a great deal of suspense about whether Mayawati would actually relinquish the post, the chief ministership was transferred to Kalyan Singh of the BJP after six months, on 21 September 1997. Within a month, the BSP withdrew its support to this government, but despite this and various other efforts to topple his government, Kalyan Singh managed to hang on.[25] Nevertheless, with the BJP's declining fortunes in the parliamentary elections held in 1999, Kalyan Singh was replaced by Ram Prakash Gupta, who in turn was replaced by Rajnath Singh. Meanwhile, Kanshiram, who was quite ill by then, decided that he would no longer be able to run the party and handed the reins over to Mayawati, the protégée he had been grooming since the very beginning of their association.[26] Inheriting the mantle of president of the BSP, Mayawati prepared hard for the 2002 assembly polls in UP and her efforts resulted in BSP capturing ninety-eight seats with 23 per cent of the vote share and emerging as the single largest party ahead of the BJP and the SP. [27] Still short of the absolute majority, the BSP struck another deal with the BJP, where Kanshiram, Mayawati, Vajpayee and Advani were involved. She was allowed to lead the government in UP for a full five-year term and was sworn in on 3 May 2002. [28]

Unfortunately, the alliance with BJP once again ran into trouble over the Taj Corridor scam, and on 25 August 2003 Mayawati severed ties with the BJP, while recommending dissolution of the assembly and the holding of fresh elections to the Governor. She thought the BJP was desperate and would ultimately support her. But she was taken by surprise when all the other parties, including the BJP and the Congress, teamed up against her and supported an alternative government led by Mulayam Singh. [29] Unluckily, at this time, she did not have the counsel of Kanshiram, as he had suffered a massive stroke that left him completely bedridden. [30]

The cracks within the BSP had begun to appear before this. As the party grew, many joined it but others left due to internal conflicts. Many activists and party workers had come close to Kanshiram over the years. Once Mayawati entered the picture and came to occupy a special place in the party beside Kanshiram, jealousies arose. Kanshiram had to face several conflicts—at the centre of which was Mayawati—the greatest being in 1994–95, when the BSP–SP alliance was in office. Mayawati had become extremely powerful within her party at that time and also kept up the pressure on Mulayam Singh.

She often came to Lucknow to review how Mulayam Singh's government was doing. Much to his annoyance, he would be obliged to give her a full report.

While the other BSP leaders objected to this, Kanshiram sided with her. He insisted that she was only acting under his instructions. It was hard for Kanshiram to manage these conflicts and to prevent trusted workers and leaders from leaving the party. One of the BSP leaders who was unhappy with Mayawati and led the faction against her was Dr Masood Ahmad, education minister in the SP–BSP combined ministry. He was a grass-roots activist of the party and had joined hands with Kanshiram in 1980. Since he had a good relationship with the Muslim community, Kanshiram took him into his fold and he soon became a close confidant. During the by-elections in Allahabad, when Kanshiram was in the running, Dr Ahmad was given the responsibility of mobilizing the Muslims, which he ably discharged. Dr Ahmad himself stood for the assembly elections from Tanda and parliamentary elections from Khalilabad. His resentment against Mayawati was taken up for discussion at the top level, despite his being a long-time loyalist, and this led to his looking towards Mulayam Singh's SP.

Seeing the gravity of the situation, Kanshiram held a closed-door meeting with all the BSP MLAs, including Dr Ahmad, which went on for nine hours. The MLAs supporting Mayawati levelled many allegations against Dr Ahmad, who in turn hit back with counter-allegations. Some MLAs claimed they had information that Dr Ahmad was being used against the party by people from several quarters, for which he was being paid. While some Muslim MLAs complained to Kanshiram that Dr Ahmad was in cahoots with the Brahmans, other leaders presented a picture of how Dr Ahmad was working against Mayawati.

Dr Ahmad had made three main allegations against Mayawati and Kanshiram stolidly defended her in every one. In reply to the first allegation, that Mayawati had called all Muslims traitors, Kanshiram said that the Muslim maulvis had spread the rumour in all the mosques that Kanshiram had said that if the BSP continued to be in power, a toilet would be constructed in place of the Babri Masjid . . . The rumours were actually false and baseless and in fact were instigated by Mulayam Singh. In reply to the second allegation, that Mayawati was living in a house worth fifty crore rupees, Kanshiram said that the house did not belong to her but was allotted to him as a parliamentarian. It would be taken back when he ceased to be one . . .

He also cleared misgivings about his relationship with industrialist Jayant Malhoutra. He said Jayant Malhoutra was offered the BSP seat in the assembly after Mulayam Singh, who had earlier promised to make him an MP, had backed out. He added that Mayawati had no role in the deal, and the allegation that she had taken money from Jayant Malhoutra for getting him a ticket to the assembly was false . . . In the meeting he insisted that whatever Mayawati did was under his instructions and also appealed to the BSP leaders and to Mayawati to work together for the welfare of the party.[31]

Kanshiram first tried to pacify Dr Ahmad, but when he did not relent, Kanshiram toughened his stand. After the meeting, he asked Mulayam Singh to immediately remove him from the ministry. He also instructed him to throw out Dr Ahmad's belongings from the official bungalow provided to him as the education minister within a few hours, by 11 p.m., and to inform the media about the incident.

Kanshiram now sought to stop other BSP leaders who were planning to desert the party. He organized a Dal Badal Virodhi (Oppose Party Defection) rally in Lucknow on 11 July 1994. Explaining the reason behind it, Kanshiram said:

> I felt the need to organize the Dal Badal Virodhi rally at that time because the crisis was threatening to engulf me. People say that when we come across people [strangers] lying injured or dead on the road in an accident we don't stop, so our work shouldn't suffer. But if we find someone from our own family lying there, we are bound to stop. This happened with me as well. When the Janata Party broke up I did not bother. When the Communist Party broke up or the independent parties broke up, even then I did not bother. But when my own party was on the verge of breaking up I had to stop and think.[32]

Kanshiram also said, 'I find it difficult to believe that our associate, who was with us for thirteen years, could carry out this act of treason.'[33] He also exhorted BSP MLAs to teach wayward party members a lesson. 'If an MLA of your community sells himself, teach him such a lesson that he forgets to do it in the future. If he does so, he should not leave unscathed but be torn to shreds. If the bahujan samaj wants to have a steadfast leader they should construct a steadfast community.'[34] The tough streak of the leader Kanshiram against perceived unfairness was being exposed.

Another conflict involved Dr R.K. Chaudhary, who was one of the front-ranking activists and among the founder members of the BSP. He had joined the movement on 30 June 1993 at the invitation of Kanshiram, setting aside home and family, and had spent nearly twenty years working to strengthen the DS4 and the BSP. Chaudhary, who belonged to the Pasi community of Faizabad, had also given up his successful legal practice. He won the elections from Manjhanpur, Kaushambi, and became cabinet minister for health and later transport, besides coordinator of the UP assembly, during the BSP regime. As a minister, he assiduously followed Mayawati's instructions and gradually grew to become her second-in-command. Soon his name started circulating as a chief ministerial candidate, which greatly angered Mayawati. On 21 July 2001 she called a press conference after throwing him out of the party. Chaudhary tried hard to placate Mayawati but with little success. When he went to Delhi to meet Kanshiram, he found him encircled by Mayawati's henchmen and was not allowed to meet him. Disappointed, he returned to Lucknow along with his supporters and formed a new party called BS4 on 30 August 2001.[35]

Whenever there was an internal conflict within the party Kanshiram would get very upset. He used to say that 'by leaving our party, our own people are causing us pain'. Anand Rahate has described this in one of his reminiscences. He wrote, 'Once before the Kolkata rally, one office bearer complained against another office bearer, saying that he had humiliated him by not sending a car to receive him. Kanshiram said, "It appears as if your eyes have still not opened. You did not feel humiliated after years of serving the Manuvadis but you are feeling humiliated because a fellow bahujan did not send a car. When will your eyes open? When will you stop fighting on small issues? You do not know but these small fights weaken our struggle.'"[36] Rahate comments that Kanshiram was very strong while fighting against the Manuvadis but came across as weak while dealing with these internal problems.

It was during such instances of growing alienation within the party that Kanshiram declared Mayawati his heir and bequeathed her the legacy of the BSP in 2001. On 25 August 2003, in the All India BSP rally organized at Dr Bhimrao Ambedkar Park, Lucknow, he defended his decision:

My efforts are now to take Mayawati beyond the stature of a chief minister. There may be many amongst all of you with whom I worked to take the movement forward. Mayawati is one of them. Keeping in mind her school and college records and also her commitment to the party, I felt that this girl is worth something. That is why I tried to groom her. I am getting aged. I am busy with my work but my capacity for work is gradually diminishing. Till I am alive, I will work, but it is my ardent desire that Mayawati carries out my unfinished work after my death.[37]

Kanshiram died in 2006 before he could see his protégée and his party reach even greater political heights, by winning an absolute majority in the 2007 assembly polls. Ironically, this victory was the outcome of the help Mayawati received from the upper castes, as part of her social engineering strategy.

Earlier, they had given political patronage to the dalits; now they themselves sought shelter and protection, politically, from an 'untouchable' dalit woman. Through Mayawati, Kanshiram had finally attained the master key that would help liberate the poor, downtrodden dalits.

~

The secret behind the attainment of the master key was Kanshiram's ability to sway and mobilize large crowds. He had a distinctive narrative style. Whenever he gave interviews or speeches and lectures, or addressed election rallies, and so on, he wove in a strong element of storytelling. His audience would be spellbound, listening with rapt attention to even simple facts. For example, he would say that 'when he left Maharashtra for north India he carried with him the turbaned Baba Phule, another turbaned Baba, namely Shahuji Maharaj, and the tie-wearing Baba Ambedkar'.[38] Using the metaphor of turbaned and tie-attired babas, or saints, in a few short sentences, he described his entire political journey, in which he had transplanted the ideology of these three social reformers from Maharashtra in the soil of north India. Similarly, whenever he wanted to express his disillusionment with Maharashtrian dalit politics, he would say in a voice dripping with sarcasm that, in fact, Ambedkar and Gandhi—the RPI and the Congress, respectively—were made to reconcile with each other many years after the Poona Pact, namely, through the seat-sharing deal in the 1970s, when the RPI was offered one seat out of 521 in the Maharashtra assembly.[39]

Since almost all of Kanshiram's speeches were meant to address the illiterate and semi-literate dalits living in rural north India, especially UP, his narratives were full of proverbs, idioms and metaphors that they could easily understand and appreciate. He used words and phrases that are commonly used by people of this region, and added his own twists to them, like *'Lokshahi mein rani aur mehtarani ki keemat ek hi hoti hai'* (In a democracy the worth of a queen and a maid is the same) and *'Congress saanp hai to Janata Dal naag hai'* (If the Congress is a snake, the Janata Dal is a cobra).[40]

Kanshiram had, from the beginning, used the word 'bahujan', denoting 'the majority', instead of 'dalit' for the untouchables and backward castes. 'Though it was a Buddhist concept reformulated by Phule, Kanshi translated it into an electoral language.'[41] Phule had used the word 'bahujan' to denote 'moolnivasi' or 'original settlers' for dalits and backwards, as opposed to the upper castes, who were Aryans who had migrated from Central Asia. But Kanshiram did not include this concept of moolnivasi in his formulation of bahujan. He used it for a broader alliance of dalits, backwards, Muslim minorities, tribals, dalit Christians and those upper castes who opposed Brahmanism. 'The Bahujan identity also rejects the mainstream formulations based on class, religion and secularism because they favour and legitimise the control of upper castes over the rest.'[42] The term bahujan was popular since it was a word that carried Buddhist memories that were still pervasive in the psyche of villagers in UP and Bihar.

Even to describe his politics he used words, idioms, phrases and metaphors linked with the local culture and people's collective memory. While Ambedkar had used the term 'master key' for politics, Kanshiram used the term 'guru killi', derived from Sikh folk culture.

There are many experiences in dalit society for which there are no Hindi words. This is because the Hindi that is commonly spoken is strongly influenced by the upper castes and reflects their desires and aspirations. So Kanshiram added several English words to his political lexicon—words for those experiences that could not be adequately explained in Hindi. For example, he often used the English word 'discrimination', finding it more appropriate than the word *bhed-bhav*. He also introduced words like 'Manuvad' to the Hindi lexicon, which were then used by other political parties in their speeches as well.

Kanshiram's style of communication was much like that of a schoolteacher explaining difficult concepts to supposedly simple-minded village children. This track helped him explain complex power relationships. He would often use the simile of the pen, as we have seen earlier, to explain the Indian social structure to people at the grass roots.

Like Ambedkar, Kanshiram too believed that politics was only about acquiring power and that power could not be acquired without struggle.[43] But for gaining power, he was convinced that it was imperative for dalits to free themselves of their dalitness. He said in a speech, 'Even more than the miserable condition of the dalits, I feel sorrowful about the dalitness of the dalits. Dalitness has become a kind of begging bowl and just as no beggar can become a ruler without liberating himself from his begging bowl, no community can become the ruling community without liberating itself from its dalitness.'[44] Saying this, Kanshiram would hold up his hands, cupped like a begging bowl, to show the prevailing attitude of the dalits. He would then slowly and deliberately invert them, as if giving away something, in order to represent the attitude he wanted to see in the dalits. He used to say that dalits should become human beings and should transform themselves into a ruling community. In his rallies he used to say that 'You all are worthless. You want reservation. I will remove your worthlessness. I will make you worthy.'[45] He used to say that 'if the dalits were worthless, the Manuvad system would continue to remain dominant and the upper castes would continue to rule. If the dalits became worthy the upper castes would be toppled.'[46] He would provoke the dalits by saying:

> They should not be content to live in poverty. 'We should try to make efforts to live in palaces and obtain all the comforts of life. The dalit society should not remain attached to huts. We should become powerful and try to live like human beings. I don't want that you remain puppets and follow the dominant sections as their tails. Our dalit society has become used to living as paupers. We are happy with whatever we have got and in whichever way we have got it. We should drop this habit and become aware of our responsibilities and duties.' He also regretted that the people who increase inequality in society were aware of these issues but the bahujan samaj was still not aware of the inequalities existing in society.[47]

Kanshiram also tried to make the dalits aware of how powerful he and the BSP were so that they realized the party was in no way inferior to those run mainly by the upper castes. He was certain this would raise their self-esteem and self-worth. In an interview published in *Maya*, a Hindi magazine, he said, 'The members of the Congress party want to meet me. I have told them that they need not come if they want to give me anything. Yes, if they want something from me they are welcome.'[48] On another occasion he said, 'When we pick up in Delhi, compared to us, the BJP will be like the salt added to wheat flour before kneading it [a mere pinchful].'[49] Later, he said, 'Except me, no one can crush the Shiv Sena. When I will go to Maharashtra I will crush them.'[50] Through such statements, Kanshiram inspired the bahujans and dalits about his leadership, raising their confidence levels in the process and urging them to fearlessly participate in politics.

Kanshiram's ambitions for the dalits were absolutely clear. There was no conflict between his practice and his preaching.

Always dressed in an ordinary bush shirt, trousers and simple slippers, his speeches were not filled with rhetoric like [those of] many others from various parties. Even when fiery and electrifying, they were delivered calmly, never aggressively or arrogantly. He would maintain a uniform tone that was soft but assertive and persuasive. This discursive style, however, did not detract from the militancy in his speeches. Each word he uttered was full of power and meant to reiterate the humiliation suffered by the lower castes for so many centuries, as well as to hit at the dominant sections of society and the social and political powers that consistently perpetrated this humiliation. This was a carefully cultivated strategy intended to displace the existing power structure and replace it with the [power structure of the] lower castes. They were simultaneously being groomed to become assertive, confident and capable of assuming positions of power. There was, however, no deliberate attempt in his words to project himself as wielding great power or to pull down the traditionally powerful community and political group so as to subvert the traditional power structure. After toppling the Mulayam Singh government, when the BJP leaders approached Kanshiram to discuss a possible alliance with the BSP, they were surprised at his civility and also his patience while handling delicate negotiations.[51]

Kanshiram also used his oratorical skills to present facts about their numbers in a manner that suggested that the BSP was financially strong and had unlimited funds to contest the elections. This was also intended to enhance the confidence of the dalits. He used to say, 'My expenses are not in thousands or lakhs but in crores. All this wealth has been obtained from the supporters of the party. I go to one meeting and bring back one lakh rupees.'[52] When he first set up BAMCEF he announced at the meetings that he would bring out a Hindi and English daily and a monthly vernacular newspaper from each state capital. This made members believe he had crores of rupees to finance the publication of so many newspapers. The parties in power and the Opposition too imagined that he was a powerful, rich and influential person. In truth, it was only his oratory at work.[53] Many critics interpreted this as pomposity and grandiosity, dismissing his speeches as empty talk. But these stirring words inspired dalits to become assertive and considerably enhanced their political participation. In one of his rousing speeches, in Lucknow, Kanshiram provoked his audience, mobilized by the BSP cadre, 'You are like animals—you have been treated like animals—and you kept suffering this. Recognize your strength now.'[54]

He once said, 'In 1996 the Narasimha Rao government approached me for an electoral alliance. I told them I would help. To solve the nitty-gritty Rao sent Sharad Pawar, who asked me how many seats the BSP wanted in UP. I told him he was speaking the language of Maharashtra. In the land of the Chamars [UP], the language of Mahars does not sound good. I added that I could humiliate him even more but was choosing not to.'[55] This rebellious streak in Kanshiram's language sprung from the reality he faced, of the centuries-old suppression and oppression of bahujan society.[56]

It is noteworthy that in the early stages of his political life, Kanshiram would deliberately use aggressive and humiliating language when dealing with Mulayam Singh, Rajiv Gandhi, Advani, Vajpayee, and so on, so that the image of these leaders as being all-powerful could be shattered. BSP slogans like *'Tilak, taraju aur talwar, joote maaro inko char'* and others were also a part of the same strategy. When Mulayam Singh and the BSP's coalition government were in power and internal conflicts surfaced, both Kanshiram and Mayawati grew hostile to Mulayam Singh, the then chief minister. In Allahabad after the Dauna case in 1994, which has been described earlier (see author's note),[57] Kanshiram, while sharing the dais with Mulayam Singh, snubbed him publicly. Kanshiram declared: 'Our ministers have no influence in the government. We will not tolerate this situation.'

Kanshiram went as far as to call Mulayam Singh a thief. These utterances led to a huge row between them, ultimately leading to the break-up of the BSP–SP coalition.[58] Kanshiram's intemperate reaction evoked a strong response from the upper castes and other dominant political sections. In the 1990s, BJP leader B.L. Sharma 'Prem' reviled Kanshiram, saying that 'this uncouthness is the result of the culture he comes from'.[59] Linking his idiom with caste culture and his parents' rustic social environment, Sharma's reaction clearly betrayed an upper-caste bias. Kanshiram was unperturbed that his language and slogans could lead to tensions. 'He believed it was just as well if that happened because it would ignite a spark in the lower castes, kindling a fire that would singe the upper castes. Only when they were reduced to ashes would there be a social equality that benefitted the lower castes.'[60] His confrontational and militant tone often rubbed the Opposition the wrong way up, raising their hackles. It was only later that Kanshiram toned down his language without compromising on its power and assertiveness.

Such a change is notably to be observed in the case of Mayawati, who earlier used extremely aggressive language with her staff and ministers. During the initial phase of her chief ministership, she projected herself as a leader by highlighting attributes of aggression and arrogance during public meetings with bureaucrats and government officials. She deliberately tried to subvert upper-caste notions of femininity and ladylike behaviour, marked by politeness and docility. Male officials and rival leaders were addressed as *tu* or *tum* (an informal—bordering on impolite—form of 'you' in Hindi), usually used to address people lower in the social hierarchy, rather than *aap*, used for addressing a superior person. She also threw in words like '*arrey*' and '*terrey*', which are generally used by upper-caste males to address people belonging to the lower castes. That was the phase when Mayawati and Kanshiram were trying hard to mobilize the bahujans, positing them against the upper castes, who had a well-defined code for addressing people belonging to different levels in the social hierarchy, which they expected everyone else to follow. Kanshiram and Mayawati's aim was to subvert this code and to humiliate the upper castes by using particular forms of address for them that were usually restricted for people lower down in the social order.

Things changed after Mayawati became the chief minister of UP on the BSP obtaining a thumping majority in the 2007 assembly elections. Her winning strategy had relied on wooing both the upper and the lower castes under the common banner of 'sarvajan' (everyone). She considerably toned down her language and behaviour at this point so that the upper-caste voters did not feel humiliated or alienated, and thereby was able to garner their votes. The example of her mentor Kanshiram was no doubt responsible for this change in Mayawati.

These changes in political style and idiom notwithstanding, over the years, like all powerful figures, Kanshiram had his share of controversy, both fair and unfair. What these criticisms were and the elan with which he countered them are described next.

6

The Critics Speak

Opportunism as a Strategy

From his political journey so far, we find that Kanshiram was constantly destabilizing centuries-old social and political arrangements with his manoeuvres and strategies. Unafraid to breach the established political etiquette, he created his own norms of political behaviour, so long as it served his aim—of winning power for the newly emerging leadership in bahujan society. He was willing to go to any extent for this, forging alliances with any party that was willing, even parties whose ideology was totally at odds with that of the BSP, even welcoming defectors from other parties, so long as they supported the BSP programme. Arif Mohammad Khan was elected to the Lok Sabha on a BSP ticket in 1998, so was Ahmed 'Dumpy'.

Akbar Ahmed 'Dumpy' came from the Congress party. He was a known Sanjay Gandhi loyalist. Ahmed 'Dumpy' stood by Maneka when Sanjay Gandhi died. He was expelled from the Congress party in March 1982 because he and Maneka had a meeting of the Sanjay Vichar Manch in Lucknow. In 1989 he rejoined the Congress after making up with Rajiv Gandhi. Two years later he left the Congress party and was persuaded by Kanshiram to join the BSP.[1]

Arif Mohammad Khan contested the first legislative assembly election from Siyana constituency of Bulandshahar on the Bharatiya Kranti Dal party's banner but was defeated. He joined the Congress party and was elected to the Lok Sabha in 1980 and 1984 from Bahraich. In 1986 he quit the Congress due to differences over the passage of Muslim Personal Law Bill which was piloted by Rajiv Gandhi in the Lok Sabha. Khan joined the Janata Dal and was re-elected to the Lok Sabha in 1989. He then left the Janata Dal to join the BSP and was again returned to the Lok Sabha in 1998.[2]

These people left their respective parties and joined the BSP because at the time the standing of these parties was waning in UP. Khan and Ahmed needed a political space for themselves. The BSP was also in need of support to increase its base among the Muslims. Thus the BSP welcomed the two politicians.

For Kanshiram the end justified the means. In this respect, he was poles apart from his mentor Ambedkar, as we have already seen.

A host of aspersions came to be cast on Kanshiram in the political arena as well as in the media. He was at various times pilloried as being a rustic, an opportunist, a collector of wealth, a dabbler in politics who was funded by the CIA, and one who allied himself with communal forces.[3] While some of these allegations appeared in newspaper articles, many were, of course, baseless rumours, both of which Kanshiram breezily dismissed, as we shall see.

In an article in the *Navbharat Times*, BJP leader B.L.

Sharma 'Prem' once described Kanshiram as rustic, uncouth and uncultured.[4] This comment reeked of personal bias, as Kanshiram had never pretended to be urbane, sophisticated or suave. He, in fact, always took great pains to nurture and cultivate this rustic persona, which was reflected in his blunt, forthright speech. It enabled him to get away with frank criticism and comments about his counterparts in politics. Stung, these people ran him down further for his rough ways.

Strongly asserting his background, Kanshiram's political vocabulary was replete with symbols and allusions that were seen as rustic. A journalist once asked him whether the BSP was in the race for forging an alliance with the Congress. Kanshiram replied, 'If the race was from the side of the BSP, I would have met you in the home or office of a Congressman. But neither do I visit anyone's home or office nor do I allow anyone to visit my home or office. The meetings are held in the fields, that is, in the home of a third person.'[5] This usage of the word 'field' is typically rural; for a farmer, any place outside his home is the field and usually meetings in rural areas take place in the fields. Such metaphors were often incomprehensible to people living in urban areas. As he said in an interview published in the newspaper *Abhay Bharti*, on 27 May 1987, 'I'm a rural person. My speeches are beyond the comprehension of city-bred people.'[6]

What few people realized, however, was that though Kanshiram asserted his rural background, he was definitely not a simple-minded villager. He was a skilled politician whose strategy aimed at the transformation of everyday local politics into affecting national politics. In the early days of the BSP, when the media was unable to understand the phenomenon of

Kanshiram's growing influence, allegations were levelled against him, of being backed by the CIA and using money supplied by them to change the face of Indian politics. Kanshiram said that the people present in power (Congress party) were accusing the BSP of taking money from the CIA.[7]

Kanshiram calmly and patiently refuted all these allegations, saying those making these accusations were ignorant and ill informed. Explaining how he raised the money to fund the elections he said:

The people with whom I am working used to live in poverty and misery till recently. But together they number nearly sixty-five crore. According to government statistics, each of them consumes food worth only Rs 1.75 each day. This means that even these poverty-stricken people together consume Rs 120 crore worth of food daily. I tell these people to go hungry at least one day in five years for their own sakes. If I have to contest for all the 542 seats in the Lok Sabha and if I spend Rs 5 lakh per person and Rs 2 crore on campaigning I will need to spend Rs 27 crore in total. So, if I keep all these people hungry even for one day I can contest four Lok Sabha elections.[8]

Elucidating the point further, Kanshiram said:

It is true that my expenditure is not in thousands or lakhs but in crores. In 1980, during the formation of BAMCEF, I spent Rs 1.87 crore. There are more than one lakh workers in my party and more than twenty-five lakh cadre members. We collect all our funds from these people. And if anyone can prove that I personally own enough land to even build a grave I am ready to face the severest punishment in India. The government is free to use its secret agencies to investigate my personal assets.[9]

In this same vein, Kanshiram succeeded in shrugging off allegations about accepting a suitcase full of money from Mulayam Singh for supporting the SP government. In 1989, a journalist of *Maya*, a Hindi magazine, once inquired whether he had forged a secret alliance with the Congress party. Kanshiram's reply contained answers not just to this query but to many more allegations against him. He said, 'What would be the use of a secret alliance to us? If our aim had been to obtain money or some other personal benefit from the party then the meaning of a secret alliance would be clear. But if the fulfilment of our mission is our objective, then a secret alliance will not be beneficial to us.'[10]

Kanshiram always detected an upper-caste bias behind the rumours about himself and the party. On another occasion, when a journalist asked about the money deal with Ghulam Nabi Azad for seat-sharing, he replied, 'I tell everyone not to come to us if they want to give us something. It is true that most people believe that our people are ready to sell themselves like animals for the smallest benefit, but I'm trying my best to change these "saleable" animals into human beings. How can I do the same thing myself?'[11] This statement also reveals Kanshiram's pain at the manner in which the upper castes stereotyped dalits and lower castes.

Branding Kanshiram as opportunistic, contriving, cunning and amoral, people failed to realize that his politics was completely different from what had been in place before him. A look at his record of electoral politics reveals that he joined up with various political parties, moved on after getting what he wanted, lent support to those governments which furthered his plans and foiled other parties' attempts at forming a government.

At the national level, he forged alliances with various political forces, broke them when they had outlived their utility, supported other governments when they aspired to form a government and also created situations so that other parties could not form the government. In this manner he 'emerged as the champion not of stability but of instability'.[12] Through this instability he and his party became even stronger.

His unique political approach could be seen in the rapid shifts in his strategies and negotiations. On 23 February 1997, Kanshiram told his legislators from UP at his Humayun Road bungalow that they should start preparing for elections, but exactly five days later he hatched a plot in Chennai with L.K. Advani, leader of the BJP, about forming a coalition government in UP. On 19 March, when Mayawati became the chief minister for the first six months in the BJP–BSP government, Kanshiram appeared to be the most composed of all the people present at the swearing-in ceremony. By contrast, the BJP leaders sitting there looked gloomy and downcast, wondering what trick Kanshiram had up his sleeve. Their chief concern was whether he would keep the BSP's side of the pact: that a BJP leader would replace Mayawati after six months and whether he would at all allow the BJP to take over the reins of the government. The party had earlier suffered at the hands of Kanshiram when Mayawati had been chief minister for four and a half months in 1995 under a similar alliance. But during that period the BSP had further strengthened its political agenda and increased its vote percentage from 10 to 20 per cent while the BJP only maintained its earlier vote percentage. This time the BJP leaders hoped that they would succeed in convincing Kanshiram to agree to an all-India alliance. As time went by, they found he'd shifted his stand.

He bluntly said he could not make any promise about future alliances. He elucidated that the BSP was only looking for opportunities to fulfil its mission: since the BJP was a Manuvadi party while the BSP was a Manavvadi [humane] party, it was not possible to forge a long-term, large-scale alliance with them . . . Whenever the BJP thought that it could get dalit votes by seeking Kanshiram's help, he shattered their hopes. When Atal Bihari Vajpayee went to Kanshiram to offer him the President's post he rejected it, saying that he wanted to become prime minister and not President.[13]

This story, of alliances formed and broken, through secret negotiations, was repeated many times by Kanshiram from 1993 onward. He once joined hands with the SP to beat the BJP while at another time he allied with the BJP against the SP. In Punjab, he allied with the Akali Dal (Badal) against the Congress party and in UP he allied with the Congress. Later, in Punjab he allied with Akali Dal (Mann) and after the assembly elections he cocked a snook at the Congress and allied with the BJP. To the charge of his being opportunistic, he replied that he did not believe in the status quo but in continuously changing his position.[14]

He also retorted that if Brahmans had marched forward through opportunistic behaviour then there was nothing wrong with the dalits doing the same.[15]

Kanshiram converted opportunism into an ideology and made practical politics his biggest principle. While allying with Gandhians he abused Gandhi; and he criticized Lord Rama, the ruling deity of the BJP during the very time Mayawati was chief minister of UP with BJP support. The latter was intended to please his dalit constituency. His politics may have appeared to be short-term, but deeper probing reveals Kanshiram's long-term agenda.[16]

To empower the powerless, on the one hand, he sought to prevent others from becoming powerful. The alliances he forged at various times with stronger or weaker parties, whatever suited his designs, were aimed precisely at checkmating the power of other parties. Alternately, he would manoeuvre to remove a party in power. On the other hand, he also sought to strengthen the weaker sections. His 'unexpected' moves sometimes left his activists and supporters confused but there was a method to his madness and continuity to his objectives.[17]

The most crucial period of Kanshiram's political career was the 1990s, when UP was ablaze with the Ram Janmabhoomi movement launched by the BJP and communal forces had a free run of the state. The BSP and SP together mobilized the lower and backward castes and defeated the BJP in November 1993. A political deal between the two parties made Mulayam Singh the chief minister of UP. Kanshiram believed this was a social and political compulsion in order to safeguard the lives, property and religious beliefs of the lower castes and minorities. However, Mulayam Singh embarked on an agenda of systematically destroying the BSP, to undercut Kanshiram's power. When Kanshiram understood his game plan, he withdrew support for the SP—just eighteen months into the government—and joined hands with the BJP, bringing down the Mulayam Singh government. Describing the situation prevailing at that time Kanshiram said, 'Mulayam's evil intentions came to the fore during the Panchayat elections and we were compelled to withdraw our support. Even the BJP was fed up with Mulayam's hooliganism and agreed to unconditionally support Mayawati's government.'[18]

Kanshiram faced the greatest flak in his political career over the BSP coming to power twice in UP with the support of the BJP. The Ambedkarites, communists, leading intellectuals and journalists with progressive views roundly condemned and criticized him and the BSP for supporting an overtly communal party. Ambedkarite K. Nath was critical that when Kanshiram formed the government for the first time in coalition with the BJP, people who were against Brahmanism and condemned Manuvad (i.e., the BSP) accepted this decision for acquiring power. 'None of the Ambedkarite leaders questioned why the BSP was compromising with the Manuvaadis.'[19] Mahipal Singh, organizer of Dalit Morcha, said 'that the elephant of the BSP is no longer the supporter of the dalits but instead it has become the Ganesha of the Manuvaadi who wants to make dalits its slave'.[20] Other Ambedkarites who criticized this move of BSP were S.R. Darapuri and Sangam Lal Vidrohi.

Kanshiram, however, was very clear that though the BJP was a Manuvadi party, he was allying with it due to political compulsions. Justifying his position he said, 'What is wrong if we used the BJP merely as a stepping stone?'[21]

Kanshiram insisted that the BSP always pushed the agenda of the lower castes and downtrodden sections of society, even when it had formed the government with the BJP's support. He declared that the first time round, for six months, poor people from the lower castes were given possession of seven lakh acres of land. Many new districts were also carved out and named after dalit saints—these include Ambedkarnagar, Phulenagar and Shahujinagar. When Atal Bihari Vajpayee requested that a new district be named after Deendayal Upadhyaya, Kanshiram scuttled the request, saying the BJP could do so when it took over from the BSP.[22] The BSP, by putting pressure on the BJP, enforced its programme of dalit empowerment, which helped the BSP to garner more dalit votes eventually. Also, Kanshiram's statement makes it clear that the BJP compromised more in this alliance than the BSP that benefited far more. Kanshiram declared that if the alliance with the BJP suited them and enabled them to form a government that would carry forward their own community's issues, they would honour it.[23]

Despite this tough talk elsewhere, Kanshiram surprisingly chose to shut his eyes to the violence perpetrated on Muslims in Gujarat in 2002, when BJP's Narendra Modi was chief minister. 'His straightforward defence was that he had no interest in Gujarat, since the Scheduled Castes comprised only 7 per cent of the state's population and he saw no possibility of building a base there.'[24] He kept silent about the injustice meted out to the Muslims, supposedly a part of the bahujan samaj.

These controversies and criticisms notwithstanding, Kanshiram stands out as a master strategist in politics, who made the BSP a force to reckon with. His sarvajana politics was built on his firm grasp of the position of the dalits in UP. In every election prior to the BSP coming to power in 2007, it received nearly 23 per cent votes. With 4 per cent votes more it could form the government. It is another matter that, though the party intended to associate all the non-dalits, it ended up focusing on only the Brahmans and Muslims. This strategy would not have worked in Punjab, where there was no independent dalit party and the Congress and the Akali Dal (with BJP) attracted the votes of Chamars, and the Valmiki and Mazhabi Sikhs respectively. Nor was it feasible in Maharashtra where the dalits were splintered into many groups, making electoral alliances with other castes problematic. And Kanshiram recognized this. Perhaps there are lessons in this for the present leadership of the BSP.

Like his life, Kanshiram's death, too, was marked by high controversy and led to a series of legal battles between various people who had vested interests. We shall examine in the next chapter the various disputes surrounding his illness and subsequent death.

7

The Last Days

Between Party and Family

As described in the first chapter, Kanshiram deliberately snapped all ties with his family and also decided to remain a bachelor so that he would not be deterred in his mission by the emotional bonds of family and marriage. Family for Kanshiram was the dalit samaj and he lived and worked for many years without any thought for his own family. He did not make any attempts to meet them after quitting his job in Poona in the mid 1960s. His family members had no clue of his whereabouts till he received media attention. In fact, Kanshiram did not recognize his youngest brother, Dalbara Singh—whom he had never seen—when the twenty-four-year-old walked up to Kanshiram at a meeting in Chandigarh and touched his feet. Kanshiram's tears welled up when the young man introduced himself.

Other family members, like his sister Sabran Kaur who met him at the residence of a common friend after many years, also had similar tales of bizarre reunions, when Kanshiram did not recognize them. Kanshiram's mother, Bishan Kaur, met him eighteen years after he had quit his job in Poona. It was a period of great agony for her, not knowing about his well-being. Her registered letters to his Poona office came back with the message that he had proceeded on five years' leave. There were rumours that he had gone abroad or disappeared. Finally, eighteen years later, when the family learnt that he was organizing employees' conferences, Bishan Kaur went to meet him at one such conference in Nagpur, but failed to convince him to return to their native village. He didn't even attend the last rites of his father, Hari Singh, though he went for the *bhog* ceremony, or funeral function.[1] By then he was an established dalit leader who had already launched BAMCEF and was preparing to launch DS4 and the BSP.

The person closest to him in his life and in politics was Mayawati, his protégée. She took upon herself the responsibility of looking after and caring for him till his death. His illness and death became the subject of a long-winded legal and political dispute between her and Kanshiram's family. In this chapter we will describe the chronology of events between 2003, when Kanshiram suffered a brain stroke, and 2006, when he passed away.

~

The feverish pace at which Kanshiram worked took a toll on his health. He developed high blood pressure and diabetes, which often interfered with his political activities. In the summer of 1995, when Kanshiram had worked out a secret plan with the BJP to prop up a BSP government (the SP–BSP alliance running the UP government with Mulayam Singh as chief minister was floundering), 'he fell seriously ill—partly due to exhaustion from travel across India, and partly due to medical complications brought on by chronic acute diabetes and hypertension'.[2] The BJP leadership had already given a letter of support to Kanshiram, but he was too frail to take on the responsibilities of chief minister. Soon news reached him that Mulayam Singh was about to break the BSP. Hurriedly, Kanshiram summoned Mayawati and convinced her to go to the Governor and hand over the papers, staking her claim to form a government. As mentioned earlier, on 3 June 1995 she was appointed chief minister of UP.[3] After recovering, Kanshiram continued working as the president of the BSP with Mayawati as the chief minister, whenever the BSP was in power.

Soon he realized that his health was rapidly failing. In 2001, he bequeathed the mantle of the BSP to Mayawati by declaring her his heir at a massive rally in Lucknow, making public his trust and faith in his protégée. The dalit community welcomed the announcement and warmly accepted the new leadership.[4] It was a timely decision as on 14 September 2003 Kanshiram suffered a severe cerebral stroke in Hyderabad. He was rushed to Apollo Hospital there, and then flown to New Delhi the next day in an air ambulance where he was admitted to Batra Hospital. He was released on 29 April 2004 but the very next day had to be readmitted. Finally, he was discharged on 1 July 2004. All these details were compiled in a press release by Dr Omkar Mittal, another doctor of the medical board set up by the Supreme Court in 2005, which submitted the final report on Kanshiram.[5]

Both times, Kanshiram was admitted for brain haemorrhage

(cerebral stroke) resulting from a sharp rise in his blood pressure. This completely paralysed the right side of his body and grossly affected his speech and comprehension. A medical report submitted on 16 June 2004 by Dr S.K. Choudhary, his neurophysician, stated that he was suffering from loss of speech ability, loss of general understanding and loss of awareness about time and space. According to the report, on 30 April 2004, when Kanshiram was admitted to Batra Hospital for the second time, he was feeling extremely giddy and had suffered a partial seizure. His paralysis had further deteriorated and his speech was grossly impaired. On 1 May 2004 an MRI revealed a fresh complication. A second report enclosed in the discharge certificate when Kanshiram left Batra Hospital on 1 July 2004 provided a clearer, more detailed picture of Kanshiram's condition.[6]

The report said that because the patient's condition was stable and had improved he was being discharged with the following remarks:

1) The present condition can remain like this for many years with the same illnesses. That is why it is advised that the patient should remain in Delhi so that he can be given immediate medical assistance in case of an emergency. He should not be allowed to travel and neither should he be subjected to any kind of stress or tension as it can badly affect his heart and brain.

2) To avoid pressure on his brain and heart it is advised that the number of people meeting him be kept to the minimum and for very short durations.

3) He should be provided adequate nursing/nursing facilities from time to time. Senior doctors will visit him whenever his attending doctor calls them.

The discharge certificate, signed by Dr M.L. Sindhwani (senior consultant) and Dr S.K. Choudhary, also advised that Kanshiram's medicines and physiotherapy should continue and that the patient should be kept in the same environment as before September 2003 when he had suffered the brain stroke. This would assist a quicker improvement in his condition. These two reports—of 16 June 2004 and 1 July 2004—make it amply clear that when Kanshiram was discharged from the hospital he had lost his abilities to speak and understand, was partially paralysed and was in no condition to express his wishes or opinions.

~

Ever since Kanshiram fell ill in September 2003, Mayawati, then chief minister of UP, undertook the entire responsibility of looking after him. When Kanshiram was discharged from hospital on 1 July 2004, she took him to her house on Humayun Road in New Delhi, where he remained till his death in October 2006.[7] Kanshiram's immediate family strongly opposed this move, insisting on taking Kanshiram back to their native village in Punjab. His brother Dalbara Singh first tried to convince Mayawati to allow his family members to take Kanshiram home from Batra Hospital in the initial period of his illness but was reportedly rebuffed. He then tried to take Kanshiram away from the hospital by force, and when he failed, he sought legal intervention to strengthen his case. However, his case was rejected by the Delhi High Court and, subsequently, the Supreme Court. He then launched a political party, carrying out a series of demonstrations with the support of some breakaway members of the BSP to force Mayawati to release Kanshiram. His efforts were in vain and Kanshiram died soon after.

Dalbara Singh documented his three-year-long struggle in a small leaflet which he circulated among the public.[8] He claimed that he had rushed to Batra Hospital on hearing the news of his brother's stroke on national television, but was refused permission to see him since Kanshiram's condition was critical. He then met Mayawati, who told him that Kanshiram would not be allowed to meet anyone for at least one month. She promised, however, to call him when the doctor allowed visitors. Hearing this, Dalbara Singh returned to his village. He later learnt through TV and radio that many political leaders had visited Kanshiram in hospital. He called Mayawati and requested permission to meet Kanshiram, but she said that since he was a family member he would not be allowed to meet Kanshiram as the sight of him might stir old memories and trigger another attack. She again promised that she would inform him when the doctors gave permission—he could then come to her house and she would herself take him to the hospital.

Dalbara Singh and his family members then filed a case in the Delhi High Court. In response to the plea, on 14 July 2004, the Division Bench of the Delhi High Court sent a judicial registrar in the capacity of local commissioner to take Kanshiram's statement. The leader was then staying at Mayawati's house, following his release from the hospital. Dr Omkar Mittal has documented the report of the judicial registrar:

I went to C-1/11 Humayun Road along with the Station House Officer. At around 2.40 p.m. I was taken to Sri Kanshiram's room on the first floor. Sri Kanshiram was sitting on a chair. A nurse and an attendant for cleaning the room were also present in the room. After entering the room I introduced myself to Sri Kanshiram. He acknowledged my introduction and greeting. I told him that I had come to record his statement and he should reply to my questions. He nodded his head in assent. I then recorded his statement. In his statement Sri Kanshiram said that he was living in C-1/11 Humayun Road on his independent wish and no one had exerted any pressure to make him live there. When I asked him directly if he was happy there he answered that he was very happy. To my question whether he wanted to continue living there he replied in the affirmative.[9]

On the basis of the judicial registrar's report the Division Bench of the Delhi High Court rejected Kanshiram's family's plea. Dalbara Singh then appealed the case in the Supreme Court with Kanshiram's mother as the principal petitioner. The Supreme Court set up a medical board to examine Kanshiram's condition which gave its preliminary report on 20 April 2005[10] and the final report on 5 December 2005.[11]

Before the Supreme Court could give its judgement based on the final report, Kanshiram's mother passed away and the judge asked Dalbara Singh's lawyer to withdraw the case as the principal petitioner was dead.

Contrary to speculations, some sections of the media believed that Mayawati did not nurse Kanshiram during his illness. Ajoy Bose, veteran journalist and author of Mayawati's biography, *Behenji*, suggests, in fact, the opposite was the case. He offers another take on the charge that she was deliberately confining Kanshiram. It was possible that Mayawati had seen the signs of the 'onset of dementia' in her mentor and 'her genuine concern for him prompted her to slowly isolate him from the outside world'. He writes:

> [Her genuine concern] became visible after he was reduced to a helpless invalid by a sudden cerebral stroke in 2003. For the three years that he lived after that in her house, Mayawati nursed him with rare devotion, quite often washing and feeding him personally with a tenderness that underlined the depth of her feelings. By then Kanshi Ram had nothing to give her and what she did was clearly out of purely personal attachment. Allegations by some members of Kanshi Ram's family that she was mistreating him, were therefore a complete travesty of the truth and obviously manipulated by her political opponents.[12]

Mayawati herself spoke to the media about Kanshiram's illness and convalescence in the NDTV programme *Walk the Talk*, telecast on 28 May 2005, when he was still in her house. When asked by Shekhar Gupta, who was conducting the programme, why there was so much controversy around this, she clarified that the members of Kanshiram's family were simple and innocent folk and some people, including from the opposition parties, were taking advantage of them, by tempting them with support, if they helped bring back Manyawar Kanshiram. She added with satisfaction that not a single person from the bahujan samaj supported them.

When Shekhar Gupta asked her whether she looked after him like his family would have, Mayawati asserted, 'I believe that I take better care of him than them. I provide him all kinds of facilities and everyone says that even a son could not have taken so much care as I am taking.'

'So you have nothing to hide about him?' Shekhar Gupta asked. To this she retorted that the AIIMS people themselves had certified that the treatment was excellent and there was no need to admit him to hospital. 'A seven-member team of specialists and doctors came and examined Manyawar over several hours. They saw all his medicines and reported to the SC that the medicines that are being administered should continue.'

While talking, they came to Mayawati's residence. As they entered Kanshiram's room, Mayawati greeted Kanshiram, saying that some people from the media had come to interview him and that he should look into the camera.

Shekhar Gupta went to Kanshiram and with a namaskar recalled their meeting with each other during a by-election in Allahabad. When Mayawati declared that Shekhar Gupta was an admirer of his, Kanshiram nodded his head in acknowledgement. When Gupta probed whether he was happy there, Mayawati laughingly repeated the question, adding that they were looking after him according to his wishes. To this Kanshiram replied yes in a low voice and nodded his head. She clarified that as he was half paralysed he could say only yes or no. Mayawati then asked whether he would like to have *chhole-bhature* or sweets with his tea. She turned to Gupta and said, 'He is very fond of chhole-bhature. Doctors have forbidden him from taking sweets so he wants to eat them.'

From this interview it is clear that Mayawati had deep concern for Kanshiram that surfaced when he was ill and helpless. Her devotion to and care of him completely vindicates the criticisms of the opposition parties and his family members that she had any ulterior motive in bringing him to her home.

~

Failing to beat Mayawati through legal action, Dalbara Singh turned to political means. Kanshiram's illness now became embroiled in politics. Along with a few breakaway members of the BSP, Dalbara Singh announced the formation of the Manyawar Kanshiram Bachao Sangharsh Committee (India) at a press conference in Lucknow on 26 March 2006. Dalbara Singh was the national chairman of the committee and the national secretary was Heera Lal Jawaddi. Addressing the press conference, Dalbara Singh announced that the committee would take action to compel Mayawati to hand over Kanshiram to his family members. It would start on 10 May 2006 with an indefinite demonstration outside Jantar Mantar near Parliament House in New Delhi.[13] On 18 July activists burnt Mayawati's effigy at the demonstration site.[14] On 11 August the committee wrote a letter to the President with the subject line: 'Liberating Manyawar Kanshiram from the personal prison of Kumari Mayawati'. The text of the letter was as follows:

Respected Honourable Sir,

We would like to bring to your notice that Manyawar Kanshiram Bachao Sangharsh Committee (India) has launched an indefinite movement since 10 May 2006 at Jantar Mantar to free Manyawar Kanshiram from the personal prison of Ku. Mayawati and has been continuously demanding that the administration intervenes to ensure that Kanshiram Sahib is hospitalized if he is ill and remains among the majority community if he is well. But unfortunately no steps are being taken by the President of the Lok Sabha or by the Leader of the Rajya Sabha or by the government to free the nationally acclaimed founder/President of the political party 'Bahujan Samaj Party' and former member of the Lok Sabha and Rajya Sabha, Manyawar Kanshiram Sahib, whom Kumari Mayawati has imprisoned in her government accommodation C-1/11, Humayun Road, New Delhi.

Therefore it is the request of the public to you to issue instructions that Manyawar Kanshiram should be freed from the personal prison of Mayawati and should be admitted to a government hospital from where medical bulletins are issued regarding his health so that the crores of sympathizers and well-wishers of Manyawar Kanshiram obtain the real facts about him.

With this hope and trust,

Sd. Dalbara Singh (President, Manyawar Kanshiram Bachao Sangharsh Committee, India)[15]

The letterhead carried the names of Dalbara Singh, national chairman, and Heera Lal Jawaddi, national general secretary, BRS Nagar, Ludhiana, Punjab.

On 15 August 2006 a cycle rally was organized and activists cycled from Auraiya to a demonstration site in Delhi. Finally, on 15 September 2006 a Vishal Kanshiram Bachao Karyakarta Mahasammelan (Massive Save Kanshiram Activists' Rally) was organized at the Roadways bus stand in Ajitmal, Auraiya. A pamphlet outlining the purpose of the massive rally was published on this occasion and it mentioned that the chief guest at the conference was Master Dalbara Singh.

The launch of a new party called Bahujan Sangharsh Party (Kanshiram) was also announced at the rally. The national president of the party was Dalbara Singh. A pamphlet circulated there had a note about the party with the title *Why only the Bahujan Sangharsh Party?* According to the pamphlet the party formed by Kanshiram was being run by its chief as a private limited enterprise, and working to 'harm the ideologies of Dr Ambedkar and Shri Kanshiram'. No poor person's son could aspire to become an MP or MLA or get a high position since the 'house of the bahujan samaj has been taken over by Brahminical murderers, mafias, robber and industrialists'.[16]

The party manifesto had twenty-one points aimed at benefiting and uplifting farmers, dalits, women, children and other weaker sections of the population towards creating an egalitarian society. It was signed by Suresh Rajput (Ferozabad by-election youth candidate, state president, UP), Brijram Singh Rathore (active in a parliamentary constituency) and Lajjaram Verma (national secretary).

However, before the party could prove its mettle in the elections, Kanshiram breathed his last on 9 October 2006, ending a major chapter in the history of dalit politics of the country.

Immediately after his death his brother Harbans Singh and sister Sabran Kaur filed a petition in the Delhi High Court that their brother's death was an unnatural one and that a post-mortem should be conducted. They also demanded that the body should be handed over to his family members for conducting the last rites. The high court did not conduct a post-mortem, nor did it allow the body to be handed over to Kanshiram's family. But it did ensure arrangements for Kanshiram's relatives to attend the funeral ceremony under police protection.

His body was taken to the BSP headquarters at 12, Gurudwara Rakabganj Road, New Delhi, for the activists and followers to have a darshan, and from there to the Nigambodh Ghat for the cremation. A huge crowd gathered at Nigambodh for the cremation, chanting slogans like 'Long Live Kanshiram', *'Bachcha Bachcha Bheem ka, Kanshiram ki team ka'* (Each and every child of Bhim is in Kanshiram's team), etc. The mortal remains of Kanshiram, covered with flowers, were taken to the platform for the last rites, accompanied by Mayawati and Kanshiram's family members. The funeral ceremony was conducted according to Buddhist rites. Although Kanshiram had followed Buddhist principles in life, he never embraced Buddhism, despite the persuasion of the majority Buddhist, dalit intelligentsia, for the reasons mentioned earlier (in chapter 3). Mayawati, who had been steadfast and loyal to Kanshiram, serving him with love and devotion till the end, lit his funeral pyre. The Buddhist priest who conducted the rites was Bhante Dhamm Virioji.[17]

The ceremony was attended by a huge crowd of ardent admirers and well-wishers of Kanshiram. Mayawati reiterated Kanshiram's wish that his ashes be placed in the party headquarters in Delhi and Lucknow and not be immersed in the Ganga, Yamuna or any other river.

Top leaders of India, across parties, and leading writers and journalists paid tribute to Kanshiram on his passing. The message from the then President of India, Dr A.P.J. Abdul Kalam said: 'The country has lost a leader who played a significant role in raising the voice of the oppressed sections of the country to demand their rights. He worked from his heart for the welfare of the people of the lower castes.' The then Vice President Bhairon Singh Shekhawat also conveyed his grave sorrow.

Dr Manmohan Singh, who was then prime minister, visited the residence of Mayawati and laid a wreath on Kanshiram's body. Congress party president, Sonia Gandhi, along with her son, Rahul Gandhi, also visited Mayawati's residence to pay her last respects to the dead leader. Later, Mrs Gandhi sent a separate condolence message to Mayawati in which she accepted openly that Kanshiram had transformed Indian politics during the last three decades. She also added that Kanshiram never accepted any political post but through his personality and ideology he had left an indelible mark on each section of society. The then chief minister of Tamil Nadu M. Karunanidhi said in his message that Kanshiram was a brave warrior who had fought for social justice and made strong efforts to elevate and uplift the exploited sections and the huge lower-caste population of the country.

Even V.P. Singh and Ram Vilas Paswan, whom Kanshiram had been critical of once, as we have seen, paid fulsome tributes to him. V.P. Singh remembered the 'reasonably good relationship' he shared with Kanshiram, and how the latter had invited him to various functions of the poor, dalits and backwards movement. 'I venerate him with full love and respect at the dedicated and sincere manner in which he fought for the poor, dalits and backwards,' he added.[18] Ram Vilas Paswan, the then Central minister of chemicals and fertilizers, recalled that his relationship with Kanshiram began in 1977. 'I learnt a great deal from him. He contributed a lot for the uplift of the dalits but unfortunately they have strayed from the path shown by him . . . I had tried to bring all the dalits together on the same platform and Kanshiram had also welcomed the effort. I felt that since Kanshiram was the most senior leader the movement should be under his leadership.'[19]

Many others, like Central ministers Shivraj Patil, Lalu Prasad Yadav, Punjab chief minister Amrendra Singh, leader of the Opposition L.K. Advani, BJP leader Arun Jaitley, ex-chief ministers of Delhi Madan Lal Khurana and Sahib Singh, also visited the residence of Mayawati to pay their last respects to Kanshiram.[20]

Remarkably, eminent social scientists and littérateurs also expressed their admiration for Kanshiram.

Ashis Nandy, recalling the new path that Kanshiram paved for dalit liberation, though leaving many unsolved questions, felt it 'is not just an irreparable loss for the dalit community but for the entire country . . . from this point [the BSP] dalit politics became a compulsion for all parties. [Kanshiram's] ideology will remain with us as his legacy but it should not remain only as his ideology.'[21]

Rajendra Yadav pointed out that '[he] was the first to transform dalit consciousness into a movement. [History would remember him] for giving practical shape to Ambedkar's ideology.'

Khushwant Singh gave a personal touch when he remembered how he had spent three days with him in a seminar of editors, governors and scholars and how Kanshiram was the odd man out. Singh said: '[He was] more comfortable in speaking with me in Punjabi . . . [and] through his conversations I could judge his angst about the condition of dalits in the country.'[22]

A pall of gloom spread over Kanshiram's village, Khawaspur, when the news of his death reached them. The alleys where Kanshiram had spent his childhood seemed desolate. In his house Kanshiram's relatives, like his sister-in-law Rajrani, his nephew Balwinder, his nieces and other relatives, were grieving before his photograph as the villagers tried to console them. The relatives were unhappy that Kanshiram had been unable to visit his mother's deathbed as he himself had been ill then.[23]

The proceedings of both the Lok Sabha and Rajya Sabha were adjourned on the first day of the next Parliament winter session, Wednesday, 22 November 2006, as a mark of respect for him.

The Bahujan Sangharsh Party (Kanshiram) once more swung into action and circulated a pamphlet posing a set of twenty-four questions to the national president of the BSP, Mayawati. Among the questions raised in the leaflet were the following:

Will Behenji take the trouble of telling us whether there is any provision in the Indian Penal Code that prevents a mother from meeting her son or a brother from meeting his brother, even if he occupies an important chair, and which forces them to take refuge in the court? All the leaders of the country are treated at the All India Institute of Medical Sciences in Delhi, so why was the founder of the BSP not taken there? The body of any deceased national leader is preserved for twenty-four hours to allow people to pay homage. Dalits and members of the oppressed communities from across India were heading towards Delhi in huge numbers to pay their respects to the great hero of the bahujan samaj—Kanshiram died at seven in the morning but you completed the entire funeral ceremony by two in the afternoon, thus hurting the sentiments of crores of dalits and oppressed. Was there any mystery behind Manyawar Kanshiram's death because of which you took such a hurried step? According to Indian culture, if a dead person does not have a son or daughter, then the brother or nephew has the right to conduct the last rites—even though Kanshiram's brothers Dalbara Singh and Harbansh Singh were present, why wasn't the dead body handed over to them? Even the bodies of dead terrorists are handed over to their family members. Will Behenji Mayawati take the trouble of telling us whether there is any provision in the Indian Penal Code and in Indian culture that a brother cannot light the funeral pyre of his brother but a woman who has no relation with the dead person can do so?

The acrimony between Mayawati and Kanshiram's family was not atypical in Indian politics. After the demise of M.G. Ramachandran (MGR), there were fist fights in public between supporters of Jayalalitha and Janaki, the wife of MGR. Allegations and counter-allegations flew thick and fast. Similar animosity was witnessed when the founder of Telugu Desam Party, N.T. Rama Rao passed away. In fact, the aftermath of Kanshiram's death was probably less ugly than what had happened in Tamil Nadu and Andhra Pradesh. These clashes ought to be seen in a larger perspective. The truth lies somewhere in between.

As far as Kanshiram was concerned, however, Mayawati was indeed his successor. This is clearly borne out by the will he left behind.

Meri khwaish hai ki Kumari Mayawati deerghaayu hokar uss mission ke liye kaam karti rahein jiske liye wo samarpit hain, lekin har aadmi ko ek na ek din marna hai. Ek din main bhi mrityu ko prapt ho jaunga aur ek din unko bhi mar jana hai. Meri khwaish hai ki mere marne ke baad meri asthiyaan Ganga-Jamuna mein na bahai jayein balki unhe Bahujan Samaj Prerna Kendra mein rakha jaye taki hamare karyakarta usse prerna le sake. Main ye khwaish bhi rakhta hoon ke mrityu ke uprant Km. Mayawati ki bhi asthiyaan meri asthiyon ke paas hi party karyalayon mein rakhi jayein. Main ummeed karta hoon ki Km. Mayawati ke mata-pita, bhai-behan Bahujan Samaj Party tatha bahujan samaj ke log meri khwaish ko poora karenge.

(It is my ardent desire that Kumari Mayawati lives a long life and continues to work for the mission to which she has dedicated herself. But each person has to die one day. One day I too will pass away and one day she too will go. My desire is that after my demise my ashes are not immersed in the Ganga or Yamuna but are kept in the Bahujan Samaj Prerna Kendra so that our activists can derive inspiration from them. I also desire that after her death the remains of Kumari Mayawati are also kept next to mine in the party office. I hope that Kumari Mayawati's parents, siblings, the party workers and the people belonging to the bahujan samaj will fulfil my desire.)

10 August 2003, New Delhi   Kanshiram,
                                            son of Late Sri Hari Singh
                                        12, Gurudwara Rakabganj Road
                                                  New Delhi 110 001

8

Long Live the Message
The Limits of Kanshiram's Politics

Aniccha vat sankhara, upadavyadhmmino
Upjjitwa nirujjhhanti esam wupsamo sukkho

(All *sanskara*s—influences of previous births—are indestructible;
to be born and to perish is Nature / To be born and to perish
is a continuous process, to imagine this is comforting)[*]

To the monks' chanting of these lines from the *Last Dhamma*, water was poured from a small lota or metal pot into a large thali or plate during the last rites of Kanshiram, performed as per Buddhist tradition. Witnessed by a large crowd of people, including admirers and political rivals, who had gathered at Nigambodh Ghat in Delhi to pay their last respects to him, Kanshiram's mortal remains were consigned to flames. With

---

[*] Translated from Pali to Hindi by Guru Prasad Madan and from Hindi to English by Arindam Roy.

him was also consumed a chapter of dalit history in UP, and indeed, India, that had been single-handedly crafted by him. After his passing away, things were never the same in the BSP camp led by Mayawati.

The BSP came to power in UP in 2007 with an overwhelming majority through Mayawati's political strategy of social engineering, whereby she tried to forge a rainbow coalition of lower castes—bahujans and the upper castes, terming them collectively 'sarvajan', or everyone. This strategy was derived from Kanshiram's concept of *bhagedari* in which all castes and communities, irrespective of their status in the caste hierarchy, were given political representation. This strategy paid off in the assembly elections (2007) but it failed to work well in the parliamentary elections (2009). Aimed at vote bank politics, the political alliance was inherently flawed because it took the form of a Brahman–dalit alliance.

'Bahujan to sarvajan' politics dilutes the feeling of bahujan identity in the dalits. This bridge can only be built when dalits enjoy the same living standards as the upper castes, a situation that exists only in the realm of imagination right now.[1] The upper castes of UP, too, cannot accept the dalits as their social equals, even if they occupy high offices, because of the vast cultural differences between the two groups. This is best illustrated by the BSP's inability to develop symbols or a vocabulary for the sarvajan, which it had successfully done for the bahujan, based on the memories of their oppressive past and their myths, legends and caste heroes.[2]

Mayawati's sarvajan politics led to dilution of the process of developing leaders among the dalit communities. To appease the upper castes, Mayawati had to give them space in her government, from the block to the state level. Moreover, this strategy stopped new castes among dalits, who had the potential of being politicized, from coming up. For Kanshiram, whose slogan was *'jati toro, samaj joro'*, casteism was intended to be a double-edged sword. He also anticipated that during the process of social change 'there may be minor turmoil in society briefly but things will become normal after some time'.[3] Casteism, which was to be used to break the dominance of the upper castes, however, also proved to be harmful later on. Casteism, in fact, closed the doors for the lower dalit castes who wanted to enter politics. The equal distribution of resources among all the dalit castes could not happen because of Kanshiram's bhagedari *siddhant* which said: *'Jiski jitni sankhya bhari uski utni hissedari'*.

The principle of participation in electoral democracy he put forth was meant to make the hierarchical Indian society more egalitarian. In the society envisioned by him, this participation included not just the dalits and the marginalized, including women, based on their numbers, but also the weaker forward castes who were numerically significant. Though radical in intent, this principle has had unintended consequences on the ground.

As far as dalits go, the downside has been the emergence of micro-inequalities among them, with those who are numerically smaller being marginalized by the numerically stronger castes like the Chamars and Pasis. Unfortunately, there isn't any visionary like Kanshiram in the BSP to handle these conflicts.

In recent years, Mayawati has also been using reservation as a strategy to mobilize dalits. This is in contrast to the vision of Kanshiram who did not encourage total dependence on the state, although he considered state power as a very important instrument of securing social justice for dalits. He wanted the dalits to go beyond the politics of reservations and to empower themselves, using their own resources. He wanted them to inculcate the concepts of self-respect and dignity and, alongside, to diversify their occupations so as not to be completely dependent on state jobs.

~

Although the BSP had a spectacular win in 2007, the party could not sustain the process of the sarvajan–bahujan mobilization begun by Kanshiram and carried forward by Mayawati. The party is slowly declining in UP, which was dramatically revealed in the 2012 UP assembly elections, when the BSP lost to the SP, its arch rival. The SP won an absolute majority with 224 seats out of a total of 403 seats, while the BSP succeeded in obtaining only 80 seats. According to me, the biggest reason for the defeat was the failure of Mayawati's sarvajan social engineering project which she had developed in 2007 through *bhaichara samiti*s at the grass roots. Dalit castes like Jatav and Chamar voted en masse for the BSP but the votes of other dalit castes like Kori, Dhobi, Pasi, Musahar and other numerically small castes were divided. The expectations of the other castes in the rainbow coalition were also not fulfilled: the Brahmans, who constitute 12 per cent of the population in UP, and had earlier voted for Mayawati, opposing the Yadav hoodlums of Mulayam Singh, were divided between the Congress, the BJP and the SP. The exception was Satish Chandra Mishra, who was close to her. The urban middle classes and the Vaishya communities who were with her in 2007 also voted against her in 2012 because of issues like corruption and poor governance. People had greater expectations from her than from Mulayam Singh, which she failed to fulfil during her tenure.

Her isolation from the voters as well as BSP cadres at the grass roots, because of a coterie of bureaucrats surrounding her, was another reason for her loss. Then there was the anti-incumbency factor. There were allegations of corruption against her and her close ministers, like Babu Singh Kushwaha, Nasimuddin Siddiqui, etc., which were well articulated in Rahul Gandhi's slogan 'Haathi paisa khata hai'. Poor governance led to the failure of development reaching all sections of society. Agents, land mafias and the elite cornered the fruits of the various development projects launched by her government. Only three or four dalit communities, like Chamars, Pasis, Koris and Dhobhis, out of a total of sixty-two dalit communities were benefited. The caste-wise analysis of the BSP government when it was in power in UP reveals that out of a total of fifty-two ministers only eight belonged to dalit castes. Five belonged to the Chamar caste, and only one each belonged to Dusadh, Pasi and Mallah castes. There was no representation in the BSP ministry from dalit castes like Basor, Dhanuk, Valmiki, Dom, Gond, Kol, Dharikar, Musahar, Beldar, Bhuaiar, Hela, Baiswar, Bansfor, Beriya, Pankha, etc. In fact, out of 403 MLAs in the Uttar Pradesh Assembly, the BSP's share of total seats was 206, out of which 100 were BSP dalit MLAs. Sadly, Mayawati's party neither addressed nor solved the problems of how to mobilize all or most of the SCs.[4]

In reservation in government jobs also such differences are visible. According to the 2001 Census report, the scheduled castes like Chamar, Dhusiya and Jatav had 59.67 per cent representation in various government jobs while the representation of other backward castes like Ahir, Yadav, Yaduvanshi and Gwala in government jobs was only 34.49 per cent.[5]

Even the initiative taken by the state government to bring about an amendment in the reservation quota in employment in 2001 could not be implemented. A Social Justice Committee was formed to make proposals on the reservation policy. It recommended in its report that the sixty-six scheduled castes in UP be divided into two groups. Amongst them 55.70 per cent population which comprises of Chamar, Dhusiya and Jatav should be given 10 per cent reservation. The remaining 44.30 per cent population comprising of other sixty-three castes should be given 11 per cent reservation. This proves the importance that some of the dominant castes like Chamar, Dhusiya and Jatav still have as compared to the other marginalized castes.[6]

This kind of discrepancy gave the Congress and other parties an opportunity to develop anti-dalit politics, which further weakened the BSP's prospects in the 2012 election. The rise of the most backward castes (MBCs) as a breakaway group from the OBCs has led to sharpening of contradictions between the dalits and OBCs, and also between dalits and MBCs, the benefit of which has been reaped by political parties other than the BSP.

The term Most Backward Classes was first used in the Kaka Kalelkar Commission in its report on the Backward Classes to identify and designate some classes based on their educational backwardness and low socio-economic status. They can be identified in the prevailing literature both in terms of caste and class. The MB *castes*, as they are commonly referred to in the literature, consist of the most backward section among the Backward Castes. They are lower *shudra* groups perched precariously on the line of pollution dividing the clean and unclean castes. Found almost entirely in rural areas, traditionally they were 'service' or artisan castes within the *Jajmani* system i.e. they provided certain services within the village system to the upper and intermediate castes (K.S. Singh 1991).[7]

The MBCs who constitute a large number among the backwards have yet to assume a distinct and collective identity . . . [These castes] such as the gadarias, jogis, dhiwars, nais, kumhars, etc, still do not have their own forum for articulation of their specific needs. [The MBCs] are large in number but scattered all over the state and hence are difficult to mobilise along political lines.[8]

In 2012, the BJP, the Congress and the SP tried to bridge the gap between the socio-economic condition of the MBCs and OBCs. The MBCs, who usually voted for the BSP, were upset that the Kurmis and other OBC communities had gained more from the fruits of development during the BSP regime than they had. Communities like the Pals and Yadavs, who had previously voted for the BSP, were alienated from them this time. The aspiration for development overtook identity politics at the grass roots. People who had previously voted for identity politics now understood the meaning and importance of development. This created an anti-BSP air prior to elections. Thus all the other parties portrayed the BSP as an anti-development and corrupt party because of which it lost votes.

After the elections Mayawati held a press conference in which she analysed the causes of her defeat. According to her, the votes of the upper castes, which had been the most important element of the sarvajan-winning alliance in 2007, had got divided while the Muslims had voted as a block for the SP because of the fear of communal violence after Uma Bharti, firebrand leader of the BJP, started communally mobilizing the OBCs in the wake of the declaration by the Congress that it would provide a quota of 4.5 per cent for Muslims within the existing OBC quota of 27 per cent.[9]

She added that some people were carrying on a propaganda campaign against her, on the ground that she has moved away from Kanshiram's path. Strongly contesting this, she declared that she was still deeply committed to his ideology and following it wholeheartedly. In the instructions issued to the party workers after the elections, she said that they should focus on strengthening the concept of bahujan for the mobilization of the BSP once again. Whenever the party was restructured at each level, it should be kept in mind that when a dalit was the president, an OBC had to be the secretary.[10]

Although Mayawati is trying to bring the BSP back on the rails, along the path shown by Kanshiram, media reports of the atrocities committed by BSP leaders in the recent past cannot be brushed aside. Three of these incidents were in the headlines for a while. In all the three cases, the BSP MLAs, two of whom were Brahmans, and their accomplices, were found guilty and convicted.

The first incident in 2007 involved Anand Sen, BSP MLA, son of a well-known SP leader and an erstwhile minister in Mayawati's cabinet, and a twenty-four-year-old dalit third-year law student, Sashi. Sashi was the daughter of BSP worker Yogendra Prasad, who had become close to Anand Sen during an election campaign. Sashi was abducted and murdered while she was returning from Saket Degree College, Faizabad. An SC/ST court in Faizabad held Anand and two others guilty in the murder case and sentenced them to life imprisonment on 16 May 2011. Earlier, Anand was dropped from the Uttar Pradesh cabinet by Chief Minister Mayawati after he had been named as an accused in the case. He was imprisoned in the Faizabad prison after his surrender in Lucknow in June 2008.[11]

In the second case, a Brahman BSP MLA, Shekhar Tiwari, along with nine of his accomplices, brutally murdered Manoj Kumar Gupta, an executive engineer of the PWD, in Auraiya, UP in 2008. Gupta refused to oblige Tiwari who had been on a fund-collection drive for the birthday celebration of the chief minister. On 6 May 2011, the additional sessions judge sentenced Tiwari and his nine accomplices to life imprisonment. The legislator's wife, Vibha Tiwari, was sentenced to two and a half years' imprisonment on the charges of destroying evidence. This case caused much embarrassment to the BSP.[12]

The third case occurred on 10 December 2010, in which a seventeen-year-old dalit girl was raped by Purushottam Naresh Dwivedi, a forty-eight-year-old BSP MLA, who represents the Naraini seat, and his three accomplices, Rajendra Shukla, Surendra Neta and Ravan Garg. The crime was committed at the MLA's residence. On 12 December, the teenager managed to escape. But Dwivedi, using his influence, falsely implicated her in a theft case and got her arrested. Following a huge hue and cry in the media, Chief Minister Mayawati had to intervene. She ordered arrest of the culprits and handed the case to CB-CID. The investigating officials found that the rape charges and the false implication in theft case were true. Dwivedi and his two aides Shukla and Neta were arrested on 13 January 2011, while the third accused Garg was reported absconding. The arrested culprits were sent to fourteen days' judicial custody by the chief judicial magistrate of Banda in January 2011.[13]

Had Kanshiram been alive today he would have been shattered by these incidents, since he could not brook atrocities on dalits and especially on women. During a rally held in Allahabad, when the BSP and the SP were jointly ruling the state, he announced clearly that 'if the SP–BSP government fails to honour the dignity of dalits, protect the minority and provide security to the people of the state, I will hold Mulayam Singh responsible'.[14] In fact, as we have seen, the first rift in the relationship between the SP and the BSP occurred after a dalit woman was paraded nude in Dauna village in UP by some upper castes and the culprits were allowed to go scot free by the Mulayam Singh government. Kanshiram immediately started taking steps to break up the alliance and did so at the first opportunity.

Kanshiram's concern for the plight of dalit women is well known. Not surprising since he had been very close to his mother. Film-maker and dalit activist Anand Rahate remembers how Kanshiram would be deeply moved when he saw women suffering.

Once Kanshiram was invited to give the opening clap for a film called *Insaaf ki Aandhi*, produced by Dilip Mendhe, which was based on the exploitation of a dalit woman. The film was based on a tribal woman living in a village called Shivri Narain. Her name was Meena Kumari Khunte and she had been gang-raped by a brahmin priest of the temple, the Thakurs and a baniya of a village called Lala Kesarwani, when she had been attending a local fair. When the terribly upset woman reached the police station to file a report, the corrupt police officers refused to file the report against the established upper castes and instead rebuked her and sent her away . . .

In the inaugural shot of the film, the heroine, Shail Jaimini, who was playing the part of the victim, and Ramesh Lakhmapure, who was playing the role of the police officer, had to perform their scene. The director, Yash Nikose, gave the clapping board to Kanshiram and asked him to give the clap to inaugurate the shooting. Kanshiram gave the clap and the shooting began. The weeping and crying Meena Kumari was standing near the police officer . . . On seeing this scene, Kanshiram's eyes filled with tears at the pathetic condition of the woman even though he knew it was only a dramatization.[15]

Rahate, who was standing next to Kanshiram, describes that he was shocked to see that Kanshiram, whose heart was strong as a rock, should melt at the sight of this helpless, downtrodden woman who was the victim of the oppressions of the upper castes.[16]

Kanshiram was also strongly in favour of women entering politics. He used to say that a Mayawati should emerge from each region of the country, one who could work for the upliftment of the dalits. He also said that he would like to make a dalit woman the prime minister of India.[17] He was also appreciative of Sonia Gandhi's entry and rise in politics, saying that she could emerge as a powerful leader and strengthen the Congress, which was declining at the hands of Narasimha Rao. (Conversely, he would also say that Rao should remain prime minister for two more years, so that the Congress would go downhill, which would be to the advantage of the BSP.)[18]

Kanshiram also celebrated the thirty-fourth year of Indian independence in 1981 as the year of Phoolan Devi, to acknowledge her struggle against the oppression of dalit women. He said that, in the coming years, Phoolan Devi would be a source of inspiration for dalit and oppressed women. Phoolan Devi, he held, 'had taught the dalits how to retaliate when dominant castes and states oppressed and subjugated them, and how to use the bullet in case of atrocities. He wondered why should the dalits wait for a devi or deva when Phoolan Devi was already there. At the same time, he cautioned dalits about balancing the use of the bullet and the ballot, so that all oppressed Indians, including they, could be uplifted as human beings.'[19] Ironically, apart from the women members of the Bahujan Volunteer Force, the BSP does not have an exclusive mass women's organization.

Mayawati's tactical retreat from sarvajan politics, post the 2012 assembly elections, and a renewed attempt to extend the dalit vote bank to the OBCs and minorities, fits into Kanshiram's original scheme of things. However, consolidating all the lower and backward castes in UP, to vote for the BSP in the next elections, will be an uphill task. Among the dalits, the Chamars are numerically strong and also dominate BSP politics. Their dominance has antagonized other numerically strong groups like Pasis, Dhobis, Koris and Valmikis. Besides, smaller groups such as Jogis, Nats, Rangrejs, Manihars, Bhangis, Helas, Nais, Dhanuks, Khatiks and Kanjars are miles away from the process of democratization. How to bring these diverse groups under the party's umbrella is a major challenge. There is room for fragmentation among dalits and, in such a scenario, there is a great possibility of them being co-opted in a Hindutva project designed to communalize the dalit identity.[20]

The BJP is trying to acquire state power by appropriating the dalits' past and identity as being a Hindu one, so as to bring the dalits within its fold. Through the dalits' own myths, heroes and caste histories, the BJP is trying to recreate the memory of various dalit castes.[21] The process by which they are doing so is fascinating. The BJP usually organizes big celebrations around each dalit male hero selected, and these are marked by a certain Hindutva aesthetic. Various kinds of badges, stickers, cards and so on are printed with the images of the dalit heroes for distribution among the people. Highly colourful and decorative, they portray them as chivalrous warriors in the image of Hindu legendary figures like Maharana Pratap.[22]

The strategy of mobilizing the various dalit castes of UP individually rather than as a consolidated whole is keeping in mind the highly caste-divided nature of the state. Winning elections in UP then depends more on the number of castes a party is able to enfold than on promises of roads, hospitals and schools that will benefit all people.[23]

The Chamar domination of the BSP is a major source of concern. Recently, 200 scheduled caste candidates were recruited in Noida Authority, out of which 199 were from the Chamar caste. The members of the other dalit castes trained their guns on Mayawati, who herself belongs to the Chamar caste, and attacked her for creating fissures in dalit unity. A programme was organized at the Charbagh Ravindralaya, in Lucknow, to bring together the neglected and deprived dalit castes spread all over UP and in different parts of the country on a common platform. One of the speakers during the event said that the BSP seems to have forgotten that all dalit castes had unified to ensure the party's victory in 2007.[24] This action will certainly serve to alienate the other dalits, to the advantage of the Hindutva forces, who too have been wooing the dalit vote bank. Kanshiram, too, had believed that Chamar dominance would form the basis of the party, and was in favour of unifying the dalits under Chamar leadership as they were more in number and strength. The present BSP furthers Kanshiram's bahujan ideology, but at the same time is faced with the challenge of uniting other strong dalit caste groups.

Kanshiram was always proud of his rural roots. He would clearly have opposed the land acquisition move by the state, using repressive measures, and the pitched battle that took place between the police and the farmers of Bhatta Parsaul village, who were protesting against land acquisition in May 2011. Many of the marginal and small farmers, including dalits, are under severe threat of losing what little land they possess. The land was ostensibly for the landless workers, mainly dalits. Kanshiram's agricultural policy was quite different. He could not imagine confiscation of land from the big or even small farmers and distributing it among the landless peasants. His slogan, *'Jo jameen sarkaari hai wah jameen hamaari hai'* (Government land is what is ours) reflects his thinking.[25] Kanshiram was of the opinion that the government, instead of taking land from the big farmers and distributing it among the landless, should take the wastelands and distribute them among the landless farmers.[26] He used his political influence in UP to give shape to this policy.

The events of Bhatta Parsaul echo what happened in Nandigram and Singur in West Bengal, which led to the defeat of the CPI(M) in 2011 and its being thrown out of office after thirty-four long years. It is feared that the atrocities against farmers for 'prized land' in UP could likewise cost the BSP. The overtures of Rahul Gandhi towards the victimized farmers in Bhatta Parsaul, with the aim of luring away the dalit vote from the BSP, has been a major cause of concern for Mayawati.

If the BSP is to rise again, it will have to return to the objective with which Kanshiram had launched the party, which was that of uplifting the dalits socially and culturally by first empowering them politically, and in the process bringing about a social transformation in UP, and in India in the long run. Its interest in fulfilling short-term political objectives, for which it is prepared to go to any extent, goes against the grain of Kanshiram's strategy. In *The Chamcha Age*, Kanshiram made a scathing attack on those dalits who had sold themselves to the upper castes for their personal gain. Sadly, the BSP today could be deemed guilty of doing the same. Though Kanshiram had no moral compunctions about using foul means to gain power, his sole aim was to turn the tables and reverse the power structure in favour of dispossessed dalits. Seeking electoral gain seemed to be the chief motive of the BSP, for which Kanshiram was often branded an opportunist, but as we have shown in the preceding chapters, he never lost sight of his long-term objective, which was that of inverting the social pyramid.

Although the BSP is one of the most important national parties of India and a dominant one in UP, which can make or break governments, it is far from fulfilling the goals with which Kanshiram launched it. To do this, it must go beyond its short-term political strategies for gaining electoral power and instead concentrate on uplifting the huge number of dalits and backward castes who, despite their political empowerment, are still languishing at the bottom of the social pyramid in north India. Only when these dalits acquire power to write their own destinies, as Kanshiram had, will his vision be fulfilled. This will be the true homage to the great dalit messiah whose entire life was dedicated to the cause of dalits.

Acknowledgements

I am thankful to Penguin Books India for graciously accepting my proposal to write this biography. I am especially grateful to Kamini Mahadevan for suggestions that helped me turn what was meant to be a personal tribute to Kanshiram into a work that encompassed some of the social and political issues of his times. Ramachandra Guha gave me the strength and support that I needed to complete this daunting task. I am deeply indebted to Professor G.K. Chadha for having inspired me and for providing me an atmosphere conducive to research at G.B. Pant Social Science Institute (GBPSSI), Allahabad. This book owes its existence also to Brijendra Gautam, Arindam Roy, Nivedita Singh, Archana Singh, Ritu Sureka and Tarushikha Sarvesh, who helped me at various stages of this project since its inception. I am also thankful to Mousumi Majumder who helped me develop the book. I am also grateful to Professor Sudha Pai and Professor Surinder S. Jodhka for their insightful comments on the manuscript which greatly helped me give a new dimension to the book.

This book owes its depth to all the people in Ropar and

Khawaspur (Punjab), like Dalbara Singh, Sabran Kaur and Ravindra Singh, and Dr Omkar Mittal from New Delhi as well as Guru Prasad Madan, R.P. Ram, R.B. Trisharan, Ramchet Ram 'Toofani' and A.R. Akela. I would like to thank all the people who provided me information about Kanshiram.

Thanks are also due to several people associated with Kanshiram—they generously allowed me to interview them and also shared their letters, diaries and personal reminiscences with me. This book owes its depth to all the people in Ropar and Khawaspur (Punjab); Lucknow, Raebareli and Allahabad (Uttar Pradesh); Poona, Mumbai, Nagpur and Chandrapur (Maharashtra); and Bapatla and Hyderabad (Andhra Pradesh). I would like to also place on record my gratitude to the director of GBPSSI, Professor Pradeep Bhargava, who provided me the necessary facilities to pursue my work on the book. Thanks are also due to the staff of the Manav Vikas Sangrahalaya, GBPSSI, for their support. Lastly, I would like to thank my family members for their moral support and cooperation.

Notes

Author's Note

1. A.R. Akela, *Kanshiram Ke Saakshatkaar* (Delhi: Manak Publications, 2007), p. 18.
2. Sudha Pai, *Dalit Assertion and the Unfinished Democratic Revolution: The Bahujan Samaj Party in Uttar Pradesh* (New Delhi: Sage Publications, 2002), p. 1.
3. *Sahara Samachar*, Lucknow, 23 January 1994, pp. 1–2.
4. R.V. Sharma, *Rag Virag* (Allahabad: Lokbharti Prakashan, 1992), p. 137.

Chapter 1. The Early Years

1. A.R. Akela, ed., *Mananiya Behan Kumari Mayawati Ke Saakshatkaar* (Aligarh: Anand Sahitya Sadan, 2008), p. 22.
2. R. Tilak, *Bharat Ki Pehli Shikshika Savitri Bai Phule* (New Delhi: Centre for Alternative Dalit Media, 2002), p. 2.
3. Mohandas Naimishraye, *Bhartiya Dalit Aandolan Ka Itihaas*, vol. 2 (New Delhi: Radhakrishna Prakashan, 2013), pp. 303–04.
4. www.ambedkartimes.com, 11 June 2012; and Mohandas

Naimishraye, *Bhartiya Dalit Aandolan Ka Itihaas*, vol. 1 (New Delhi: Radhakrishna Prakashan, 2013), p. 480.

5. Bharat Patankar and Gail Omvedt, *The Dalit Liberation Movement in Colonial Period* (New Delhi: Critical Quest, 2004), p. 13.

6. Mark Juergensmeyer, *Religious Rebels in the Punjab: The Ad Dharm Challenge to Caste* (New Delhi: Navayana Publishing, 2009), p. 90.

7. Patankar and Gail, *Dalit Liberation Movement*, p. 13.

8. Suratha Malik, 'Analysing Dalit Movement: Interpreting the History', p. 4, https://www.academia.edu/3849348/analysing_dalit_movement.

9. R.K. Kshirsagar, *Dalit Movement in India and Its Leaders* (New Delhi: M.D. Publications Pvt. Ltd, 1994) p. 345.

10. Nandini Gooptu, *Swami Acchutanand and the Adi Hindu Movement* (Cambridge: Cambridge University Press, 2006), p. 14.

11. Ibid., p. 12.

12. Badri Narayan and A.R. Mishra, eds., *Multiple Marginalities: An Anthology of Identified Dalit Writings* (New Delhi: Manohar, 2004), p. 105.

13. Gooptu, *Swami Acchutanand*, p. 13.

14. Dr Rajpal Singh 'Raj', *Swami Acchutanand Harihar* (Delhi: Rajlakshmi Prakashan, 2002), p. 28.

15. Narayan and Mishra, *Multiple Marginalities*, pp. 105–06.

16. Ibid., p. 107.

17. Kshirsagar, *Dalit Movement*, p. 398. Other leaders included Prithvi Sing Azad (Ambala), Prabhati Ram (Amritsar), Kartar Chand Sulekh (Jalandhar), Mihan Singh (Patiala), Nanak Chand Rattu (Hoshiarpur), Keharsing Choturam Gondi (Rohtak), Charan Singh (Shimla), Chanan Ram (Shimla), Chand Ram (Rohtak), Prabharam Boudh (Panipat).

18. Ronki Ram, 'Untouchability, Dalit Consciousness, and the Ad-Dharm

Movement in Punjab', *Contributions to Indian Sociology*, n.s., 38, no. 3 (2004): 327. Posted on www.ambedkartimes.com on 11 June 2012.

19. Naimishraye, *Bhartiya Dalit Aandolan Ka Itihaas*, vol. 1, pp. 420–21.

20. Kshirsagar, *Dalit Movement*, p. 93.

21. Juergensmeyer, *Religious Rebels*, p. 38.

22. S.L. Malhotra, 'Hindu Politics and Untouchability in Punjab, 1900–1935', *Social Science Research Journal* 1 (1976): 74–88.

23. Juergensmeyer, *Religious Rebels*, pp. 47–49.

24. Eleanor Zelliot, *Dr Ambedkar and the Mahar Movement* (Philadelphia: University of Pennsylvania Press, 1969).

25. Gail Omvedt, *Dalits and the Democratic Revolution: Dr Ambedkar and the Dalit Movement in Colonial India* (New Delhi: Sage Publications, 1994), pp. 223–59.

26. Dalbara Singh, interview by Brijendra Gautam in Khawaspur, 22 October 2010. Sabran Kaur, interview by Brijendra Gautam at Kanshiram's birthplace in Bunga Sahib on 23 October 2010.

27. S. Singh, *Bahujan Nayak: Kanshiram* (New Delhi: Samyak Publications, 2005), p. 14.

28. Ibid., p. 18.

29. Ibid., p. 20.

30. S.S. Gautam, *Bahujan Nayak Manyavar Kanshiram Smriti Granth* (New Delhi: Gautam Book Centre, 2006), p. 55.

31. Sabran Kaur, interview by Brijendra Gautam.

32. Singh, *Bahujan Nayak*, pp. 20–21.

33. Ibid.

34. Y.K. Yaad, *Samajik Parivartan Ke Mahanayak Manya Kanshiram Sahab* (Lucknow: Bahujan Sahitya Sanstha Ltd, 2005), p. 9.

35. Singh, *Bahujan Nayak*, p. 22.

36. Ibid., p. 21.

37. Yaad, *Samajik Parivartan*, p. 9.

38. Ibid., p. 8.

39. M.P. Ahirvaar, '*Manyavar Kanshiram: Tathya Evam Bhrantiyaan*', *Ambedkar in India*, October 2008, p. 7.

40. Ibid.

41. Singh, *Bahujan Nayak*, pp. 22–24.

42. Ibid., p. 24.

43. Yaad, *Samajik Parivartan*, pp. 26–27.

44. Ibid., p. 12.

45. Ibid.

46. Kshirsagar, *Dalit Movement*, pp. 415–16.

47. Yaad, *Samajik Parivartan*, p. 13.

48. Ibid.

49. Ibid., p. 14.

50. Singh, *Bahujan Nayak*, pp. 27–28; and S. Sonik, *Yug Purush Kanshiram Ka Bahujan Sangharsh* (Delhi: Siddhartha Publication, 2007), p. 39.

51. Singh, *Bahujan Nayak*, p. 28.

52. Ibid., p. 28–29.

53. Singh, *Bahujan Nayak*, pp. 29–30; and Yaad, *Samajik Parivartan*, p. 14.

54. V. Kumar, '*Aadhunik Bhartiya Rajneeti Ke Mahan Nayak*', *Ambedkar in India*, March 2010, pp. 8–9.

55. Ibid.

56. R.P. Ram, a BSP political activist, who worked with Kanshiram, interview by Brijendra Gautam on 5 November 2010 in Raebareli, UP.

57. Kumar, '*Aadhunik Bhartiya Rajneeti*', pp. 8–9.

Chapter 2: Seeking the 'Master Key'

1. A. Mukul, '"Maya Jaal" Spreads over Maharashtra', *Times of India*, 17 June 2004.

There has been some debate on what was the 'master key' for Ambedkar. Bhagwan Das holds that Ambedkar is being misquoted as saying that political power is the master key. This was meant for the audience of political leaders that he addressed at a particular time. Ambedkar did not emphasize political power alone. He felt that the weakness within society was as important and had to be overcome by promoting education. Without a sound ideology, political power would amount to nothing. (Bhagwan Das, interviewed by Vidya Bhushan Rawat, http://www.countercurrents.org/rawat021007.htm, 2 Oct 2007.)

K.C. Das suggests that Kanshiram turned the above view of the master key on its head—and thus subverted its spirit. He says this was because Kanshiram had observed in UP that the Chamars, and also the Pasis and Koris, had produced an educated class from within the castes, thanks partly to the welfare policies initiated by the government. Kanshiram's problem was, therefore, to campaign for these dalit castes to acquire political power, not education. (Reply to above at http://www.countercurrents.org/rawat021007.htm, 2 Oct 2007.)

2. Ibid.
3. A.R. Akela, *Kanshiram Ke Saakshatkaar* (Delhi: Manak Publications, 2007), p. 115.
4. Ibid., p. 263.
5. A.R. Akela, ed., *The Oppressed Indian: Mananiya Kanshiram Saheb Ke Sampadakiya Lekh* (Aligarh: Anand Sahitya Sadan, 2012), p. 81.
6. Harish S. Wankhede, 'Dalit/RPI Politics in Maharashtra', Dalit Perspectives blog, 28 April 2012, dalitperspectivejnu.blogspot.in/2012/04/dalitrpi-politics-in-maharashtra.html.
7. Ibid.
8. Ibid.

9. A.K. Dubey, *Kanshiram: Ek Alochanatmak Adhyayan* (New Delhi: Rajkamal Prakashan, 1997), pp. 40–41.

10. Wankhede, 'Dalit/RPI Politics'.

11. Ibid.

12. Harish S. Wankhede, 'The Political and the Social in the Dalit Movement Today', *Economic and Political Weekly* 43, no. 6 (2008): 52.

13. L. Murugkar, *Dalit Panther Movement in Maharashtra* (Bombay: Popular Prakashan, 1991), p. 51.

14. Anand Teltumbde, 'Crisis of Ambedkarites and Future Challenges', CounterCurrents.org, 22 April 2011, www.countercurrents.org/teltumbde220411.htm.

15. Murugkar, *Dalit Panther Movement*, p. 91.

16. Gail Omvedt, 'Ambedkar and After: The Dalit Movement in India', in *Dalit Identity and Politics*, ed. Ghanshyam Shah (New Delhi: Sage Publications, 2001), p. 53, quoted in Wankhede, 'The Political and the Social', p. 53.

17. Ibid.

18. Christophe Jaffrelot, *India's Silent Revolution* (New Delhi: Permanent Black, 2006), p. 390, quoted in Wankhede, 'The Political and the Social', p. 53.

19. Sudha Pai, 'Kanshi Ram: The Man and His Legacy', *eSocialSciences*, 13 October 2006, http://www.esocialsciences.org/Articles/ShowArticle.aspx?acat=Current+Affairs&aid=639.

20. S.S. Gautam, *Bahujan Nayak Manyavar Kanshiram Smriti Granth* (Delhi: Gautam Book Centre, 2006), p. 56.

21. Ibid., pp. 59–60.

22. *Bahujan Sangathan*, 27 February 1989, quoted in R.K. Singh, *Kanshiram Aur BSP: Dalit Aandolan Ka Vaicharik Aadhar Brahmanvaad Virodh* (Allahabad: Kushwaha Book Distributors, 1994), p. 30.

23. Akela, *Kanshiram Ke Saakshatkaar*, p. 13.
24. Y.K. Yaad, *Samajik Parivartan Ke Mahanayak Manya Kanshiram Sahab* (Lucknow: Bahujan Sahitya Sanstha Ltd, 2005), p. 15.
25. Ibid., p. 16.
26. Ibid.
27. Ibid., p. 46.
28. A. Kumar, ed., *Bahujan Nayak Kanshiram Ke Avismarniya Bhashan* (Delhi: Gautam Book Centre, 2007), p. 89.
29. Yaad, *Samajik Parivartan*, p. 17.
30. Ibid., p.18.
31. Ibid.
32. Ibid.
33. Akela, *Kanshiram Ke Saakshatkaar*, p. 256.
34. Gautam, *Bahujan Nayak*, p. 70.
35. Ibid., p. 64 and p. 68.
36. Ibid., p. 70.
37. Ramchet Ram, interview by Brijendra Gautam, 13 March 2011.
38. Badri Narayan, *The Making of the Dalit Public in North India: Uttar Pradesh, 1950–Present* (New Delhi: Oxford University Press India, 2011), pp. 35–58.
39. Akela, *Kanshiram Ke Saakshatkaar*, p. 256.
40. Yaad, *Samajik Parivartan*, p. 18.
41. Ibid., pp. 18–19.
42. Dubey, *Kanshiram*, p. 50.
43. Yaad, *Samajik Parivartan*, p. 19.
44. S.D. Gulde, *Jai Bheem Jagriti Geetmala* (New Delhi: Samyak Prakashan, 2000), p. 11.
45. R.B. Trisharan, *Bhim Ekta Geet* (Basti, UP: Samaj Sudhar Prakashan, 1994), p. 16
46. Yaad, *Samajik Parivartan*, p. 19.
47. Ibid., pp. 19–20.

48. Kamlakant, *Daliton Ke Messiah Kanshiram* (Delhi: Raja Pocket Books, 2006), pp. 10–11.

49. Dubey, *Kanshiram*, p. 51.

50. Ibid., pp. 52–53.

51. Ibid., p. 53.

52. S. Singh, *Bahujan Nayak: Kanshiram* (New Delhi: Samyak Publications, 2005), p. 35.

53. Kamlakant, *Daliton Ke Messiah Kanshiram*, p. 15.

54. Akela, *The Oppressed Indian*, p. 227 and pp. 228–29.

55. Ibid., p. 11, p. 12 and p. 14.

56. Ibid., pp. 230–32.

57. Singh, *Bahujan Nayak*, pp. 36–37.

58. Ibid.

59. K. Bharti, *Kanshiram Ke Do Chehre* (Rampur, UP: Bodhisattva Prakashan, 1996), p. 13.

60. Dubey, *Kanshiram*, p. 53.

61. Ibid.

62. Ajoy Bose, *Behenji: A Political Biography of Mayawati* (New Delhi: Penguin, 2008), p. 40.

63. Mayawati, quoted in A.R. Akela, ed., *Mananiya Behan Kumari Mayawati Ke Saakshatkaar* (Aligarh: Anand Sahitya Sadan, 2008), pp. 49–50.

64. Ibid., p. 149.

65. Ibid., pp. 21–22.

66. Ibid., p. 65.

Chapter 3: The Chamcha Age

1. Nicolas Jaoul, 'Political and "Non-political" Means in the Dalit Movement', in *Political Process in Uttar Pradesh: Identity, Economic Reforms and Governance*, ed. Sudha Pai (New Delhi: Pearson Education, 2007), p. 194.

2. Prasanna Kumar Choudhary and Srikant, *Swarg Par Dhawa: Bihar Mein Dalit Aandolan 1912–2000* (New Delhi: Vani Prakashan, 2005), p. 280.

3. K.C. Das, *Indian Dalits: Voices, Visions and Politics* (Delhi: Global Vision Publishing House, 2004), p. 217.

4. *The Telegraph*, 3 December 1989.

5. *The Week*, 16 April 1992.

6. *Surya India*, 1992.

7. Kanshiram, *Chamcha Yug: An Era of the Stooges*, translated into Hindi by Moses Michael (New Delhi: Samyak Prakashan, 2008), p. 72.

8. Ibid., pp. 76–77.

9. Ibid., p. 77.

10. Ibid.

11. Ibid., pp. 82–86.

12. Ibid., pp. 86–87.

13. Ibid., pp 107–08.

14. Ibid., pp 109–10.

15. A.R. Akela, ed., *The Oppressed Indian: Mananiya Kanshiram Saheb Ke Sampadakiya Lekh* (Aligarh: Anand Sahitya Sadan, 2012), p. 191.

16. Ibid., p. 211.

17. A. Kumar, ed., *Bahujan Nayak Kanshiram Ke Avismarniya Bhashan* (Delhi: Gautam Book Centre, 2007), pp. 77–78.

18. Dhananjay Keer, *Dr. Ambedkar: Life and Mission* (Bombay: Popular Prakashan, 1971), p. 124 and p. 491.

19. B.R. Ambedkar, *The Annihilation of Caste* (New Delhi: Arnold Publishers, 1990).

20. Ibid., p. 63.

21. Ibid., p. 54.

22. Ibid., p. 64.

23. Ibid., p. 81.

24. Ibid., p. 83.

25. Ibid., p. 84.

26. Ibid.

27. Ibid., pp. 83–84.

28. Ambedkar, *The Annihilation of Caste* (annotated and extended version by The Multimedia Study Environment), available online at http://ccnmtl.columbia.edu/projects/mmt/ambedkar/web/section_21.html.

29. Ibid.

30. Kumar, *Bahujan Nayak Kanshiram*, p. 71.

31. Kanshiram, cited in Kumar, *Bahujan Nayak Kanshiram*, pp. 69–70.

32. B.R. Ambedkar, '*Gaon*', translated in English as *Poems of Ambedkar* in Badri Narayan and A.R. Mishra, eds., *Multiple Marginalities: An Anthology of Identified Dalit Writings* (New Delhi: Manohar, 2004), p. 229.

33. S. Singh, *Bahujan Nayak: Kanshiram* (New Delhi: Samyak Publications, 2005), p. 122.

34. Cited in A.R. Akela, *Kanshiram Ke Saakshatkaar* (Delhi: Manak Publications, 2007), p. 34.

35. Ibid., p. 25.

36. Singh, *Bahujan Nayak*, p. 123.

37. A.R. Akela, *Mananiya Kanshiram Saheb Ke Saakshatkaar* (Aligarh: Anand Sahitya Sadan, 2009), p. 194.

38. Badri Narayan, *Women Heroes and Dalit Assertion in North India* (New Delhi: Sage Publications, 2006), p. 81.

39. Ibid., p. 77.

40. S.S. Bechain, *Hindi Ki Dalit Patrakarita Par Patrakar Ambedkar Ka Prabhav* (Delhi: Samta Prakashan, 1997), p. 137.

41. Ibid., p. 187.

42. Ibid., p. 185.

43. Ibid., p. 219.

44. Jean Drèze, 'Dr Ambedkar and the Future of Indian Democracy', South Asia Citizens Web, 31 January 2012, www.sacw.net/article2523.html.

45. Anand Teltumbde, *Ambedkar in and for the Post-Ambedkar Dalit Movement*, originally presented as a paper in a seminar on the post-Ambedkar dalit movement, Department of Political Science, University of Pune, 27–29 March 1997 (Pune: Sugawa Prakashan), p. 19.

46. D. Keer, *Dr. Babasaheb Ambedkar: Jeevan Charit* (New Delhi: Popular Prakashan, 2006), p. 477.

47. Akela, *Kanshiram Ke Saakshatkaar*, p. 232.

48. Ibid., p. 229.

49. A.R. Akela, ed., *Mananiya Behan Kumari Mayawati Ke Saakshatkaar* (Aligarh: Anand Sahitya Sadan, 2008), pp. 164–65 and p. 171.

50. Cited in H.L. Dusadh, *Bahujan Samaj Ka Hit Bhagedaari Siddhant Mein: Kanshiram Ke Aarthik Darshan Par Ek Addhyayan* (New Delhi: Bahujan Diversity Mission, 2007), p. 26.

51. Ibid., p. 29.

52. Cited in Akela, *Kanshiram Ke Saakshatkaar*, p. 256.

53. Ibid., p. 257.

54. Akela, *Mananiya Kanshiram Saheb Ke Saakshatkaar*, pp. 350–51.

55. Ibid., p. 352.

56. Ibid.

57. Akela, *Kanshiram Ke Saakshatkaar*, p. 270.

58. Ibid., p. 265.

59. Ibid.

60. R.K. Singh, *Kanshiram Aur BSP: Dalit Aandolan Ka Vaicharik Aadhar Brahmanvaad Virodh* (Allahabad: Kushwaha Book Distributors, 1994), p. 30.

61. Ibid., p. 31.

62. Dusadh, *Bahujan Samaj Ka Hit*, p. 39.

63. Akela, *The Oppressed Indian*, p. 134.

64. Ibid., pp. 46–47.

65. Ibid., p. 39.

66. Ibid.

67. Ibid., pp. 84–85.

68. Akela, *Kanshiram Ke Saakshatkaar*, p. 19.

69. Teltumbde, *Ambedkar in and for the Post-Ambedkar*, p. 17.

70. Kanshiram, cited in Akela, *Kanshiram Ke Saakshatkaar*, p. 59.

71. Ibid., p. 69.

72. Ibid., p. 106.

73. S.S. Gautam, *Bahujan Nayak Manyavar Kanshiram Smriti Granth* (Delhi: Gautam Book Centre, 2006), p. 62.

74. Akela, *The Oppressed Indian*, p. 223.

75. Ibid., p. 243.

76. Raj Sekhar Vundru, 'The Other Father', *Outlook*, 20 August 2012, pp. 46–47.

Chapter 4: The Elephant Rises

1. *Reservation as a Welfare Measure*, Report of the National Commission for Religious and Linguistic Minorities, chapter 8, *Communalism Combat*, April 2010, p. 14, http://www.sabrang.com/cc/archive/2010/apr10/chapter8.pdf.

2. G.K. Lieten and R. Srivastava, *Unequal Partners: Power Relations, Devolution and Development in Uttar Pradesh* (New Delhi: Sage Publications, 1999), pp. 57–58.

3. A.K. Verma, 'Uttar Pradesh: Politics of Social Polarisation and its Limits', *Journal of Indian School of Political Economy* 15, nos. 1 & 2 (2003): 252.

4. Ibid., p. 253.

5. Harish K. Puri, 'Scheduled Castes in Sikh Community: A

Historical Perspective', *Economic and Political Weekly* 38, no. 26 (2003): pp. 2693–701.

6. Inderjit Singh, 'Bahujan Samaj Party in Punjab: Organization, Support Base and Performance' (unpublished thesis, Punjabi University, Patiala, 2011), chapter 6, p. 243, http://shodhganga. inflibnet.ac.in/bitstream/10603/4286/13/13_chapter% 206.pdf.

7. Ibid., pp. 244–47.

8. Owen M. Lynch, *The Politics of Untouchability* (New Delhi: National Publishing House, 1974), pp. 67–68.

9. B.S. Hans, *Gau Brahmin Namo-Namo: Ko Rakshati Vedah* (Patna: Ambedkar Mission Prakashan, 2003), p. 77.

10. Owen M. Lynch, *The Politics of Untouchability* (New York: Columbia University Press, 1969), p. 95.

11. Ibid.

12. Ibid., p. 86.

13. A.R. Akela, *Kanshiram Ke Saakshatkaar* (Delhi: Manak Publications, 2007), p. 20.

14. R. Patel, *Mahamana Ram Swaroop Verma Ka Sankshipta Jeevan Parichay* (Basti, UP: Samta Prakashan, 2001), p. 6.

15. R.K. Singh, *Kanshiram Aur BSP: Dalit Aandolan Ka Vaicharik Aadhar Brahmanvaad Virodh* (Allahabad: Kushwaha Book Distributors, 1994), p. 93.

16. S. Singh, *Bahujan Nayak: Kanshiram* (New Delhi: Samyak Publications, 2005), p. 41.

17. Ibid.

18. Ibid., p. 42.

19. Singh, *Kanshiram Aur BSP*, p. 95.

20. Maikulal Varishtha Chintansheel Nagrik, *Gurudev Bhagwan Ravidas Ka Sankshipta Jeevan Parichay* (Lucknow: Maikulal Varishtha Chintansheel Nagrik, 2005), p. 3.

21. Badri Narayan, *Women Heroes and Dalit Assertion in North India* (New Delhi: Sage Publications, 2006), p. 53.
22. Compiled from *Jansatta*, 28 July 1997; B.S. Visharad, *Virangana Jhalkari Bai* (Aligarh: Anand Sahitya Sadan, 1964); R.K. Choudhary, *Pasi Samrajya* (Lucknow: Shruti Prakashan, 1997); and M.R. Vidrohi, *Dalit Dastavej* (New Delhi: Samyak Prakashan, 2004).
23. Vidrohi, *Dalit Dastavej*, pp. 74–82.
24. R.P. Saroj, *Krantiveer Madari Pasi Evom Eka Aandolan* (Lucknow: Sushila Saroj, 1997), p. 27.
25. Vidrohi, *Dalit Dastavej*, p. 176.
26. Ibid., p. 81.
27. Narayan, *Women Heroes*, pp. 140–41.
28. Ibid., p. 71.
29. Badri Narayan, *Fascinating Hindutva: Saffron Politics and Dalit Mobilisation* (New Delhi: Sage Publications, 2009), p. 86.
30. D.C. Dinkar, *Swatantrata Sangram Mein Achhuton Ka Yogdan*. (Lucknow: Bodhisattva Prakashan, 1990), p. 23.
31. S.S. Bechain, *Hindi Ki Dalit Patrakarita Par Patrakar Ambedkar Ka Prabhav* (Delhi: Samta Prakashan, 1997), p. 145.
32. Badri Narayan, *Documenting Dissent: Contesting Fables, Contested Memories and Dalit Political Discourse* (Shimla: Indian Institute of Advanced Study, 2001), p. 144.
33. A.R. Akela, ed., *The Oppressed Indian: Mananiya Kanshiram Saheb Ke Sampadakiya Lekh* (Aligarh: Anand Sahitya Sadan, 2012), p. 83.
34. Ibid., pp. 100–02.
35. Ibid., p. 83.
36. Ibid., p. 103.
37. Akela, *Kanshiram Ke Saakshatkaar*, p. 8.
38. Singh, *Kanshiram Aur BSP*, pp. 89–90.
39. Ibid., p. 90.

40. Ibid., p. 94.

41. Ibid.

42. Ibid.

43. Ibid., p. 86.

44. *Amrit Prabhat*, 2 June 1988, Allahabad.

45. Singh, *Kanshiram Aur BSP*, p. 96.

46. Ibid., p. 95.

47. A.K. Dubey, *Kanshiram: Ek Alochanatmak Adhyayan* (New Delhi: Rajkamal Prakashan, 1997), p. 70.

48. Singh, *Kanshiram Aur BSP*, p. 95.

49. Ibid.

50. Ibid., p. 96.

51. A. Kumar, ed., *Bahujan Nayak Kanshiram Ke Avismarniya Bhashan* (Delhi: Gautam Book Centre, 2007), p. 80.

52. K. Bharti, *Kanshiram Ke Do Chehre* (Rampur, UP: Bodhisattva Prakashan, 1996), p. 14.

53. Ibid. The Khoti system was a system of land tenure in the Konkan region, which treated agricultural tenants as serfs. Zamindars gave the land to farmers to cultivate, and in return the farmers became their slaves for generations as they could not claim any right on the produce of the land. Ambedkar introduced a bill in 1937 to abolish this system.

54. Ibid., p. 15.

Chapter 5: The Bid for Power

1. A.K. Dubey, *Kanshiram: Ek Alochanatmak Adhyayan* (New Delhi: Rajkamal Prakashan, 1997), p. 57.

2. Ajoy Bose, *Behenji: A Political Biography of Mayawati* (New Delhi: Penguin, 2008), p. 64.

3. Dubey, *Kanshiram*, pp. 82–83.

4. Kamlakant, *Daliton Ke Messiah Kanshiram* (Delhi: Raja Pocket Books, 2006), pp. 17–18.
5. Dubey, *Kanshiram*, p. 58.
6. Ibid., pp. 66–67.
7. Ibid., p. 67.
8. Kamlakant, *Daliton Ke Messiah Kanshiram*, p. 18.
9. Ibid., p. 31.
10. Ibid., p. 30.
11. Bose, *Behenji*, pp. 70–71.
12. Ibid., p. 79.
13. Kamlakant, *Daliton Ke Messiah Kanshiram*, p. 32.
14. Dubey, *Kanshiram*, p. 68.
15. Ibid., p. 69.
16. Ibid., p. 104.
17. Ibid., p. 105.
18. Ibid., p. 106.
19. Bose, *Behenji*, pp. 73–74.
20. Ibid., pp. 74–75.
21. Ibid., pp. 75–77.
22. Ibid., p. 95 and p. 101.
23. Ibid., p. 109.
24. Ibid., pp. 122–24.
25. Ibid., p. 126.
26. Ibid., p. 141.
27. Ibid., p. 143.
28. Ibid., p. 146.
29. Ibid., pp. 161–62.
30. Ibid., p. 165.
31. A.R. Akela, *Kanshiram Ke Saakshatkaar* (Delhi: Manak Publications, 2007), pp. 171–72.
32. Ibid., p. 168.

33. Ibid., p. 171.

34. Ibid., pp. 168–70.

35. Nisar Ahmed Quraishi, *Safar DS-4 Se BS-4 Tak* (Lucknow: BS4 UP unit, n.d.), p. 4 and p. 5.

36. S.S. Gautam, *Bahujan Nayak Manyavar Kanshiram Smriti Granth* (Delhi: Gautam Book Centre, 2006), p. 66.

37. A.R. Akela, ed., *Mananiya Behan Kumari Mayawati Ke Saakshatkaar* (Aligarh: Anand Sahitya Sadan, 2008), front flap cover.

38. Akela, *Kanshiram Ke Saakshatkaar*, p. 260.

39. Ibid., p. 263.

40. K. Bharti, *Kanshiram Ke Do Chehre* (Rampur, UP: Bodhisattva Prakashan, 1996), p. 62.

41. Kancha Ilaiah, 'A Paradigm Shift Called Kanshi Ram', http://roundtableindia.co.in/index.php?option=com_content&view=article&id=4813:a-paradigm-shift-called-kanshiram&catid=127:post-ambedkar-leaders&Itemid=158).

42. Harish S. Wankhede, 'The Political and the Social in the Dalit Movement Today', *Economic and Political Weekly* 43, no. 6 (2008): 53.

43. Akela, *Kanshiram Ke Saakshatkaar*, p. 13.

44. A. Kumar, ed., *Bahujan Nayak Kanshiram Ke Avismarniya Bhashan* (Delhi: Gautam Book Centre, 2007), pp. 82–83.

45. Gautam, *Bahujan Nayak*, p. 102.

46. Ibid.

47. H.L. Dusadh, *Bahujan Samaj Ka Hit Bhagedaari Siddhant Mein: Kanshiram Ke Aarthik Darshan Par Ek Addhyayan* (New Delhi: Bahujan Diversity Mission, 2007), p. 31.

48. Akela, *Kanshiram Ke Saakshatkaar*, p. 36.

49. Ibid., p. 26.

50. Bharti, *Kanshiram Ke Do Chehre*, p. 62

51. Dubey, *Kanshiram*, p. 27.

52. Akela, *Kanshiram Ke Saakshatkaar*, p. 15.

53. Bharti, *Kanshiram Ke Do Chehre*, p. 62.

54. Ajay Singh, editor, *Governance Now*, interview by Brijendra Gautam, New Delhi, 23 March 2011.

55. Akela, *Kanshiram Ke Saakshatkaar*, p. 263.

56. Bharti, *Kanshiram Ke Do Chehre*, p. 63.

57. A. Singh, 'Caste in Their Eyes', *The Telegraph*, 1995.

58. Bharti, *Kanshiram Ke Do Chehre*, p. 63.

59. Ibid., p. 64.

60. Akela, *Kanshiram Ke Saakshatkaar*, p. 25.

Chapter 6: The Critics Speak

1. Priya Sahgal, 10 Questions: Akbar Ahmad Dumpy, *Outlook*, 18 February 2002, www.outlookindia.com/article.aspx?214613.

2. Ibid.

3. Anand Teltumbde, *Ambedkar in and for the Post-Ambedkar Dalit Movement*, originally presented as a paper in a seminar on the post-Ambedkar dalit movement, Department of Political Science, University of Pune, 27–29 March 1997 (Pune: Sugawa Prakashan).

4. K. Bharti, *Kanshiram Ke Do Chehre* (Rampur, UP: Bodhisattva Prakashan, 1996), p. 64.

5. '*Mere Sahare Bina Koi Gaddinashi Nahi Ho Sakega*', *Maya*, 30 September 1989, cited in A.R. Akela, *Kanshiram Ke Saakshatkaar* (Delhi: Manak Publications, 2007), p. 35.

6. Kanshiram, interview published in *Abhay Bharti*, 27 May 1987, cited in Akela, *Kanshiram Ke Saakshatkaar*, p. 17.

7. Kumari Mayawati, *Mere Sangharshmaya Jeevan Evam Bahujan Movement Ka Safarnama Part 1* (New Delhi: BSP, 2006), p. 129.

8. '*Varga Sangharsh Chidne Ke Dar Se Main Chup Nahi Rahunga*', *Abhay Bharti*, 27 May 1987, cited in Akela, *Kanshiram Ke Saakshatkaar*, p. 20.

9. '*BSP Inka Ke Liye Naya Khatra*', *Maya*, first fortnightly, 1986, cited in Akela, *Kanshiram Ke Saakshatkaar*, p. 15.

10. '*Mere Sahare Bina Koi Gaddinashi Nahi Ho Sakega*', *Maya*, 30 September 1989, cited in Akela, *Kanshiram Ke Saakshatkaar*, p. 35.

11. Ibid., p. 36.

12. A.K. Dubey, *Kanshiram: Ek Alochanatmak Adhyayan* (New Delhi: Rajkamal Prakashan, 1997), p. 21. See *Outlook*, 2 April 1997, for aspersions on Kanshiram being an opportunist.

13. Ibid., p. 20. See also Bhavdeep Kang, 'Will the BJP-BSP Coalition Last beyond Mayawati's Six Months as Chief Minister?' *Outlook*, 2 April 1997.

14. Ibid., pp. 20–21. See also Kang, 'Will the BJP-BSP Coalition'.

15. A. Kumar, ed., *Bahujan Nayak Kanshiram Ke Avismarniya Bhashan* (Delhi: Gautam Book Centre, 2007), p. 71.

16. Dubey, *Kanshiram*, p. 21.

17. Ibid., p. 22.

18. Bharti, *Kanshiram Ke Do Chehre*, p. 66 and p. 69.

19. K. Nath, 'Shant Ho Gaya Dalit Aandolan', *Dalit Today*, August 2009, p. 20.

20. 'Dalit Morcha Ki Chetavani,' *Dalit Today*, May 2008, p. 25.

21. A.R. Akela, *Mananiya Kanshiram Saheb Ke Saakshatkaar* (Aligarh: Anand Sahitya Sadan, 2009), p. 327. See also '*Bhajpa Ka Kewal Seedhi Ke Roop Mein Istemaal*', *Aaj Ka Surekh Bharat*, Nagpur, October 2002.

22. Akela, *Kanshiram Ke Saakshatkaar*, p. 238.

23. Ibid., p. 237.

24. Ibid., p. 239. See also '*Uttar Pradesh Mein Baspa Ka Agenda Laagu Hoga: Kanshiram*', *Aaj Ka Surekh Bharat*, Nagpur, May 2002.

Chapter 7: The Last Days

1. S. Singh, *Bahujan Nayak: Kanshiram* (New Delhi: Samyak Publications, 2005), p. 29.
2. Ajoy Bose, *Behenji: A Political Biography of Mayawati* (New Delhi: Penguin, 2008), p. 94.
3. Ibid., pp. 94–95.
4. Kamlakant, *Daliton Ke Messiah Kanshiram* (Delhi: Raja Pocket Books, 2006), p. 80.
5. The details of all the reports on Kanshiram's medical condition were part of the press release prepared by Dr Mittal. The press release was given by Kanshiram's brother Dalbara Singh to Brijendra Kumar Gautam who went on a field visit to Kanshiram's home in Ropar district, Punjab.
6. Ibid. According to this report his neurological status was 'a) Right ataxic hemiparesis; b) Speech: in monosyllables—only "yes"'. The report also included a list of questions which Kanshiram was asked at the time of his discharge. These were:

   1) Have you eaten? Answer: yes
   2) Have you not eaten? Answer: yes
   3) Do you want to eat? Answer: yes
   4) Do you want to go back home? Answer: yes
   5) Do you want to stay in the hospital? Answer: yes

7. Kamlakant, *Daliton Ke Messiah Kanshiram*, p. 81.
8. Dalbara Singh, *Bahujan Samaj Party Ke Rashtriya Sansthapakadhyaksh Manyavar Kanshiramji Ki Bimari Va Jail Ke Teen Saal*, a leaflet written by Kanshiram's brother.
9. Ibid.
10. From the press release prepared by Dr Mittal:

    Kanshiram had been suffering from high blood pressure and diabetes for many years. He has triple vessel disease in his heart for which stenting and Coronary Artery Bypass Graft Surgery (CABG) had been done in the year 2004. He had cerebrovascular accident twice in 2004. While examining him it was found that he was conscious and cooperative. His understanding was not good. He could understand only simple oral instructions. He had emotional instability and frequently answered only the single words 'yes' and 'no' and that too without comprehension. Both his sides were paralysed, right side 1/5, more than the left side which was 3/5, along with spasticity. He needed assistance for standing and walking. There were no injury marks on his legs. The opinion of the medical board is that Sri Kanshiram does not need hospitalization at present. He should be treated at home with medicines and nursing. *(Translated from Hindi)*

11. Ibid.

Sri Kanshiram had been a patient of high blood pressure and diabetes and had also suffered from cerebrovascular accident. A detailed medical, psychiatric and neuropsychological examination was carried out. In the examination it was found that his right side was paralysed with spasticity and the right side of his face was also affected. In the examination it was found that he displayed symptoms of frontal lobe release. The patient was also undergoing treatment for thyroid deficiency. At the time of the examination it was found that the patient was conscious but he had no sense of time, place, etc. He had very short attention span and his cooperation was sometimes less sometimes more. He had global aphasia. He had a very limited vocabulary. He did not have the ability to understand questions and give proper replies and was also unable to concentrate and express his opinion in words. The medical board is of the opinion that in view of his present condition the patient was unable to comprehend the questions which the Supreme Court had asked him and in their context, to express his independent wishes and implement them. *(Translated from Hindi)*

12. Bose, *Behenji*, p. 50.

13. Singh, *Kanshiramji Ki Bimari*, p. 14.

14. Dalbara Singh, *Mayawati Ki Niji Jail Se Manyavar Kanshiram Ko Mukt Karane Hetu Ek Jut Ho*, a pamphlet printed by Manyawar Kanshiram Bachao Sangharsh Committee (India) in Khawaspur.

15. Ibid.

16. Dalbara Singh, *Bahujan Sangharsh Party (Kanshiram) Hi Kyon?*, a pamphlet printed by Manyawar Kanshiram Bachao Sangharsh Committee (India) in Khawaspur.

17. S.S. Gautam, *Bahujan Nayak Manyavar Kanshiram Smriti Granth* (Delhi: Gautam Book Centre, 2006), p. 127.

18. *'Garibon Ke Andaaz Mein Ladi Garibon Ki Ladai'*, *Rashtriya Sahara*, 10 October 2006, quoted in Gautam, *Bahujan Nayak*, p. 168.

19. *'Vishal Hridaya Ke Neta'*, *Rashtriya Sahara*, 10 October 2006, quoted in Gautam, *Bahujan Nayak*, p. 168.

20. *'Baspa Sansthapak Kanshiram Ka Antim Sanskaar'*, *Jansatta*, 10 October 2006, quoted in Gautam, *Bahujan Nayak*, p. 99.

21. *'Sapno Ke Aage Choti Padi Umar'*, *Rashtriya Sahara*, 10 October 2006, quoted in Gautam, *Bahujan Nayak*, p. 168.

22. *'Daliton Ki Awaaz To Kanshiram Hi Thhe'*, *Hindustan*, Delhi, 10 October 2006, quoted in Gautam, *Bahujan Nayak*, p. 87.

23. *'Paitrik Gaon Mein Chhaya Maatam'*, *Amar Ujala*, Roopnagar, 10 October 2006, quoted in Gautam, *Bahujan Nayak*, p. 100.

Chapter 8: Long Live the Message

1. Badri Narayan, *'Asmita Ke Baad Chahiye Nayi Rajneeti'*, *Hindustan*, 25 May 2009.

2. Badri Narayan, *Women Heroes and Dalit Assertion in North India* (New Delhi: Sage Publications, 2006), pp. 133–49.

3. A. Singh, 'Mulayam Government a Failure So Far: Kanshi', *Telegraph*, Lucknow, 6 April 1995.

4. This is based on the field data collected by the Dalit Resource Centre, at the G.B. Pant Social Science Institute, Allahabad.

5. 'Jitna Chahiye Usse Adhik Mil Chuka Hai Aarakshan', *Amar Ujala*, 12 September 2013.

6. '*Failon Mein Kaid Hai Aarakshan Mein Sanshodhan*', *Hindustan*, 13 September 2013.

7. Sudha Pai, 'Understanding "Backwardness" for Affirmative Action: The Most Backward Castes/Classes in Uttar Pradesh', *mySOCIETY* 1–4 (2008–09): 33–54, http://www.scribd.com/doc/62215475/Mysociety-2008-2009.

8. Sudha Pai and Jagpal Singh, 'Politicisation of Dalits and Most Backward Castes: Study of Social Conflict and Political Preferences in Four Villages of Meerut District', *Economic and Political Weekly* 38, no. 23 (7 June 1997).

9. '*Bhajpa Aur Congress Ke Karan Haare: Mayawati*', *Amar Ujala*, Lucknow, 8 March 2012, p. 16.

10. '*Rajya Sabha Nahi Jayenge Shashank Shekhar*', *Amar Ujala*, Lucknow, 13 March 2012, p. 10.

11. M.M. Rai, 'BSP Legislator Anand Sen Gets Life Sentence for Dalit's Murder', *Economic Times*, 18 May 2011.

12. M.M. Rai, 'BSP MLA, Shekhar Tiwari Gets Life Imprisonment in PWD Engineer Murder Case', *Economic Times*, 7 May 2011.

13. Headlines Today Bureau, 'SC to Hear Plea for Judicial Probe into Banda Girl Rape Case', New Delhi, 17 January 2011, http://indiatoday.intoday.in/story/sc-to-hear-plea-for-judicial-probe-into-banda-girl-rape/1/126892.html.

14. A. Singh, 'Kanshiram Tears Apart Mulayam', *Telegraph*, Allahabad, 5 March 1995.

15. S.S. Gautam, *Bahujan Nayak Manyavar Kanshiram Smriti Granth* (Delhi: Gautam Book Centre, 2006), pp. 57–58.

16. Ibid.

17. Ibid., p. 126.

18. '*Rao Do Saal Aur Rahen Taaki Congress Tabah Ho Jaaye*', *Nayi Zameen Weekly*, 28 September to 4 October 1993, compiled in A.R. Akela, *Kanshiram Ke Saakshatkaar* (Delhi: Manak Publications, 2007), p. 96.

19. A.R. Akela, ed., *The Oppressed Indian: Mananiya Kanshiram Saheb Ke Sampadakiya Lekh* (Aligarh: Anand Sahitya Sadan, 2012), p. 125.

20. Badri Narayan, 'Message for Mayawati', *Times of India*, 1 July 2009.

21. Badri Narayan, *Fascinating Hindutva: Saffron Politics and Dalit Mobilisation* (New Delhi: Sage Publications, 2009), p. 8.

22. Ibid., p. 9.

23. Ibid., pp. 9–10.

24. '*Baspa Ne Daliton Ki Eka Todi*', *Hindustan*, Lucknow, 25 May 2011, p. 2.

25. H.L. Dusadh, *Bahujan Samaj Ka Hit Bhagedaari Siddhant Mein: Kanshiram Ke Aarthik Darshan Par Ek Addhyayan* (New Delhi: Bahujan Diversity Mission, 2007), p. 33.

26. Ibid., p. 32.

Bibliography

Ahirvaar, M.P. '*Manyavar Kanshiram: Tathya Evam Bhrantiyaan*'. *Ambedkar in India*, October 2008.

Akela, A.R. *Kanshiram Ke Saakshatkaar*. Delhi: Manak Publications, 2007.

———, ed. *Mananiya Behan Kumari Mayawati Ke Saakshatkaar*. Aligarh: Anand Sahitya Sadan, 2008.

———. *Mananiya Kanshiram Saheb Ke Saakshatkaar*. Aligarh: Anand Sahitya Sadan, 2009.

———, ed. *The Oppressed Indian: Mananiya Kanshiram Saheb Ke Sampadakiya Lekh*. Aligarh: Anand Sahitya Sadan, 2012.

Ambedkar, B.R. *The Annihilation of Caste*. New Delhi: Arnold Publishers, 1990.

Bechain, S.S. *Hindi Ki Dalit Patrakarita Par Patrakar Ambedkar Ka Prabhav*. Delhi: Samta Prakashan, 1997.

Bharti, K. *Kanshiram Ke Do Chehre*. Rampur, UP: Bodhisattva Prakashan, 1996.

Bose, Ajoy. *Behenji: A Political Biography of Mayawati*. New Delhi: Penguin, 2008.

Choudhary, P.K., and Srikant. *Swarg Par Dhawa: Bihar Mein Dalit Aandolan 1912–2000*. New Delhi: Vani Prakashan, 2005.

Das, K.C. *Indian Dalits: Voices, Visions and Politics.* Delhi: Global Vision Publishing House, 2004.

Dinkar, D.C. *Swatantrata Sangram Mein Achhuton Ka Yogdan.* Lucknow: Bodhisattva Prakashan, 1990.

Diwakar, R.A. '*Samaj Vigyaani Manyavar Kanshiram*'. *Kameri Duniya*, March 2010.

Dubey, A.K. *Kanshiram: Ek Alochanatmak Adhyayan.* New Delhi: Rajkamal Prakashan, 1997.

Dusadh, H.L. *Bahujan Samaj Ka Hit Bhagedaari Siddhant Mein: Kanshiram Ke Aarthik Darshan Par Ek Addhyayan.* New Delhi: Bahujan Diversity Mission, 2007.

Gautam, S.S. *Bahujan Nayak Manyavar Kanshiram Smriti Granth.* Delhi: Gautam Book Centre, 2006.

Gooptu, Nandini. *Swami Acchutanand and the Adi-Hindu Movement.* Cambridge: Cambridge University Press, 2006.

Gulde, Shayar D. *Jai Bheem Jagriti Geetmala.* New Delhi: Samyak Prakashan, 2000.

Hans, B.S. *Gau Brahmin Namo-Namo: Ko Rakshati Vedah.* Patna: Ambedkar Mission Prakashan, 2003.

Ilaiah, Kancha. 'A Paradigm Shift Called Kanshi Ram'. Round Table India, 15 March 2012. http://roundtableindia.co.in/index.php?option=com_content&view=article&id=4813:a-paradigm-shift-called-kanshiram&catid=127:post-ambedkar-leaders&Itemid=158.

Jaffrelot, Christophe. *India's Silent Revolution.* New Delhi: Permanent Black, 2006.

Jaoul, Nicolas. 'Political and "Non-political" Means in the Dalit Movement'. In *Political Process in Uttar Pradesh: Identity, Economic Reforms and Governance*, edited by Sudha Pai. New Delhi: Pearson Education, 2007.

Juergensmeyer, Mark. *Religious Rebels in the Punjab: The Ad Dharm Challenge to Caste.* New Delhi: Navayana Publishing, 2009.

Bibliography

Kamlakant. *Daliton Ke Messiah Kanshiram.* Delhi: Raja Pocket Books, 2006.

Kanshiram. *The Chamcha Age: An Era of the Stooges.* New Delhi: Kanshiram, 24 September 1982.

———. *Chamcha Yug: An Era of the Stooges.* Reprint, Nagpur: Samta Prakashan, 1998.

———. *Chamcha Yug: An Era of the Stooges.* Translated into Hindi by Moses Michael. New Delhi: Samyak Prakashan, 2008.

Katiyar, B.S. '*Samajik Parivartan Ke Yugpurush Manyavar Kanshiram*'. *Ambedkar in India,* October 2008.

Keer, Dhananjay. *Dr. Ambedkar: Life and Mission.* Bombay: Popular Prakashan, 1971.

———. *Dr. Babasaheb Ambedkar: Jeevan Charit.* New Delhi: Popular Prakashan, 2006.

Kshirsagar, R.K. *Dalit Movement in India and Its Leaders.* New Delhi: M.D. Publications Pvt. Ltd, 1994.

Kshirsagar, Ramchandra. *Political Thought of Dr Baba Saheb Ambedkar.* New Delhi: Intellectual Publishing House, 1992.

Kumar, A., ed. *Bahujan Nayak Kanshiram Ke Avismarniya Bhashan.* Delhi: Gautam Book Centre, 2007.

Kumar, V. '*Aadhunik Bhartiya Rajneeti Ke Mahan Nayak*'. *Ambedkar in India,* March 2010.

Lieten, G.K., and R. Srivastava. *Unequal Partners: Power Relations, Devolution and Development in Uttar Pradesh.* New Delhi: Sage Publications, 1999.

Lynch, Owen M. *The Politics of Untouchability.* New York: Columbia University Press, 1969.

———. *The Politics of Untouchability.* New Delhi: National Publishing House, 1974.

Maikulal Varishtha Chintansheel Nagrik. *Gurudev Bhagwan Ravidas Ka Sankshipta Jeevan Parichay.* Lucknow: Maikulal Varishtha Chintansheel Nagrik, 2005.

Malhotra, S.L. 'Hindu Politics and Untouchability in Punjab, 1900–1935', *Social Science Research Journal* 1 (1976): 74–88.

Murugkar, L. *Dalit Panther Movement in Maharashtra*. Bombay: Popular Prakashan, 1991.

Naimishraye, Mohandas. *Bhartiya Dalit Aandolan Ka Itihaas*. Vols. 1 and 2. New Delhi: Radhakrishna Prakashan, 2013.

Narayan, Badri. *Documenting Dissent: Contesting Fables, Contested Memories and Dalit Political Discourse*. Shimla: Indian Institute of Advanced Study, 2001.

———. *The Making of the Dalit Public in North India: Uttar Pradesh, 1950–Present*. New Delhi: Oxford University Press India, 2011.

———. *Women Heroes and Dalit Assertion in North India*. New Delhi: Sage Publications, 2006.

Narayan, Badri, and A.R. Mishra, eds. *Multiple Marginalities: An Anthology of Identified Dalit Writings*. New Delhi: Manohar, 2004.

Omvedt, Gail. 'Ambedkar and After: The Dalit Movement in India'. In *Dalit Identity and Politics*, edited by Ghanshyam Shah. New Delhi: Sage Publications, 2001.

———. *Dalits and the Democratic Revolution: Dr Ambedkar and the Dalit Movement in Colonial India*. New Delhi: Sage Publications, 1994.

Pai, Sudha. *Dalit Assertion and the Unfinished Democratic Revolution: The Bahujan Samaj Party in Uttar Pradesh*. New Delhi: Sage Publications, 2002.

———. 'Kanshi Ram: The Man and His Legacy'. *eSocialSciences* (13 October 2006), http://www.esocialsciences.org/Articles/ShowArticle.aspx?acat=Current+Affairs&aid=639.

———. 'Understanding "Backwardness" for Affirmative Action: The Most Backward Castes/Classes in Uttar Pradesh'. *mySOCIETY* 1–4 (2008–09): 33–54. http://www.scribd.com/doc/62215475/Mysociety-2008-2009.

Pai, Sudha, and Jagpal Singh. 'Politicisation of Dalits and Most Backward Castes: Study of Social Conflict and Political Preferences in Four Villages of Meerut District'. *Economic and Political Weekly* 38, no. 23 (7 June 1997).

Patankar, Bharat, and Gail Omvedt. *The Dalit Liberation Movement in Colonial Period.* New Delhi: Critical Quest, 2004.

Patel, R. *Mahamana Ram Swaroop Verma Ka Sankshipta Jeevan Parichay.* Basti, UP: Samta Prakashan, 2001.

Puri, Harish K. 'Scheduled Castes in Sikh Community: A Historical Perspective'. *Economic and Political Weekly* 38, no. 26 (2003): 2693–701.

Ram, Ronki. 'Untouchability, Dalit Consciousness, and the Ad-Dharm Movement in Punjab'. *Contributions to Indian Sociology,* n.s., 38, no. 3 (2004): 323–49.

Saroj, R.P. *Krantiveer Madari Pasi Evom Eka Aandolan.* Lucknow: Sushila Saroj, 1997.

Sharma, R.V. *Rag Virag.* Allahabad: Lokbharti Prakashan, 1992.

Singh, Inderjit. 'Bahujan Samaj Party in Punjab: Organization, Support Base and Performance'. Unpublished thesis, Punjabi University, Patiala, 2011. http://shodhganga.inflibnet.ac.in/bitstream/10603/4286/13/13_chapter%206.pdf.

Singh, R.K. *Kanshiram Aur BSP: Dalit Aandolan Ka Vaicharik Aadhar Brahmanvaad Virodh.* Allahabad: Kushwaha Book Distributors, 1994.

Singh, S. *Bahujan Nayak: Kanshiram.* New Delhi: Samyak Publications, 2005.

Sonik, S. *Yug Purush Kanshiram Ka Bahujan Sangharsh.* Delhi: Siddhartha Publication, 2007.

Teltumbde, Anand. *Ambedkar in and for the Post-Ambedkar Dalit Movement.* Originally presented as a paper in a seminar on the post-Ambedkar dalit movement, Department of Political Science, University of Pune, 27–29 March 1997. Pune: Sugawa Prakashan.

————. 'Crisis of Ambedkarites and Future Challenges'. CounterCurrents.org, 22 April 2011. www.countercurrents.org/teltumbde220411.htm.

Tilak, R. *Bharat Ki Pehli Shikshika Savitri Bai Phule*. New Delhi: Centre for Alternative Dalit Media, 2002.

Trisharan, R.B. *Bhim Ekta Geet*. Basti, UP: Samaj Sudhar Prakashan, 1994.

Verma, A.K. 'Uttar Pradesh: Politics of Social Polarisation and Its Limits'. *Journal of Indian School of Political Economy* 15, nos. 1 & 2 (2003): 249–77.

Vidrohi, M.R. *Dalit Dastavej*. New Delhi: Samyak Prakashan, 2004.

Wankhede, Harish S. 'Dalit/RPI Politics in Maharashtra'. Dalit Perspectives blog. 28 April 2012. dalitperspectivejnu.blogspot.in/2012/04/dalitrpi-politics-in-maharashtra.html.

————. 'The Political and the Social in the Dalit Movement Today'. *Economic and Political Weekly* 43, no. 6 (2008).

Whalley, P. 'Places and Names in the United Provinces of Agra and Awadh'. *Journal of United Provinces Historical Society* 4 (1928): 91–129.

Yaad, Y.K. *Samajik Parivartan Ke Mahanayak Manya Kanshiram Sahab*. Lucknow: Bahujan Sahitya Sanstha Ltd, 2005.

Zelliot, Eleanor. *Dr Ambedkar and the Mahar Movement*. Philadelphia: University of Pennsylvania Press, 1969.

Index